THE FIRESIDE BOOK OF
GUNS
BY LARRY KOLLER

THE FIRESIDE BOOK OF GUNS

By **LARRY KOLLER**

HAROLD L. PETERSON, *Historian*   **HERB GLASS,** *Gun Consultant*

A RIDGE PRESS BOOK

SIMON AND SCHUSTER · NEW YORK

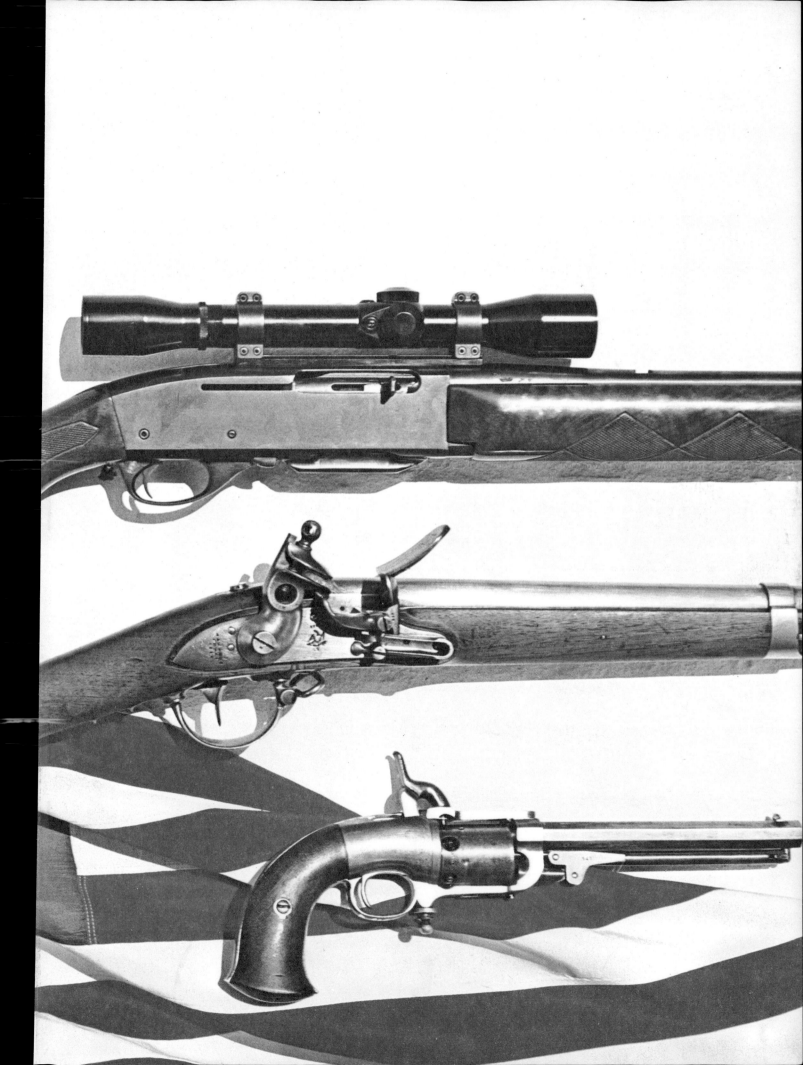

CONTENTS

Editor-in-Chief: JERRY MASON
Editor: ADOLPH SUEHSDORF
Art Director: ALBERT A. SQUILLACE
Project Editor: DON MYRUS
Associate Editor: RUTH BIRNKRANT
Art Researcher: JOZEFA STUART
Art Associate: ALBERT KAMP

*Book-jacket guns are Remington
Model 740 autoloader, Harpers Ferry
Model 1835 flintlock musket, and
Butterfield patent percussion revolver.
Photograph by Robert Mottar*

*Prepared and produced by
The Ridge Press, Inc. and
the Artists and Writers Press, Inc.
Printed in the United States
of America by Western Printing and
Lithographing Company.
Published by Simon and Schuster, Inc.
Rockefeller Center,
New York 20, New York
Third Printing*

BOOK ONE | WORK AND WAR

BOOK TWO | ROUGH AND READY

BOOK THREE | GAME AND TARGET

INTRODUCTION

■ For most men, a gun is an irresistible object. Whatever its age or condition, it calls forth an almost instinctive response. It must be picked up, hefted, balanced, and cocked. A rifle must be raised to the shoulder and sighted, a handgun gripped and aimed. Then, ineffable moment, the trigger is squeezed and the hammer, swiftly obedient, clicks sharply, the no-nonsense sound of oiled steel on steel. The gun is lowered, examined keenly once more, and returned to rest, the gun handler absorbed for the moment in private visions or longings inexpressible. With an old gun there is an additional, intermediate, essential step. The examination continues until the mystery of the mechanism is understood, the meaning of its function possessed, and, often, the power of its heritage evoked.

This response, it can be said with certainty, is world-wide, although in other countries only a select group, comprising the sporting upper classes and the professional soldier, is likely to have the background and the freedom to support its enthusiasm. In America it has always been otherwise. Men of all degrees of wealth and lineage have used guns to survive, to protect the republic, and to sport. Many of the great have been familiar with the gun—George Washington, Abraham Lincoln, Theodore Roosevelt. And so have been the forgotten and the unknown who made everyday phrases of such technical expressions as "flash in the pan," "going off half-cocked," and "lock, stock, and barrel." Gunmakers Eliphalet Remington II and Sam Colt have won honored places beside other captains of industry. Gun users like Daniel Boone and Wyatt Earp have become folk heroes.

The fascination of guns and shooting is the subject of this volume. It is expressed through words, historical paintings, and contemporary photographs. Because category-of-use seemed the best way to present the wealth of material, the volume has been divided into three parts.

WORK AND WAR tells how the ingenuity of gunmakers met the clamorous demand for ever better firearms to wrest a beachhead in the New World, to conquer the Indian, to fashion a colonial empire; how Americans labored, with guns at the ready, to gather furs and hides, land and gold, how they founded an independent nation in one war and preserved it in another.

ROUGH AND READY tells how firearms, mostly handguns, served gentlemen and more commonly bred hotheads in settling affronts to honor; how, in the hands of pirates, rustlers, and stagecoach robbers, they became a law unto themselves; and how, in the hands of peace officers (who also used shotguns and did not always fire face to face), they brought peace to the West.

GAME AND TARGET tells how, since the beginning of America, men have been sporting with guns by shooting either at game or targets; how firearms and cartridges have been brought to their final stage of practical development; and how to hit what you aim at.

THE AUTHOR, Larry Koller, is a noted hunter of American game. During World War II he worked as a gunmaker. Since then he has written a number of highly regarded books and articles about guns, hunting, and the outdoors. Historian Harold L. Peterson, author of the definitive *Arms and Armor in Colonial America* and the *Encyclopaedia Britannica* article on firearms evolution, authenticated the text. Herb Glass guided the selection of the guns to be photographed and checked the facts about them. He is a recognized expert in the specialized field of gun consultation and has helped develop many of the distinguished gun collections in the United States.

ACKNOWLEDGMENTS

Although specific acknowledgment of source is made under each photograph, the editors are especially grateful to the following persons and organizations for their co-operation in making guns available: Miss Rose Briggs and Warren Sampson of Pilgrim Hall, Plymouth; Colt's Patent Firearms Mfg. Co.; William F. Florence; Gerald Fox; Gerald Stowe of the West Point Museum; William O. Sweet; Remington Arms Co.; Sturm, Ruger and Co., Inc.; Winchester Repeating Arms Co. Special thanks also are given to Harold McCracken for permission to reproduce illustrations from his "Portrait of the Old West," and to Thomas E. Hall for helpful suggestions on the manuscript of Book III.

BOOK ONE | WORK AND WAR

CHAPTER ONE

OLD GUNS IN A NEW WORLD

And we are sixteen, and they are but seven hundred

at the most; and assure yourselves, God will so assist us, that if you dare

stand but to discharge your pieces the very smoke will be

sufficient to affright them. CAPTAIN JOHN SMITH

They debarked from their fat-bellied ships and came ashore, saturnine soldiers of Spain burning with the fervor of conquest and impatient for gold. The westerly wind was spilled from the slatting sails emblazoned with the Cross. The fiery gleam of Caribbean sunlight was caught and reflected by breastplate and morion, by sword pommel and by halberd, and here and there, on those sixteenth-century mornings in the New World, the sun shone equally on the iron mountings of muskets.

They were low on firepower, these primitive guns, and short on man-killing accuracy. But they could cough with a roar and spit white smoke, and possession of them meant mastery.

Not immediately. Not always. For two centuries, ambush and massacre threatened the trails that led inland from the sea. But eventually and inevitably, on one front after another, the gun became the acknowledged weapon of survival and success, and a determinant in the history of a continent.

From the first landings of the earliest explorers to the end of the war that established a nation and set it free, few days seem to have passed without the firing of a gun to advance the claims of a conqueror or to defend—or wrest away— what he had taken. It was a large country, vaster

PAGES 14 AND 15: *Well-preserved Pilgrim arms and armor*
include Italian musket with lever-action trigger;
steel morion and breastplate; halberd from John Alden house
GUNS COURTESY OF PILGRIM SOCIETY, PILGRIM HALL
PHOTO BY ROBERT MOTTAR

RIGHT: *Splendidly-garbed musketeer of early 1600's positions*
cumbersome matchlock as specified in manual of arms: "Hold your
musket in your rest and with the left hand onely in Ballance."
COURTESY STEPHEN V. GRANCSAY

Columbus brings Christianity and matchlocks to the New World. The discoverer's weapons, however, were even more primitive than the musket, below, which was made in Europe in the early 1600's. Inside detail of matchlock mechanism shows cord wick attached to serpentine which, in turn, is connected to link, sear, and spring.

MUSKET: T. E. HALL;
MECHANISM: WINCHESTER MUSEUM

even than its discoverers dreamed. Yet it was not large enough to contain the many rivals who contended for it. The Spanish, moving up from the Caribbean, secured the Florida coast, penetrated the Southwest, and cruised the great rivers of the South. The English ranged the eastern seaboard from New England to Virginia, their holdings interrupted only by colonies of Dutchmen and Swedes clustered in New Jersey, Pennsylvania, Delaware, the Hudson Valley, and Manhattan. The French, losing out to Spain in the South, settled along the St. Lawrence and sent their scouts and missionaries deep into the Midwest. Wherever these Europeans met they clashed, and at other times there was always the common foe, the savage Indian, to fight.

In time, guns decided the course of empire in the New World. They echoed the voice of insurrection and rebellion against despotic colonial governors. In the hands of the militiaman and the backwoods marksman they helped win the Revolutionary War. The long rifles of the pioneers pointed the way west, cleared and held Bloody Kentucky, followed the great watercourses and swept the plains. Guns hurled back the Mexicans in the Southwest and acquired California. They stirred up lawlessness in the rawboned West and, in the end, they established law.

Ultimately, too, they decided the unremitting, bitter conflict with the Indians. Although the Indian's use of the gun undoubtedly prolonged his resistance to the whites, ironically it also predestined the outcome of the struggle. For it was never a battle of equals. Long before defeat was final, the Indian's defeat was certain. The gun was the white man's weapon. He invented it. He understood it. He was capable of improving it. He had the facilities to produce it. For the Indian, it was a prize to be captured, traded for, or stolen. Once he learned to need it, his ability to clothe and feed himself by hunting, to enrich himself in the fur trade, and to triumph in war

was imperiled. Without a gun, he was prey to hunger, poverty, and death.

The story of the gun in America is fitful. The early firearm was by turns an astounding success and a ludicrous failure. But it was no freak. If its action was slow and clumsy, its range short, and its accuracy unpredictable, its potential was lethal and there was nothing wrong with it that someone, sooner or later, could not fix. It was as though everyone who used it knew in his bones what it could be. It persisted.

THE MATCHLOCK

The guns that came ashore with the Spaniards were matchlocks—"lock" meaning the mechanism that fires a gun, "match" designating the system of ignition. There were two kinds: the arquebus and the musket. Both were simple devices, quite as lacking in ingenuity as in precision. Their barrels were long, heavy iron tubes,

smoothbored and fastened to a crude stock with a huge butt. The arquebus had been in use since about 1450; it was about .72-caliber, shot a .66-caliber ball, and was held against the chest in firing. It weighed ten or eleven pounds. The musket was developed about a hundred years later in Spain; it was a twenty-pound monster with a 10- or even 8-gauge barrel and was fired from the shoulder with the aid of a forked rest to steady it.

Both were muzzle-loaders. A fat charge of loose black powder, a lead ball, and a wad of tow or paper were dropped down the barrel and tamped home with a ramrod. Next, at the firing end, a small pan fixed to the barrel was filled with fine priming powder, and the glowing match, a wick of loosely braided cord impregnated with saltpeter, was clamped in a serpentine, which had roughly the same function as the modern gun's hammer.

To fire his piece, the musketeer — or arque-

19

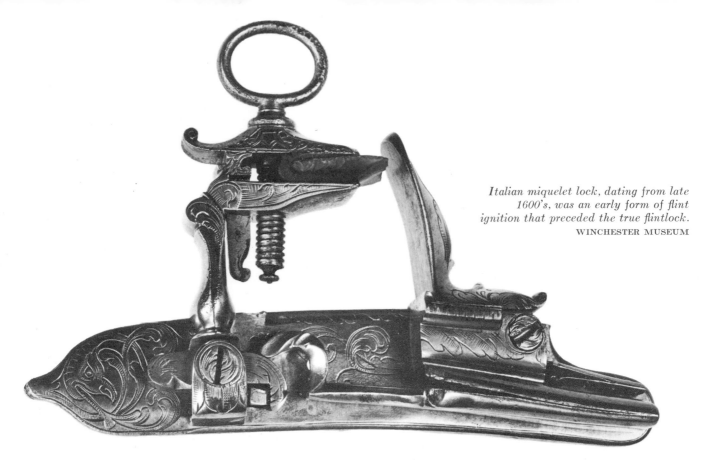

Italian miquelet lock, dating from late 1600's, was an early form of flint ignition that preceded the true flintlock. WINCHESTER MUSEUM

On a journey down the Mississippi in 1682, La Salle—armed with a fuzee—discusses the gun trade with the chief of the Taensas. PAINTING BY GEORGE CATLIN. THE GOLDEN BOOK OF AMERICA AND AMERICAN HERITAGE

busier—squeezed the trigger (in early guns it was a lever that was clutched upward toward the stock), the serpentine swung forward on its pivot to bring the match into contact with the priming powder, and the resulting flame spurted through a touch hole above the pan and ignited the main charge. If all went well, the gun discharged with a great belch of fire and smoke, and the ball sailed off, reluctantly, on a maximum flight of about three hundred paces.

After firing, the gunner removed the match to avoid an accidental explosion during reloading, poured in a new charge of powder and ball, reprimed the pan, reclamped the match, and turned again to face the foe.

It is a wonder that anyone ever stood still for the first shot—and that musketeers ever lived to fire a second. Still, the matchlock saw service in America for nearly a century and a half after the first landings of the Spaniards in the 1520's. And for seventy five of those years from 1550 to 1625—it was the most important weapon on the continent. Despite its inadequacies, its power when it hit was devastating and its performance against the Indian was better than that of the pike, lance, or crossbow. Gradually, the white colonist-adventurer began to shuck his armor, discard the tactics of formal combat, and shape his campaigns around the gun.

War in the New World presented new problems. In well-ordered battles between stately masses of soldiery on the plains of Europe, the fighting generally took place by daylight, in good weather, and with the target in plain sight and within range. Along the coast of America the battlefields were densely forested and the red-skinned enemy struck swiftly and stealthily with limber bow and silent arrow.

"They never stand still," complained one of De Soto's companions, "but are alwaies running and traversing from one place to another: by reason whereof neither crossebow nor arcubuse can aime at them: and before one crossebowman can make one shot, an Indian will discharge three or foure arrows; and he seldom misseth what he shooteth at."

De Soto himself could attest to that. During one skirmish he rose in his saddle to impale an Indian with his lance and exposed the unarmored seat of his pants. Another Indian, observing the target, let fly. The great man took a shaft in his fundament, forcing him to fight the rest of the battle standing up in his stirrups.

Guerrilla warfare quickly exposed other failings of the gun. Inescapably, the slow-match had to be kept burning at all times—and at both ends, so that one could relight the other, if necessary—or the gun could not be fired. Yet at night its glow betrayed the white man's position and at any time its smoky fumes might tinge the air and signal his presence. Rain doused the matches and dampened powder. Fouling of barrel or touch hole resulted in misfires and explosions.

All this the Indian noted and turned to his advantage. In 1609, Hendrik Hudson and his men took a fearful drubbing from Indians when their matchlocks were made impotent by a storm. Two years earlier, Englishmen cruising in a small boat off the coast of Maine had the firebrand that lit their matches snatched away and thrown overboard by an Indian who waded out, feigning friendliness, to ask a light for his pipe. The crew leveled its matchless weapons at the other Indians now clustering on the beach while one intrepid soul dashed ashore for another brand. He returned empty handed, but the Indians, still not certain the firesticks were powerless, faltered momentarily in their attack, which enabled the English to escape.

Finally, there was the hazard of accidental ignition of the loose powder the musketeer carried. Captain John Smith of Jamestown Colony writes most vividly of the painful consequences:

"Either by accident, or maliciously of purpose (which I know not, nor will presume to judge, but the good God, He knows), someone fired my powder pouch, which tore the flesh from my body and thighs, nine or ten inches square, in a most pitiful manner. Awakened from my sleep in this rude way, being dazed and yet in intolerable agony, to quench the tormenting fire, which was frying me in my clothes, I leaped overboard into the deep river, in which I was near drowned ere they could recover me. It was a very grievous wound, and I was in the sorest pain, yet in this state, without either surgeon

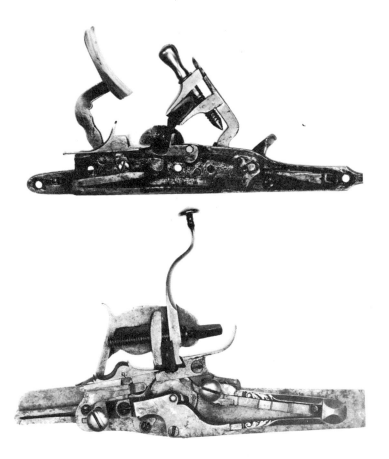

Inside views of two seventeenth-century locks: top, a Dutch snaphaunce; bottom, a Swiss wheel lock. WINCHESTER MUSEUM

or surgery, I had to go near a hundred miles."

But bulky and balky as it was, the matchlock roared its defiance of the Indian onslaughts, and its monstrous ball sank home just often enough to inspire respect. Its thunder and flame were awesome, and in the stunning aftermath of its discharge the gunner readied his second shot.

Occasionally, too, the firestick dealt a truly remarkable blow on behalf of the invaders. Perhaps the most resounding shot was fired by Samuel de Champlain while exploring, in the name of New France, the beautiful lake that bears his name. In July, 1609, accompanied by friendly Hurons, Algonquians, and Montagnais, he encountered a war party of hostile Iroquois at a cape near Crown Point. The two groups skirmished until dusk. In darkness, the Iroquois —some two hundred of them—landed and threw up a barricade. Next morning, according to Champlain's drawing of the event, the forces opposed each other on the beach, with the explorer and his arquebus in the forefront and two French companions covering him from the bush. Three tall Iroquois chiefs stood before their redoubt. Champlain advanced, waiting for the Indians to make the first move. At a range of thirty yards, the chiefs raised their bows. Champlain hoisted his arquebus and fired.

Wham! Down went the three chiefs, two of them dead, the other mortally wounded. It was a preposterously wonderful shot, even when it is known that Champlain had had the foresight to stuff his piece with four balls.

"The Iroquois," Champlain tells us with relish, "were greatly astonished, seeing two men killed so instantaneously, notwithstanding they were provided with arrow-proof armor woven of cotton thread and wool; this frightened them very much. Whilst I was reloading, one of my companions in the bush fired a shot which so astonished them anew . . . that they lost courage, took to flight, and abandoned the field and their fort, hiding themselves in the depths of the forest, whither pursuing them I killed some others. Having feasted, danced, and sung, we returned three hours afterwards with ten or twelve prisoners. I named the place where this battle was fought Lake Champlain."

It was, as matters turned out, a hollow victory. Smarting from their defeat, the Iroquois became implacable enemies of the French and in years to come helped to dislodge them from the New World forever.

Over the years there were changes in the design and nomenclature of the matchlock. The trigger action began to develop in the direction of the modern gun; the trigger guard appeared. And the stock took on a more recognizably modern shape. The name "caliver" came into use for the lighter, arquebus-type of weapon and later "fusil" or, corruptly, "fuzee."

Curiously, there was through all these turbulent times a better gun than the matchlock available to the colonists. This was the wheel lock, which had been known in Germany as early as 1520. Instead of the pesky match, the wheel lock had a small, rough-edged wheel that revolved under spring tension against a lump of iron pyrites, somewhat as cigarette lighters do today. The resulting shower of sparks ignited the priming charge and fired the gun. Its lock worked faster and more reliably than the matchlock, thus improving the accuracy of aimed firing, and it even functioned to some degree in light rain and snow. It had disadvantages as well. It cost twice as much as a matchlock and was a more complicated mechanism to repair. The spring was wound with a small spanner wrench, or key. If it were lost, the gun was *kaput*.

Surviving records mention the wheel lock infrequently, but it may have been more widely used than appears. It overcame several basic

Dutch flintlocks, like this .78-caliber musket, were traded for twenty beaver skins. WINCHESTER MUSEUM

23

flaws in the matchlock and on this score would have appealed strongly to gun-conscious colonists, regardless of expense. Wheel locks are listed among the armament of the tragic English settlement at Roanoke Island in 1585, lock fragments and spanners have been excavated at Jamestown, and the Spanish explorer Don Juan de Oñate, kin to Cortez, carried them on his expedition to colonize the area north of the Rio Grande in 1597. And it seems likely that they were the "firelocks" occasionally referred to in documents of the period.

Still, the conservative Spaniards seem to have clung mostly to their matchlock muskets in waging war against the French and the Indians on the Florida mainland and against French and English freebooters offshore. It was the weapon of the first French and Dutch and Swedes. And the English employed it to gain footholds at Roanoke, Jamestown, Plymouth, and Massachusetts Bay.

But when survival demanded something better than the matchlock, it was the flintlock that answered the challenge.

THE FLINT ARM

Change came gradually and competing weapons overlapped in time until the law of natural selection asserted itself and the supremacy of one was established. The matchlock served its time. The wheel lock never quite made it. The flintlock emerged and dominated its world. Gathering momentum after its first appearance

valiant, who was thought to be their captain, stood behind a tree within half a musket-shot of us, and there let his arrows fly at us. He was seen to shoot three arrows, which were all avoided, for he at whom the first was aimed stooped down and it flew over him. He stood three shots of a musket. At length one took full aim at him, after which he gave an extraordinary cry, and away they went, all. We followed them about a quarter of a mile. Then we shouted altogether several times, and shot off a couple of muskets, and so returned. This we did that they might see we were not afraid of them nor discouraged."

Standish's gun was very likely an English lock, one of the five types of flint arms which preceded the true flintlock.

First came the snaphaunce, which was developed in Scandinavia and the Low Countries about 1550. Its operation, like that of the wheel lock, was based on the principle of striking sparks with flint and steel to kindle a fire. The flint was held in a viselike arm called a cock, which pivoted on a pin to strike a bar of steel called the battery, against the force of a mainspring. The sparks dropped directly into a flashpan below the battery—which was provided with a sliding cover to retain the powder until the shooter was ready to fire—igniting the priming charge there and, through the touch hole, the main charge. Its name, deriving from the Dutch *snap-haan,* or "snapping cock" (the German *schnapp-hahn,* or "pecking fowl"), is a fairly vivid image of the action of its hammer. Like all great notions, it was as simple as it was ingenious. It did away with the bothersome match. It had none of the wheel lock's complexity. It

early in the seventeenth century, it forged into prominence as the American gun, and its use as a military weapon did not end until after the Civil War.

Flint arms were not unknown to the early settlers. Captain Miles Standish, for instance, is reputed to have carried one—and used it well —when Pilgrims surveying Cape Cod for a proper site to settle on met hostile Indians, probably Wampanoags or Nausets, near Wellfleet.

"Captain Miles Standish made a shot," writes Edward Winslow, an eye-witness who later became governor of Plymouth, "and after him another . . . there were only four of us which had their arms ready, and stood before the open side of our barricade . . . .

"There was a lusty man, and no whit less

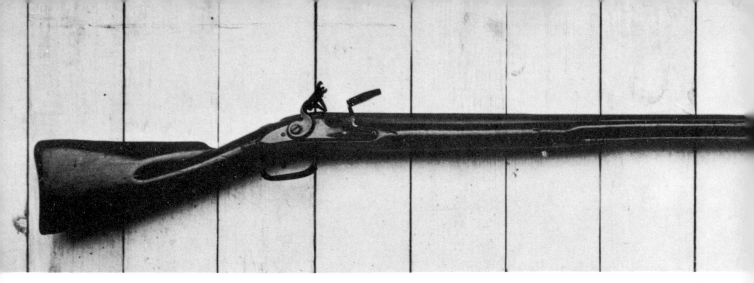

Hudson Valley long fowler—with five-foot barrel and heavy breech—was a good gun for hunting and fixed defense.

was a gun that could be loaded and carried at the ready for hunting or defense. The gunner could use both hands to hold his weapon steadily on target and he could reload more swiftly.

Although popular in Europe, a true snaphaunce was a rarity in America, principally because British gunsmiths, by the time of the Plymouth landing, had come forward with an improved English lock and its variant, the dog lock. On these new locks, the pan cover and battery were one piece—called a frizzen—which pivoted so that the cover lifted automatically when flint struck steel. Although some snaphaunces also had this automatic action, many others were manual—and an embarrassment to the shooter who forgot to open the pan before pulling the trigger.

The frizzen, however, posed another problem. It had no safety. With a snaphaunce the battery could always be flipped out of striking position. Now, if the pan cover was closed—as it had to be when the gun was primed—the battery was poised for action. The English lock offered a not quite satisfactory solution; the more popular dog lock achieved the same end with a manually operated "dog catch" which hooked into a notch on the backside of the cock.

The miquelet lock, notable principally for having its mainspring on the outside of the lock plate, was a Spanish development almost as old as the snaphaunce. Evidence of them in

America is slight, although specimens have been found in Virginia, Georgia, Florida, and the Southwest. Finally, there was the Scandinavian "snaplock," which apparently was used only by the Swedes along the Delaware River.

Of the five types, the dog lock gained greatest acceptance. Between 1625 and 1675 it was the predominant gun in America, gradually supplanting the matchlock and then giving way to the true flintlock.

The flintlock was the end point, the ultimate evolution, in the development of flint-and-steel weapons. To France goes the credit for devising it. It appeared shortly before 1615 and held undisputed sway for more than two hundred years. It was not a highly original design, but it combined the best features of what had gone before into a safe and reliable weapon, inexpensive to manufacture and simple to repair. The Colonies were acquiring them in quantity by 1660. In 1665, the Carignan-Sallieres regiment in Canada became the first French army unit equipped with flintlocks as the standard weapon. By 1700 it was the paramount arm everywhere.

HANDGUNS

The coming of flint gave a boost to the development of the handgun. Huge wheel-lock pistols with long barrels and straight grips had been a cavalry weapon in Europe since the

GUN COURTESY HAROLD PETERSON. PHOTO BY ROBERT MOTTAR

1520's, and the earliest flint models followed this design. Shortly after 1600, however, the notion of the pistol as a side arm was more strongly established and the curved grip that prevails today was introduced.

Records make scant mention of pistols until the eighteenth century when officers in the French and Indian War used them with fair regularity. But it is known that Roanoke Island had some and that Captain John Smith wielded a French snaphaunce bravely in the scuffle that led to his capture by Chief Powhatan and the death sentence from which he was melodramatically saved by the princess Pocahontas. A doglock pistol from the Plymouth Colony survives. And as early as 1648, British troops were issued a government-model flintlock.

One continuing mystery is the derivation of the name "pistol." One of several possibilities is the fact that as a cavalry weapon it was carried in a long, large holster lashed to the dragoon's saddle pommel, or *pistallo*.

THE STRUGGLE FOR THE CONTINENT

More than blankets, more than gewgaws and gimcracks, more even than fascinating, friendly, beguiling rum, the Indian wanted the gun. It was a revolutionary technological advance in the art of war. To assert and maintain himself, he had to have it.

Aside from land and liberty, the white settlers wanted furs. There was a ready market for them in chill and drafty Europe. Trimmings, edgings, and linings of fur had always been a mark of prestige as well as of comfort, and the rising middle class of the Old World could now afford to indulge itself in both.

Thus began the fur trade. And out of competition for the furs erupted the bitter, brutal little wars that determined the fate of nations and started the Indian on the retreat across the continent that would end with his eclipse.

The furs were beaver. The guns were flintlocks. The matchlock was the invasion weapon, the weapon that secured the beaches and demonstrated to the Indian that there was something new under the sun. It was distributed to friendly Indians to win them as allies against hostile tribes. On a restricted basis it was traded. Early in the game, however, it did not seem sensible to give too freely of the vital weapon. With it the Indian became a more potent foe of the white man and one never knew when, in the checkered pattern of events, yesterday's gift would be firing back at the giver today. Further, the Indian was not too fond of the heavy matchlock. It was the flint arm that struck his fancy, particularly the short, lightweight carbines and musketoons which began to appear during the first half of the seventeenth century and which set the pattern for subsequent trade guns.

27

Trade on a large scale began with the canny
Dutch. The Spaniards arrived first, of course,
but throughout their tenancy of the South and
Southwest they adhered quite strictly to a no-
trade policy. The facile French penetrated far-
thest with the gun trade; they were everybody's
friend. But in the end, it was the English who
had the staying power, and the best guns.

The Dutch agents operating in New Jersey
and as far north as Albany were doing a thriving business in long-barreled matchlocks with
their particular friends, the Iroquois, in the
early 1640's. The exchange rate was twenty
beaver skins for one "firelock." In their activities was established the inevitable cycle that gun
trading was to follow. They armed the Iroquois
at the expense of alienating all the other tribes
in the area. They muscled in on British trade
with the Mohawks, fiercest of the six Iroquois
nations. And they paid an appalling price in
Dutch lives after their callous director-general,
William Kieft, seeking to strengthen his position and his profits with the Iroquois, attacked
inoffensive Algonquian refugees fleeing from
Mohawk terror. In 1643, his troops crossed the
river to Pavonia, New Jersey, and massacred
about a hundred Algonquians as they slept in
their tents. Outraged and seeking vengeance,
the other tribes in the area rose as one and
savaged the Dutch settlements for two years.
Left untouched, lest the gun supply be cut off,
were the trading posts of the *bosch-lopers*, or
woodsrunners, whose gun business was at the
root of the trouble.

Kieft was not well loved, even by the Dutch.
One of his countrymen, Maryn Adrianzen, tried
to assassinate him with a flintlock pistol, but
failed when a bystander jammed his thumb between hammer and frizzen and prevented it
from firing.

Kieft eventually was deposed and replaced by
Peter Stuyvesant, who attempted to restore
good relations with all the Indians and thereby
retrieve the Dutch position. He was too late.

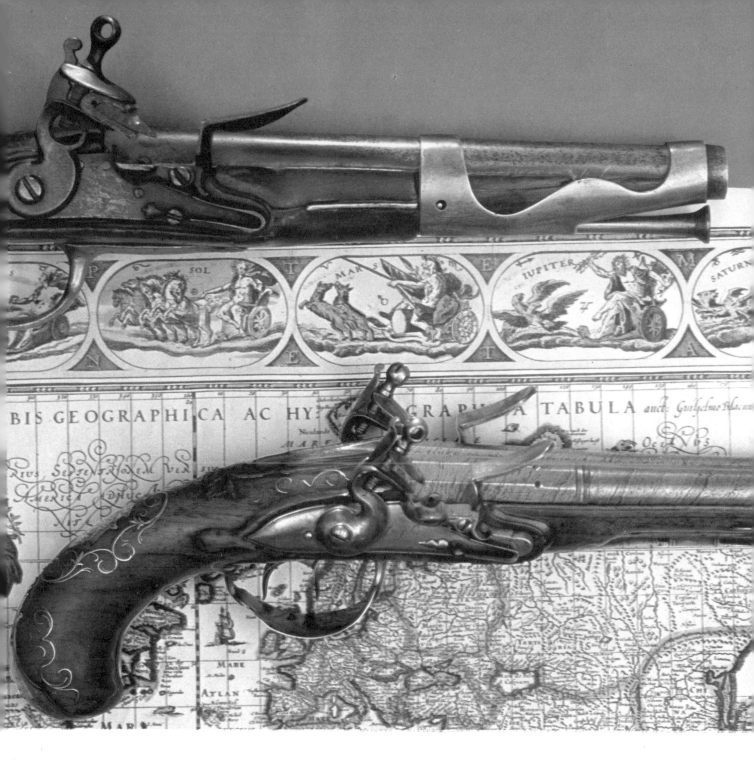

In 1664, an English fleet besieged Manhattan and forced a surrender by which the Dutch lost all possessions and influence in America.

The French, trading the more highly favored flintlock at more generous prices of two to five beavers, swept far and wide from their bases along the St. Lawrence. First to be supplied were the Hurons, the Ottawas, the Algonquians, and the Montagnais, and when the redoubtable Iroquois — remembering Champlain — literally decimated these tribes, the French moved further west. They infiltrated into Lake Michigan and through what are today the states of Michigan, Minnesota, Wisconsin, Illinois, and Indiana. They coursed the valley of the Mississippi to the Gulf and reached out into Arkansas and Texas.

And they brought back a treasure in furs.

The great French explorer, René Robert Cavelier, Sieur de La Salle, noted wryly, "The savages take better care of us French than of their own children. From us only can they get guns."

The English, who encountered fierce resistance from the first, came more slowly to the gun trade. At Jamestown, save for a peaceful interval after pioneer tobacco planter John Rolfe married Pocahontas, the settlers were under constant attack, first by Powhatan and then by his brother, the virulent Opechancanough. It was Opechancanough who, in 1622, sent his warriors into the settlement to palaver and trade and then, on signal, to slaughter some three hundred and fifty whites. And it was Opechancanough, aged and confined to a litter, but still bright-eyed with hate, who struck again twenty-two years later to kill five hundred more.

At Plymouth the situation was little better. Excursions and alarms were frequent. By the time of the Pequot War in 1637, quarter was neither asked nor given. In the battle near Groton, Connecticut, which ended the conflict, the English and their Indian allies slew eight hundred Pequots in one bloody hour.

Yet despite the harrowing lessons of experience, the attraction of profits in the fur trade was irresistible. By the 1640's Plymouth and Boston merchants were beginning to trade. With the fall of New Netherlands in the 1660's they took over the Dutch trade with the Iroquois. In 1670 the Hudson's Bay Company was founded. Meanwhile, Englishmen to the south, no more mindful of the bloody past—and heedless of the bloody future to come—pushed out from Virginia and the Carolinas, along the Appalachian trails, arming Choctaws and Chickasaws, Creeks and Cherokees as they went. And as the traders broke new ground, new settlements took root and grew.

By the 1670's, in the Northeast, the pressure of the white population was great and the Indian's grievances were many. His lands had diminished, frequently taken from him by trickery and guile. The burgeoning cattle of the settlers overran their bounds and trampled Indian corn. Tribes were displaced westward into wilderness country the white man had not yet learned to covet. Or if they stayed, they found themselves held to account by the white man's laws, yet rarely the beneficiary of his justice. Bitter in their hearts, the surviving Indians grew restive.

Alarmed, the English attempted to reinforce the laws—long overlooked and ignored—prohibiting the delivery of firearms to the savage, particularly the nearby Wampanoags of King Philip, successor to Massasoit, the Englishman's friend. Philip protested. It was now possible for Indians dependent on guns to starve for lack of them. The English turned a deaf ear.

In 1675, the Algonquians of southern New England formed an alliance—one of the greatest efforts toward cooperative action in Indian history—and turned ruthlessly on the whites. Thus began King Philip's War, a devastating conflict in which more than six hundred settlers, one-sixth of the male population of the region, were killed. But the English muddled through. With the help of their flintlocks and the inability of the Indians to provision themselves adequately for a long campaign, they won out. King Philip was trapped in the Assowomsett Swamp, in Massachusetts. According to an eye-witness account, it was a misty morning when they shot him with an old-style, dog-lock musket.

By the early years of the eighteenth century, the Atlantic slopes of the mountains from Maine to Florida were rid of hostile Indians and firmly in the hands of the settlers. Now the battle line moved west, and here the advancing English

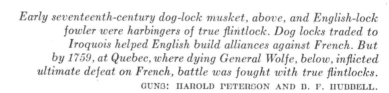

Early seventeenth-century dog-lock musket, above, and English-lock fowler were harbingers of true flintlock. Dog locks traded to Iroquois helped English build alliances against French. But by 1759, at Quebec, where dying General Wolfe, below, inflicted ultimate defeat on French, battle was fought with true flintlocks.
GUNS: HAROLD PETERSON AND B. F. HUBBELL.

bellied up against the entrenched French. A series of brushfire wars was fought: King William's, Queen Anne's, King George's. And then, on May 28, 1754, as a twenty-two-year-old soldier named George Washington led a company of Virginians to victory over a small French unit near Great Meadows, Pennsylvania, the French and Indian War began.

Nine years it lasted, for the mother countries quickly sensed that this was the battle that would decide all. Regulars of the armies of Britain and France were poured into the Colonies. Settlers fought, and backwoodsmen. And, fighting first on one side and then on the other, were the Indians of a score of tribes.

In the West it was wilderness war—raid and ambush, the intaking of strategic forts and the pinching off of trade routes. It was full-dress rehearsal for the Revolutionary War ahead, had the British professionals chosen to heed the signs. Rogers' Rangers came to prominence in the North as the first of America's guerrilla fighters. The luckless General Braddock, en route to seize Fort Duquesne, learned what could happen to parade-ground formations seeking to fight a stand-up battle on a forest trail.

Yet the important campaigns were in the East. General Jeffrey Amherst (who, among other things, suggested that Indians be given blankets infected with smallpox germs) and General James Wolfe captured the key fortress of Louisburg; then Fort Frontenac fell and Canada was cut in two. The end came with young Wolfe's brilliant victory over Montcalm on the Plains of Abraham, before Quebec, in 1759. ("They run! See how they run!" cried the English. "Now God be praised," murmured Wolfe, thrice wounded and ebbing fast. "I will die in peace.") New France was done.

But the fighting would not down. With French guns no longer available and the English now refusing to trade, the Algonquians, Wyandots, and Senecas formed a confederation under Chief Pontiac of the Ottawas to get weapons. He and his warriors were finally driven off to the Illinois territory in the 1760's. The flintlock and the English were masters of the continent.

Throughout a century or more of war, the gun had proved itself the tool of survival. The better the gun, the better a man's chances of seeing another day. Frontiersmen, gunsmiths, and manufacturers were beginning to bend themselves to the task of improving the Colonies' most vital implement. Through the French and Indian War there were no radical changes in flintlock design, although slight improvements were made to increase range and accuracy. Deadliness of fire also increased when it was found that several buckshot could be rammed in with the ball.

Perhaps the most significant change was the development of fixed ammunition. Powder charges were wrapped in tubes of paper and packed in cartridge boxes, which facilitated loading. Next, the ball was attached to the paper powder container, so that the entire charge could be seated at one thrust.

The Kentucky rifle had appeared and was making its mark, although in this period it was neither the standard weapon of the professional soldier nor a trade gun for the Indian.

Now history rushed toward a new war whose opening shot would be heard 'round the world. The American and his gun would be ready.

Queen Anne musket, right, built about 1690, preceded the Brown Bess, left. Early Brown Bess (1725-60) was later modified, served both sides in the Revolution with deadly distinction and, then, the British Army for fifty years more.
GUNS: HAROLD PETERSON. PHOTO BY ROBERT MOTTAR

CHAPTER TWO TOOLS

OF SURVIVAL

These are an excellent species of light infantry. They use a peculiar kind of musket, called a rifle. It has circular . . . grooves within the barrel, and carries a ball with great exactness to great distances. JOHN ADAMS

PAGES 34 AND 35: *An American arm of Revolution was the French Charleville musket. Later Kentucky rifle (shown with tiger-stripe maple stock) was used in War of 1812. Stone wall is on Sugar Loaf Hill, New York, site of patriot fort.*
GUNS: WEST POINT MUSEUM.
PHOTO BY ROBERT MOTTAR

ABOVE: *Frontiersmen lived by the gun. Buckskin-clad hunters return with whitetail deer buck and wild turkeys, taken with Kentucky rifles.*
LITHOGRAPH BY CURRIER AND IVES.
COURTESY KENNEDY GALLERIES

On the eve of the Revolution, life in the Colonies was rigorous but thriving. Primarily it was an agricultural economy. Tobacco was the big crop in Virginia and Maryland, rice in the Carolinas, elsewhere wheat and corn. Manufactures —some necessities and most niceties—still came from England and there was a brisk mercantile trade with the homeland, although under onerous tariffs and restrictions that would become one of the prime causes of the war.

New England ships dotted the seas, laden with American exports: tar, pitch, turpentine, indigo, furs, dried meat, salt fish, boxes and barrels, and even a sectional house, an early pre-fab. They returned with molasses from the

West Indies for the distillation of potent New England rum and they hauled African slaves into the southern states. By 1775, there were half a million Negroes in America, representing about twenty per cent of the population.

There was work for everyone. Artisans were in great demand: carpenters, smiths, coopers, wheelwrights, and stonecutters. And in the growing cities, where fortunes were being made and society was taking on a patina of English gentility, the craftsmen — silversmiths, glass blowers, clock- and cabinet-makers — were enhancing the grace of colonial homes with articles of consummate taste and skill. This was the time when today's antiques were fresh-minted.

It was a life that had its charm, although it demanded much and hazard was never far off. Pirates found haven in New York harbor. Merchants and sea captains engaged in smuggling to circumvent British law and keep their trade flourishing. And off beyond the rural village, a hard-won patch of civilization, was wilderness and the Indian. Farmers plowed with muskets at hand. Communities formed a militia of citizen-soldiers and many a village green had its powder house. "Muster days" were required by law and every adult male was expected to answer the call with musket, powder, ball, and cartouche box in which he carried the paper cartridges he made.

The frontiersman lived in the backwoods
with none of the amenities. For him life was
what it had been for the settlers who landed
a century or more before. Homesite and farm-
land had to be cleared from virgin fields and
forest. The treacherous Indian was full of vin-
egar and might strike at any hour. Here was the
picket line, the edge of the battle.

These pioneers were plain, taciturn men, jeal-
ous of their independence and ready to work or
fight to preserve it. Time has invested them
with a glamor they probably did not have. But
no romantic imagination could summon up a
dream of freedom more complete than the actu-
ality of their daily lives. They lived mainly on
game, using the large-caliber smoothbore musket with fine shot for birds and small animals,
and with a single ball for bigger game—and Indians. The rifle was highly desirable because of its
greater accuracy, but it was costly and in short
supply. The frontiersman who owned only the
musket yearned for the day when he could add
the deadlier, long-range rifle to his armament.

THE KENTUCKY RIFLE

The concept of the rifle—cutting spiral grooves
in the barrel to impart spin to the ball and, thus,
greater accuracy over longer range—was not new
in the frontiersman's day. Rifling—from the German *riefeln*—had been known in Europe as far
back as the late 1400's. But in its primitive forms
the rifle was not popular.

As always, the new-found advantage had
attendant disadvantages that temporarily canceled it out. Cutting the grooves was quite
expensive. The tight fit of the ball, which was
essential to the rifle's efficiency, made loading
a slow and laborious process that frequently
resulted in a snapped ramrod and, consequently, a useless gun.

Yet it was from this pack of problems that
the lovely Kentucky rifle eventually emerged.
For undeniably the rifle was accurate, and it
was this factor that German and Swiss armorers,
settling around Lancaster and Reading in the
1720's, started with. Slowly, over a period of
fifty years or more, the cumbersome rifle was
altered and refined by the pressures and requirements of the frontier.

The early Kentuckys showed their German ancestry in a fairly straight stock that was quite thick through the grip and the entire butt section. Calibers ranged from .45 to .60. Gradually, however, the demand increased for a rifle of lighter weight and higher velocity. The frontiersman traveled on foot; he wanted a weapon that handled easily in the woods, extended the effective range without sacrificing accuracy, and economized on powder and ball, which was expensive to buy and heavy to carry.

The gunsmiths responded by reducing the bore and the over-all diameter of the barrel. By the end of the Revolution, the popular calibers were .40 to .45. The smaller bores lessened recoil and permitted the heavy butt plate to be dis-

carded. The stock was slimmed to a minimum and the graceful forms of the classic Kentuckys began to appear.

The slender barrels were lengthened to as much as forty-eight inches in order to assure complete consumption of the powder charge, although these extreme lengths were soon found to be unwieldy in timberland and brush and were cut back, often by the rifleman himself. The popular standard became about forty-two inches, give or take a little.

Heavier powder charges were used. Daniel Boone, loading his flintlock with "six fingers" of black powder to discomfit Indians who thought themselves out of range, quite possibly achieved a muzzle velocity of better than 2,000 feet per

Gunsmiths, migrating from the Rhenish Palatinate to Pennsylvania.
brought heavy hunting rifles, like gun, above. From it
developed graceful Kentuckys, like the silver-inlaid rifle, top,
and the maple-stocked, brass-mounted pistol, bottom right.
PHOTO DETAIL BY ARNOLD NEWMAN. COURTESY LIFE

second—a speed not appreciably increased until the development of smokeless powder and jacketed bullets about a century later.

Of course, only so much black powder would burn in a barrel of practical length. Overloads were avoided not because they necessarily endangered the barrel, but because excess powder simply would be blown out, unburned. Smart riflemen utilized this fact to gauge maximum powder charges precisely. They would fire various loads over a clean expanse of snow until they found one that did not speckle the whiteness with unburned powder grains.

The ball was just slightly smaller than the bore. To assure a snug fit, it was wrapped in a patch of greased linen or very thin buckskin that accommodated itself to the rifling as the charge was pushed home with a thin hickory rod. When fired, the patch rotated with the rifling, spun the ball on its way to the target, and dropped off immediately after leaving the muzzle. An additional function of the patch was to provide a gas-seal between ball and bore in order to give full impetus to the shot. Insertion of a patch with each load also helped to clean caked powder from the rifling, although, even so, the bore had to be swabbed with a water-soaked patch after ten or a dozen shots to keep

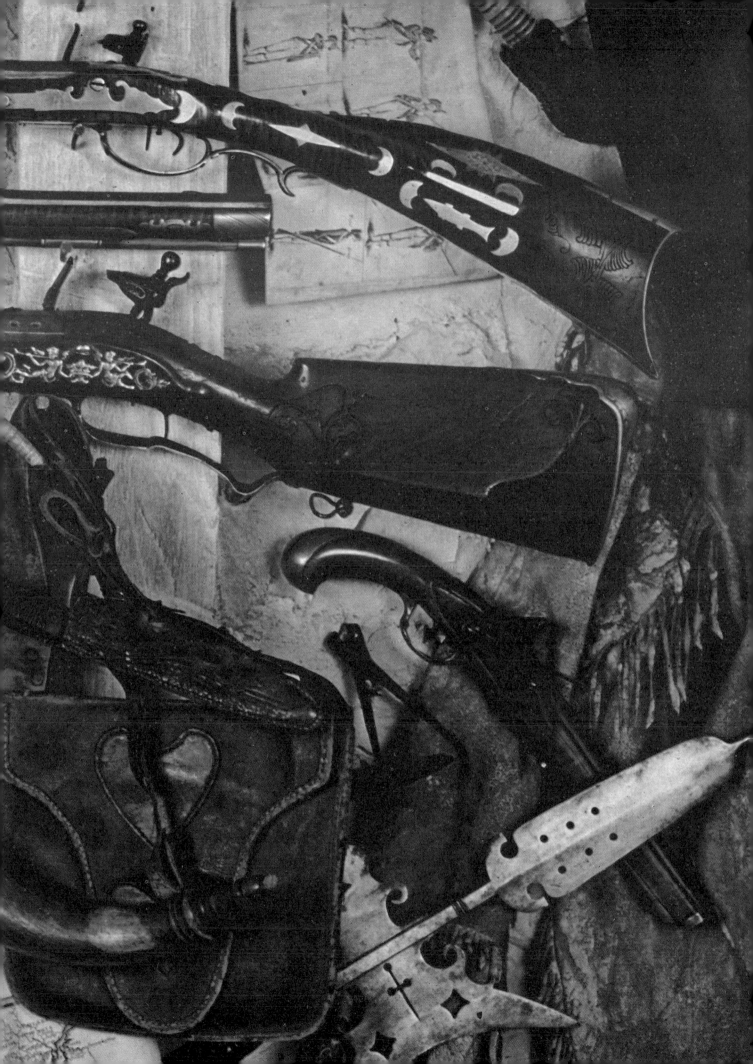

the barrel from fouling. Patches were kept in a box set into the stock. The ramrod, when not in use, was held to the underside of the barrel by two or three metal tubes called thimbles.

The Kentucky was Pennsylvania-born and universally used along the frontier. Kentuckians had no claim on it that others did not enjoy. In its day it was simply the long rifle. It was designated as "the Kentucky" by gun lovers after the Civil War, most likely because of the exploits of Dan'l Boone, who used it most effectively in opening up the Kentucky territory. In any event, the Pennsylvania-Kentucky rifle was and still is an efficient weapon, and for the century of its greatest use it was without doubt the most accurate long-range rifle in the world. In the hands of a man who knows how to load and shoot it, it still can give many modern rifles a run for their money. The frontiersman could, with ease, pot a squirrel high in an oak tree or drop a deer at 100 yards and he thought nothing of putting a ball through a redskin's head at 200 yards under good conditions.

It was the target shooter who coaxed the Kentucky rifle to its ultimate pinnacle as a weapon of accuracy and precision. In the second half of the eighteenth century "shooting at a mark" was a national pastime.

For the pioneer lad the mark was a chip from a log or a knot on a tree. He began shooting as soon as he could hold a rifle and he learned to load and fire well enough to kill game for the family table by the age of twelve.

For the menfolk, there were turkey shoots and beef shoots, events important enough to be declared holidays and to draw every male in the area into competition. Live turkeys, tied to a stake, were fired at from distances of fifteen rods (about 250 feet) offhand or twenty rods (330 feet) from a rest. The first man to draw blood won the bird.

In beef shooting, each competitor furnished his own target, a board with a cross marked on its center. One shot was fired for the first choice cut of the beef, the winner, of course, being the man closest to the center of his cross. A second shot was fired for the second-best cut, and so on, until the animal was reduced to hide and hoofs.

These backwoodsmen became excellent shots. When uncouth companies of riflemen from Virginia, Pennsylvania, and Maryland rallied to Boston at the beginning of the Revolution, they took the city folk's breath away with the accuracy of their shooting. One Virginian plunked eight consecutive shots through a five-by-seven-inch target at sixty yards. And an entire company placed shots, one after another, into a seven-inch target at 250 yards.

For the skilled rifleman of the time, proficiency in aiming and firing his weapon was not enough. He also had to be an expert in loading, the fussy talent that lay at the heart of accuracy. He cast his own balls, carefully trimming off the "sprue," the small irregularity left where the hot metal entered the mold. Finicky shooters placed the trimmed spot upward when the ball was seated, so that the "true" surface would rest against the powder. Patches were carefully cut from "shirt-bosom" linen, generally conceded to be the best, or linen-rag paper. Bear oil and tallow were used to coat the patches.

In seating the ball, great care was taken not to rap the charge too hard with the ramrod, lest the contour of the ball be damaged and accuracy thereby lessened. Yet the fit had to be snug. A considerable nicety of touch had to be developed.

The type of powder used was of great importance. Black powder of FFG or FFFG granulation was the rule, and great store was set on powder compounded with willow charcoal. The finer the granulation, the more certain the ignition. When fine powder was unavailable, the

Indians, ever envious of the white man's weapons, got their arms
by bartering furs or allegiance. To gain warrior's friendship,
the British provided guns like English trade musket of 1760, top;
Americans made the carbine or Indian musket, Model 1807,
distributed by the Indian Department of young U.S. Government.
Peace pipe tomahawk was used for ceremony and war.
GUNS: GERALD FOX. TOMAHAWK: WILLIAM SWEET.

PHOTO BY ROBERT MOTTAR

frontiersman would crush his coarse powder with a rolling pin, or with mortar and pestle.

Good, stable gunpowder whose granules of charcoal, saltpeter, and sulphur were well mixed, that did not congeal, and that burned evenly and completely, was hard to come by. Further, the prohibitive taxes imposed on it by the British before the Revolution prompted the colonists to undertake elaborate ruses and evasions.

In calculating the size of a load, one of the precepts was: "One and a half calibers of powder for rifles under 70 gauge (.40-caliber) and two calibers for those over that gauge." Thus, a .36-caliber rifle would use thirty-six plus eighteen, or fifty-four grains of powder. A 52-gauge (.45-caliber) gun would use ninety grains. For the backwoodsman who could not weigh out a charge, the rule-of-thumb was to place a ball on the palm of the hand and pour out a cone of powder sufficient to cover it. This method gave good results, although the charge works out to something less than the amount prescribed by the caliber rule.

At their best, the "Kaintuck" rifles were supreme examples of the gunsmith's art. Great care was lavished on them; they were a proud personal possession and never traded with the Indian. The hills of Pennsylvania were scoured for the finest "tiger-stripe," or flame-grained curly maple, for stocks. Birch and cherry also were highly regarded native woods and occasionally black walnut was used. Brass mountings gave beauty and serviceability to the piece. They were craftsmanlike as well, although critics have pointed out that the workmanship of even the best American-made Kentucky locks was inferior to that available in fine London-made weapons of the time. The truth is that most Kentuckys were made with locks purchased from English makers.

Perhaps the most remarkable feature of this famous and influential weapon was its complete lack of uniformity. Of the many hundreds that survive in museums and collections, no two are ever alike. While conforming to a general pattern, they all vary in details.

These rifles were highly prized by their owners and a gratifyingly large number of them has been preserved, in excellent condition, by museums and collectors. All of them are redolent of

the frontier and the stern purpose of the men who carried them. No weapon, before or since, has been so imbued with an American character, an American personality.

THE FLINTLOCK: MUSKET OR RIFLE?

The Kentucky rifle was the wilderness weapon. Fine performer though it was, it made little headway in the established settlements of the Colonies where the field tactics of the British regular were the accepted military doctrine and were assiduously copied by the militiamen and their leaders.

These tactics were admirable in conception and wrung a maximum of effectiveness from the Redcoat's basic arm, the famous Brown Bess musket. By the late 1770's, this was a .75-caliber, smoothbore flintlock with a round barrel thirty-nine inches long. Its stock was walnut, its mountings brass, and its ramrod of iron. An acid bath pickled the unfinished barrel iron and left it the uniformly brown color from which its name derived. "Blueing," as we know it today, did not exist. The original model, somewhat longer in

the barrel, was selected by John Churchill, Duke of Marlborough, in the reign of Queen Anne, and with only minor modifications it served the British army well for more than a hundred years.

It weighed about ten pounds with bayonet and was neither handy nor particularly accurate. With a close-fitting ball it could do quite well, but with the undersized ball and paper cartridge of the eighteenth century it was fairly wild.

Major George Hanger, an intelligent and observant British officer whose interest in firepower problems was somewhat ahead of his time, rated the musket as accurate between 80 and 100 yards, but said: ". . . a soldier must be very unfortunate indeed who shall be wounded by a musket at 150 yards . . . and as to firing at a man at 200 yards . . . you may just as well fire at the moon and have the same hopes of hitting your object."

This was not a serious deficiency. In the battles it fought, the musket was not required to function at much more than 100 yards. The objective was a hail of fire, not pinpoint accuracy. Infantrymen in those days stood shoulder to shoulder in files, two or three lines deep, with file-closers grouped behind, ready to step into the places of the fallen. They fired straight ahead, or to right or left, on command and then charged, with bayonets fixed. Or, on defense, they reloaded as fast as possible and ripped off another volley.

To load, the musket man simply plucked a cartridge from the container—a box or a pouch—at his waist, bit off the end, sprinkled some powder into the flash pan for priming, dumped the rest of the charge into the muzzle, together with the paper and the ball, and rammed it home. A well-trained soldier could load and fire four shots a minute. At this rate, a regiment of 500 riflemen could fire two volleys of a thousand balls into an enemy before he had advanced a hundred yards. For even denser fire, buckshot could be loaded with ball. General Washington recommended that his troops use "one musket ball and four or eight buck Shott, according to the strength of their pieces."

Fighting this kind of war, the rifle was at a distinct disadvantage. It was not fitted for a bayonet, and loose powder and ball were a much slower load than the all-in-one paper cartridge. Washington, deploring the lack of a bayonet, insisted that Colonel Daniel Morgan's Virginia riflemen carry spears. Military writing of the time is full of firmly stated opinion condemning the rifle except for scouting, sniping, or light-infantry use.

Major Hanger, reporting a clash between Morgan's men and a Colonel Abercrombie's

light infantry in Pennsylvania during the Revolution, had this to say:

"Not one [rifleman] out of four had time to fire, and those that did had no time given them to load again: the light infantry not only dispersed them instantly, but drove them for miles over the country. They never attacked, or even looked at, our light infantry again without a regular force to support them." Regular force, of course, meant regulars equipped with fast-firing muskets. (Aside from the musket's tactical superiority, there was involved here the amateur's awe of the disciplined professional. The Americans continually were amazed at the hard-nosed British regular's unflinching poise in the face of massed gunfire and at his standing firmly in ranks when it might suit him better to run.)

On the other hand, Hanger acknowledged the rifle's astonishing accuracy. On one occasion, a marksman at a distance Hanger later paced off as "a full 400 yards" fired a shot that passed between the Major and his Colonel and felled the horse of a bugler stationed behind them. It is not likely that the horse was the primary target, but the fact that anything at all could be hit at that range inspired respect.

"I am certain," Hanger wrote, "that, provided an American rifleman was to get a perfect aim at 300 yards at me standing still, he most undoubtedly would hit me, unless it was a very windy day."

THE WAR OF INDEPENDENCE

The issue was never resolved. By and large, the Revolution was a war fought by smooth-bore muskets and at close quarters, in the European manner. "Don't fire until you see the whites of their eyes," Colonel William Prescott's immortal order at Bunker Hill, had at least as much to do with the range and accuracy of his

men's muskets as with the fact that they were short of powder and ball. The rifle played its part, but mostly in a supporting role. It was paramount only in a few engagements where terrain favored the hit-and-run tactics and bull's-eye marksmanship of the frontier.

Not only tactics, but convention dictated the use of the musket. It had been the prevailing gun in the Colonies for many years, the gun most colonists were most familiar with. This is not to say that American arms were in any way standardized, but simply that they were flintlock muskets, usually of British make. Calibers varied. Repairs frequently were made with parts salvaged from guns of an earlier vintage, or forged according to the whim or the ingenuity of the colonial gunsmith.

It was a motley collection of weapons that stood against the Redcoats at Concord, Lexington, and Bunker Hill, and the Continental Congress quickly empowered local Committees of Safety to spur the production of arms for the patriots who were mobilizing.

The so-called "Committee of Safety muskets" are a rarity today. Essentially they were a stop-gap effort, and not many of them could have been made by the Colonies' relatively few gunsmiths in the three-year period (1775-78) before Committee functions were absorbed by other agencies of the young government. But it is interesting to note that, despite minor variations, the weapon the Committees so desperately sought was a .75-caliber flintlock with a forty-two- to forty-six-inch barrel that in all ways resembled the Brown Bess.

Meanwhile, emissaries of the Congress were dealing for guns in Holland, Belgium, and most importantly France. To the end of the French and Indian War, of course, France had been an enemy and many of the Revolution's leaders had fought to bring about her downfall. Now, however, the logic of politics dictated that she should befriend the struggling colonists, and befriend them—in hopes of belting Britain and preserving French holdings in Louisiana—she did. All told, some 100,000 French arms were provided the Continentals at about $5 apiece, about a quarter of them being smuggled in even before the alliance was a fact.

For the most part, these were Model 1763 "Charleville" muskets of .69 caliber, which had a forty-four-and-a-half-inch barrel and weighed about ten pounds. The first regulation French musket was the Model 1717, which subsequently endured fifteen design changes, most of them minute; Charleville was one of several government arsenals. It is clear, therefore, that the term "Charleville musket" covers several possible models and sources.

The French product was a good weapon, quite on a par with the Brown Bess, and the Americans were sufficiently pleased with it to make it the prototype of their own first regulation weapon, the U.S. Model 1795 musket.

Throughout the war there were many engagements that illustrated clearly the special advantages of musket and rifle.

The rifleman's greatest success was at King's Mountain, near the border between North and South Carolina, in October, 1780. Here, a force of 1,100 American Loyalists under a capable Scots Major named Patrick Ferguson was surprised on a wooded plateau by nine hundred dead-eye backwoodsmen. The riflemen called

Flintlocks for war: Scottish Black Watch
pistol, 1760, top; cavalry musketoon, 1680, left;
British enlisted man's sword; American blunderbuss, 1725,
center; Committee of Safety musket, 1775, right.
GUNS: HAROLD PETERSON, EXCEPT MUSKETOON—HERB GLASS.
PHOTO BY ROBERT MOTTAR

General Daniel Morgan
INDEPENDENCE HALL

Morgan's Virginia rifle corps—plus a brigade of New Hampshiremen—that pinned down the British flank while Benedict Arnold led a hell-for-leather attack on the center. The British broke and "Gentleman Johnny" Burgoyne surrendered. The Americans reaped some six thousand prisoners, forty-two cannon, five thousand muskets, and stores of ammunition One of Morgan's men put the rifle's stamp on the battle by killing the able British General, Simon Fraser, with a shot from 300 yards.

The finest example of expert utilization of musket and rifle together was the Battle of Cowpens in January, 1781, another instance of the genius of Daniel Morgan. General Nathaniel Greene was fencing with Lord Cornwallis in the Carolinas and as part of the maneuvering Morgan was sent to threaten British outposts in the western part of the states. Cornwallis dispatched Colonel Tarleton after him with 1,100 men. They met at the Cowpens, in South Carolina, a few miles southwest of King's Mountain and just west of the Broad River.

The battlefield was a long slope leading to a rise. Behind this was a depression, then another rise, 150 yards beyond, and then the river, cutting off all hope of retreat. It was singular terrain for a rifleman to choose, but Morgan was rarely orthodox. His force of nine hundred included many militiamen, and as he viewed the field he is reported to have said that he could ask for only one thing better: to be surrounded by the enemy, so his fellows couldn't run.

When Tarleton hove to, Morgan placed his skirmishers 150 yards in front of the first rise and ordered them to fire at least two accurate rifle volleys before retreating. On the first hill he stationed his Maryland and Delaware regulars and some militia, all armed with muskets. Behind the second hill he placed his cavalry, under Colonel William Washington, the General's bold

the tune. In familiar fashion, they crept through the forest fringing the plateau and picked off the beleaguered Tories, one by one.

Ferguson, believing with reason that the frontiersmen would run for cover before a charge, attempted to get out of the trap behind a wave of bayonets. It worked, but only briefly. Melting into the trees, the riflemen again took up their stand and chopped the enemy from long range. Among those who fell was Ferguson. Realizing that the battle was lost, he tried to cut his way through the American lines and escape. A rifle ball stopped him. As he fell from his horse at least seven more sharpshooters' bullets found their mark and he died ignobly, with one foot still caught in his stirrup.

The Tories surrendered. In one hour of fighting, two hundred and fifty of them had been killed and one hundred and sixty-three wounded. Seven hundred and fifteen were taken prisoner. The Americans suffered twenty-eight dead and sixty-two wounded.

The Second Battle of Saratoga, in October, 1777, also saw a prominent part played by the rifle. Here it was the brisk shooting of Daniel

and able second cousin.

The British advanced. The riflemen stood their ground and brought off several volleys with fine effect. Then they retired to the left, around the shoulder of the hills, where they re-formed.

The British left reached around the right flank of the Maryland regulars, who shifted with it. Tarleton decided the rebels were retreating and hustled his men forward in some disorder. At that moment, Colonel Washington's horse came wheeling around from the left, to pass through the skirmishers' original position and take the British from the rear. The riflemen, regrouped, swarmed around on the right to meet the British left flank. The musket men poured a volley at thirty yards' range and then charged down the slope with bayonets fixed.

The British collapse was immediate and complete. Tarleton came within a whisker of being cut down by the saber of Colonel Washington himself, but escaped with remnants of his force.

Some two hundred and seventy of his 1,100 men were killed and wounded, and six hundred taken prisoner. Two fieldpieces and eight hundred muskets also fell to the Americans. Morgan's losses were twelve killed and sixty-two wounded.

These battles were elements of the major campaigns that crisscrossed the settled East. But the Revolution was also fought beyond the mountains, among the forts and back-country outposts of the trade routes and trappers' trails. Here, some thirty thousand Indian warriors of a dozen tribes, armed with British guns, fought to uphold the British King. They opposed the settlement of Kentucky and disrupted American shipping along the Ohio River.

Beating them back was work for the rifle. In a familiar setting against a familiar foe, the rifle held its own. Chief among the campaigners were the rugged backwoodsmen of General George Rogers Clark who scored their greatest triumphs at Vincennes with long Kentuckys that found

Minute Man—Committee of Safety musket in hand—hastens to call of war. Wife fastens his knapsack.

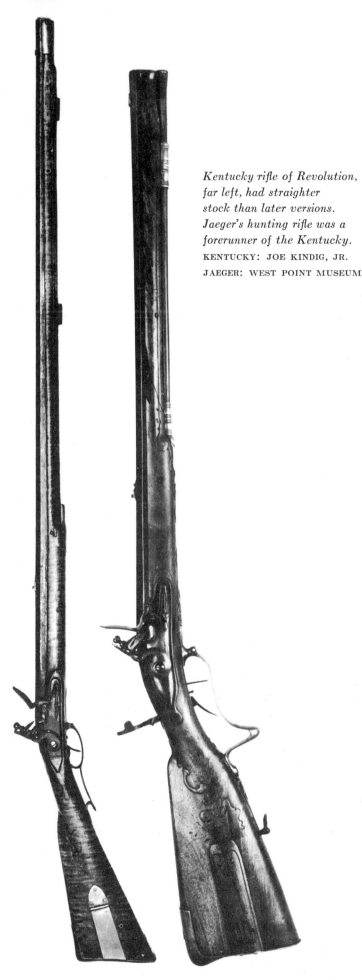

their mark through embrasures and gun slits in the fortress walls. Clark's series of scuffles with the British and their Indian allies, if not decisive, at least thwarted the effort to contain the Americans on the eastern seaboard and left the way clear for the postwar migrations of the citizens of the United States.

In addition to the American rifle and the standardized infantry muskets used on both sides, there was a spate of other weapons that saw service during the Revolution.

British officers carried the fusil, rather than the musket, in the field. It differed from the standard weapon only in being lighter, somewhat better made, and likely to have its mountings ornamented or engraved. British troops occasionally were armed with smoothbore carbines, or musketoons, the terms being used interchangeably and signifying, again, a musket conforming generally to the infantry standard, but with a .66-caliber bore and a barrel drastically shortened to twenty-eight and a half inches.

French officers also were provided with fusils and musketoons and these weapons appeared on the American side after 1777, when France became an ally. The French musketoon, which was standardized in the Model 1763, had a round, thirty-one-inch barrel stocked along its entire length. The stock subsequently was shortened, and the barrel lengthened slightly to thirty-three and a half inches.

German muskets and rifles also appeared with the mercenaries enlisted in the British cause. The world remembers these troops as Hessians, although many a German princeling besides the Margrave of Hessen-Kassel impressed his subjects for a price to meet Britain's need for manpower. The German weapons were as varied in quality as the troops that carried them; the common features of most of them were a heavy stock and a sizable butt, a large lock, and an elliptical brass front sight. German riflemen were a different matter. The *Jaeger* was a trained woodsman and an expert shot. The gun he carried was shorter than its American counterpart, generally measuring only forty-four or forty-six inches over all, and had a bigger lock, like the German musket. Otherwise it loaded like an American rifle, performed about as well, and was used under similar conditions—as support for musketry.

The bell-mouthed blunderbuss saw action principally as a naval weapon. All art and literature to the contrary notwithstanding, this was not the weapon of the Pilgrims. Certainly the passengers and crew of the *Mayflower* never saw one. It was little used before 1700 and attained its greatest prominence during the eighteenth century. It took an enormous load of "buck Shott" and cut a devastating swath over a wide area at close range. It was used to quell uprisings or repel boarders at sea.

BREECHLOADERS AND REPEATERS

The men who conceived the gun dreamed from the very beginning of an ultimate firearm that could fire multiple shots without pause and be charged more quickly than the muzzle-loader. And while it was not until nearly the middle of the nineteenth century that the combination of quick loading and rapid fire was incorporated into truly efficient and reliable weapons, inventors were remarkably close to the solution nearly three hundred years before.

Cannon that loaded at the breech were in use before the development of the handgun, and the first repeating weapons appeared in the first part of the sixteenth century. The mechanisms were primitive, yet the principles were sound and clearly anticipated the magazines and revolving cylinders that eventually would realize the intention. The problem that plagued the designers

and confounded their efforts was the leakage or gas and flame from the joints and seams of the breech, which dissipated the thrust behind the ball and frequently ignited the other charges in the breech to the great detriment of the shooter. These early designs also were guns of great bulk and extremely clumsy to use since each chamber in the big cylinder required a separate frizzen and flash pan.

In America, the first breech-loading repeater, known as the "Cookson type," appeared in the early eighteenth century. Manufactured by John Cookson of Massachusetts, it was, however, apparently the model devised by an earlier John Cookson of London, who seems to have copied the mid-seventeenth-century British patent of one Abraham Hill.

The Hill mechanism employed a vertical cylinder in the breech which conducted powder and ball from separate cavities in the butt to the bore. By seesawing the muzzle up and down as the cylinder was rotated from magazine to bore,

George Washington's silver-mounted flintlock pistols were made by Hawkins of London. Pewter plate was used in Washington household at West Point. GUNS: WEST POINT MUSEUM. PHOTO BY ROBERT MOTTAR

a kind of gravity feed introduced the charge, in proper sequence, to the barrel, filled the priming pan, and set the piece at half-cock.

It was an ingenious weapon, although requiring craftsmanship of a high order to make the moving parts align exactly and fit tightly. Consequently, it was too expensive for all but the wealthy sportsman.

The only breechloader that saw service during the Revolution was an exceptional rifle designed by the redoubtable Major Patrick Ferguson, who died at King's Mountain. The action was breath-takingly simple. Instead of a cylinder, the Ferguson had a vertical screw-plug which could be lowered by the turning of a lever to expose a chamber in the breech. The ball was inserted and rolled forward until stopped by the lands (the raised tracks) of the rifled barrel; the powder charge followed. When the plug was screwed back to seal the breech and the pan

primed, it was ready to fire.

It weighed only seven and a half pounds, was sighted for ranges of from 100 to 500 yards, and could be fired six times a minute. Given an opportunity to demonstrate its capabilities before a military board in England, Ferguson, for openers, fired for four or five minutes, in a high wind and pelting rain, at the steady rate of four shots a minute. He then advanced the rate to six shots a minute, and for a clincher fired four times a minute while advancing at the rate of four miles an hour. As for accuracy, he missed the target, at 200 yards, only three times throughout the entire demonstration.

It was an incredible performance, one calculated to upset contemporary military doctrine completely. Equally incredibly, however, its use by the British during the Revolution was confined to one or two hundred men of Ferguson's own command. The thought of an alert high command in London ordering an immediate switch from the Brown Bess to the Ferguson for the Redcoats in America leads to some frightening conjectures as to the possible subsequent course of the Revolutionary War.

The rifle was not Ferguson's only chance to alter history. The story is told that at Brandywine he was ranging ahead of the British lines with three of his best Ferguson-armed riflemen when he heard hoofbeats approaching and took cover. Peering out, he saw a pair of Continental officers, one wearing a "remarkable, large cocked hat" and obviously of high rank, the other in the uniform of a French hussar.

Ferguson's first impulse was to snipe at the horsemen from ambush, and he so ordered his men. Then his sporting instincts got the better of him and he canceled the order. A Scotsman raised in the best tradition of the Highland grouse moors, he knew that no gentleman ever potted a sitting bird. He next decided to capture the pair. Stepping from cover, he ordered the Continentals to dismount. The hussar cried a warning. The officer in the large hat wheeled and made off. Even then, Ferguson's marksmen had the target dead in their sights, but, as the Major later reported the incident, "I let him alone, disgusted with the idea of firing at the back of an unoffending individual who was acquitting himself very coolly of his duty." And that is how General George Washington did not get shot in September, 1777.

HANDGUNS

In handguns as in muskets, Britain set the style. The Americans copied it. And French models were an afterthought that was prompted by the convenience of association.

Pistols were the province of no one rank. Enlisted men carried them as well as officers, with the difference that the officers' weapons were personal side arms and accordingly were better made and more handsomely decorated.

The standard British military pistol had a nine-inch barrel, a .69-caliber bore, and a lock similar to that of the Brown Bess musket.

In Highland regiments, such as the Black Watch, every man jack carried the so-called Scottish pistol which was notable mostly for being made entirely of metal (the stock was brass), for having a bulbous trigger without a guard, and for a unique butt of fishtail, kidney, or ram's-horn design.

American pistols imitated British models closely. The only distinctly American type was the Kentucky pistol, which was rifled and, unlike foreign pistols, had sights. The others were distinguishable only by workmanship and by the indigenous American woods—maple, cherry, walnut—that were used for the stock.

French pistols were not standardized until 1763, but it was the model of 1777 that found most favor in America. It was of .69 caliber and had a seven-and-a-half-inch barrel; after the war it served as the model for the first handguns contracted for by the United States Government.

The War of Independence lasted for six years. It was an uphill struggle by civilians against the disciplined Redcoats of one of Europe's finest armies. If distressing numbers of militiamen took advantage of short enlistments to leave off fighting, it was also true that they often were underfed, underequipped, seldom paid, and in constant danger of losing their farms and families as the battle swept over their homeland. The wonder of it is, not that there were defections and despair, but that so many of them clung together for the common purpose, so dimly seen yet so strongly felt.

They were men used to the gun as a tool of survival, and they used it well.

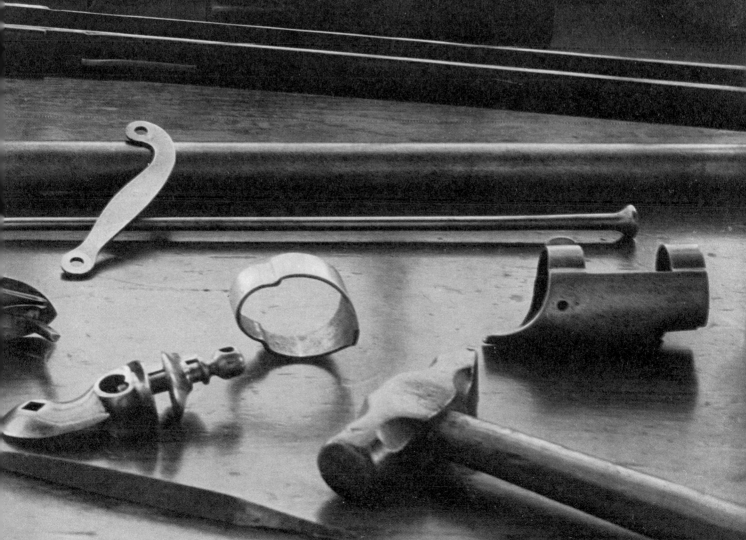

CHAPTER THREE

ARMS FOR A NEW NATION

A well-regulated militia being necessary

to the security of a free state, the right of the people

to keep and bear arms shall not be infringed.

ARTICLE II, THE BILL OF RIGHTS

Independence brought responsibilities. The United States had no sooner drawn its first heady breath as the newest of the world's nations than it found itself faced with accompanying national responsibilities. Among them was the constitutional requirement to "provide for the common defense."

All was by no means serene. The army that had won the War of Independence had melted away. In 1789 it totaled a mere eight hundred and eighty-six officers and men. In the pleasant aftermath of victory, this was not a grave concern; for the moment there was no significant land enemy in sight. British gun traders still roamed the Northwest Territory. A few isolated British garrisons remained. Indians in the Ohio country and in the South were hostile, often encouraged by these remaining Redcoats.

Nevertheless, it was not the intention of the young Government to saddle itself with a large standing army. It would be far too expensive, and large debts still hung over from the war. The defense of the several states would be left to a trained militia with assistance from the small Regular Army.

Somewhat more pressing was the threat from abroad. By 1793, England was at war with the newly arisen French Republic, and the effects were quickly felt by American ships carrying goods to and from Europe, as each of the contenders sought to limit the other's trade. Barbary pirates also complicated the situation by

PAGES 54 AND 55: *Desperate for arms, the new Government contracted with Eli Whitney to build muskets of 1798. In fulfilling order, he adapted the concept of interchangeable parts and assembly-line production to guns.* GUN: JACK CALLAN. GUN PARTS: HERB GLASS. EIGHTEENTH-CENTURY TOOLS: ROCKWELL GARDINER, STAMFORD, CONN. PHOTO BY ROBERT MOTTAR

RIGHT: *Resourceful Seminole warrior, Osceola, led two-year rebellion in Florida against United States. Gun is a Kentucky.* PAINTING BY W. M. LANING. COLLECTION OF EDGAR WILLIAM AND BERNICE CHRYSLER GARBISCH, NATIONAL GALLERY OF ART

raiding cargo vessels in the Mediterranean and demanding tribute for safe passage.

Such emergencies—and there would be more in the years ahead—demanded more and better arms. The nation met the challenge. Its new arms industry was launched in 1795 with the beginning of musket manufacture in the first Government armory at Springfield, Massachusetts. It was expanded in 1798 when Congress authorized the purchase of 40,200 muskets from twenty-seven private manufacturers. The weapon was the U.S. Model 1795, a musket patterned closely after the French Model 1763 "Charleville" of Revolutionary War fame. It was .69 caliber, a half-inch shorter than five feet overall, and two ounces under nine pounds in weight. It was to be delivered for $13.40.

Until this time, with a few notable exceptions, gunsmithing had been primarily a household industry practiced by a few hundred craftsmen who combined the arts of blacksmith, locksmith and cabinetmaker—men, in short, who could make "lock, stock and barrel." Their output during the Revolution, even with the encouragement of bounties and exemptions and some ingenious experiments in the use of unskilled labor to mass-produce sub-assemblies, had been nowhere near enough to prosecute the war. Imports from France had saved the day, but now France was hostile. The armory at Springfield would not achieve a capacity of even 5,000 muskets a year until 1799. The output of the Harpers Ferry armory in Virginia was even less. The United States faced the task of arming itself.

MASS PRODUCTION

Among the twenty-seven contractors was Eli Whitney, who had operated a two-man nail factory during the war and subsequently become famous as the inventor of the cotton gin. Although he had had no experience with firearms, he was a mechanical genius of the first order and had been tinkering for years with the notion of "labor-saving" machinery and the mass production of industrial items. Now impoverished by unsuccessful lawsuits to fight infringements on his cotton-gin patent, he sensed in the Government's need for muskets in quantity an opportunity both to apply his theories and recoup his finances. He entered a bid and was awarded a contract for 10,000 muskets, more than three times the number allotted any other manufacturer. Furthermore, he promised delivery by September 30, 1800—a little over two years—a remarkably swift performance.

Whitney's hope lay in the concept of interchangeable parts. This idea had been tried with some success in France, and American clock makers also were experimenting with the technique. Whitney believed that he could make the elements of a musket in multiples so nearly identical that the pieces of any set could be replaced by like pieces from other sets without loss of efficiency in the action of the assembled weapon. At a time when the parts of a gun were hand-forged and hand-filed to join and fit only with each other, this would be a major innovation.

It would be pleasant to report that Whitney's system enabled him to complete his order in record time, but the fact is that it took him ten years—until 1809—to finish the job. The Government was extremely lenient, for his reputation as a quality manufacturer remained good despite bugs in his production methods. Extensions were granted as needed, one of them after a dramatic demonstration in Washington before the Secretary of War and members of the Army's high command. On a table Whitney placed the parts for ten muskets, one pile for each component. Choosing pieces at random from the piles, he assembled the guns. The

Gun technology was revolutionized by Eli Whitney in this New Haven factory, where, for first time, unskilled workers were involved in gun assembly.

standardized parts meshed. Each gun was uniform in appearance and action.

A few years later, Captain John H. Hall, a canny inventor from Yarmouth, Maine, advanced farther into the machine age. In 1811, he and William Thornton patented a breech-loading flintlock rifle. After exhaustive tests, the Army adopted the gun—its first official breech-loader—and hired Hall at a salary of $60 a month plus a royalty of $1 per gun to supervise its production at Harpers Ferry. There Hall developed machinery to manufacture standardized parts with tolerances finer than Whitney's and to achieve complete interchangeability of parts.

Step followed step in the rapid advance toward true assembly line production. One of the most important was taken by Thomas Blanchard of Massachusetts, who worked at the Springfield Armory. An all-purpose inventor with a stammering tongue and a nimble mind, Blanchard was issued his first patent at the age of thirteen for an apple-peeling machine. From this it apparently was a short step to a remarkable barrel-turning lathe that could shape both the cylindrical portions of a gun barrel and the flat and oval sections at the breech in a single, almost continuous action. He then created an eccentric

lathe — "Blanchard's self-directing machine" — that could duplicate irregular shapes, among them gunstocks. The Government paid him a royalty of nine cents for each gun made with it.

At this time, too, emerged the first of the famous men whose names still grace American arms today: Eliphalet Remington, II. His story illustrates the way the private gun industry was burgeoning from the one-man shop to the full-scale factory with an assembly line to meet the demand for both civilian and military arms.

"Lite" Remington had a keen shooting eye, an engulfing curiosity about gun design and construction, and the inborn wizardry of a master mechanic. In an era when the sun shone brightly on the gunmaker, he was one of the best.

A forge was at hand. "Lite's" industrious father had built one, sometime between 1812 and 1814, near the family farm at Herkimer, New York, to repair his tools and those of his neighbors. Here, in 1815, young Remington began building flintlocks by hand methods.

The barrel came first—a slow and difficult job. A rod of iron, about .40 caliber, served as the core, or mandrel. Around it "Lite" wound a strip of soft iron, about half an inch square. The strip was heated bright red, then spiraled around the core for a few inches. Sand and borax were sprinkled over the seams and the hammer completed the weld. Then the process was repeated. Eventually, the mandrel was totally entwined in the strip. Over-all length: forty-two inches.

Remington lacked the machinery to ream and rifle his barrel, so he walked it to Utica, fifteen miles away, and had it done there. Returning home, he fitted the breech plug, ground the eight "flats" (surfaces) that would give his barrel an octagonal shape, made and fitted the lock, and shaped and fitted the stock. That he always finished his guns handsomely is a matter of record. In the shooting matches of that autumn, his work caused a stir and brought a number of orders for more, "just like that one."

By 1816, he was set up in the arms business at nearby Ilion Gorge. In 1828, he built a forge and factory on the banks of the Mohawk, to take advantage of the fast transportation afforded by the new Erie Canal, where he soon installed the precision machinery developed by Hall and Blanchard. Texas achieved its independence in 1836, and increasing threats of war with Mexico accelerated arms production throughout the United States. In the midst of the clamor for guns, Remington obtained his first Government contract. In 1845 John Griffiths, a Cincinnati manufacturer, defaulted on a contract for 5,000 "Harpers Ferry" Model 1841 rifles, and "Lite" was able to take over for him. Shortly thereafter, Remington also succeeded in taking over an incompleted contract for a breech-loading carbine invented by William Jenks.

The large orders for both of these arms forced an expansion of the Remington factory. More floor space was needed, as were more and better machines to complete the work faster. The armory that he built served the firm until 1915. The machines he developed were milestones in the history of firearms manufacture. Edging machines were adapted to carry forward the work of the Blanchard lathe and produce the first completely machine-made gunstocks. More important still, Remington designed special drilling equipment that revolutionized the techniques of barrel-making. With his new equipment he could make the barrel by drilling through a solid bar of cast steel. Gone forever was the laborious process of lap-welding strip iron around a core rod. The new process was faster and better, yet it produced a barrel that was infinitely stronger and could stand up under the heaviest charges of black powder—or the high-pressure smokeless powders to come.

Such were the restless and fertile minds that started America on the long march toward technological perfection. Milling machines, triphammers, boring rigs, and cutting tools were now commonplace. The handcraftsman was doomed and so were the simple weapons he constructed. Anything was possible now.

PERCUSSION IGNITION

Even as the machines of mass production began to turn, a fundamental and long-standing problem of the gun was solved with the invention of percussion ignition.

Although firearms had been in use for some five hundred years, the system for igniting the charge still was an uncertain and unsatisfactory piece of business. Even with a sharp flint and a clean touch hole, the military flintlock was not expected to fire more than seven times out of ten. The highest-quality sporting arms did well to fire a dozen shots in succession. Dampness always plagued the flintlock shooter. He trusted in God and tried to keep his powder dry.

The flintlock also was subject to hangfire. The trigger would be pulled, the priming powder would ignite, but the main charge in the breech would fail to explode. (From this performance, promising much and delivering little, came the expression "flash in the pan.") Then, as the exasperated shooter lowered the weapon from his shoulder and stared at it balefully, it would fire. In the case of a misfire, of course, the gun would not go off at all until it was reprimed and another attempt made. Both these exasperating occurrences were frequently caused by powder fouling or blocking the touch hole.

Misfire and hangfire were serious shortcomings in an implement on which so much depended. In 1805, as Eli Whitney struggled to produce 10,000 muskets, a Scots Presbyterian

*Contemporary caricature of 1830
militia, above. Matched pair of Hall
breech-loading flintlocks—two
of four such pistols
known—bracket Model 1819 rifle.*

RIFLE: WEST POINT MUSEUM.

PISTOLS: HERB GLASS.

PHOTO BY ROBERT MOTTAR.

CARICATURE: GOLDEN BOOK OF AMERICA
AND AMERICAN HERITAGE

minister, the Reverend Alexander John Forsyth, of Belhelvie, found the answer. It seems a curious avocation for a clergyman, but the fact is that Dr. Forsyth, between sermons, was a tireless experimenter on the problem of firing guns. His starting point was the well-known fact that certain chemicals would explode if struck a sharp blow with a blunt instrument. A chemical that was powerful, reliable, and safe, he reasoned, should do very well in a gun. After some trial and error, he settled on a potassium-chlorate compound. He devised a lock with a tube that led to the bore and through which the flash would travel when his compound was detonated by the hammer, thus igniting the main charge.

The Forsyth system was not without flaws. Its potential, however, was so obvious that gunmakers and inventors everywhere turned to with a will to iron out the defects. An immediate objection was the danger that the entire packet of sensitive powder might explode when the gun was fired. Forsyth countered this hazard by installing a blow-out plug, somewhat like that in a pressure cooker, in his priming box.

Other inventors found different ways to handle the compound. Some rolled it into pills or pellets. Some enclosed it in paper, like a small boy's roll of caps. These efforts led to the percussion cap, a major advance now attributed to several inventors, possibly because the most likely one, Joshua Shaw, an Englishman living in Philadelphia, was an alien and therefore could not obtain a patent in the United States.

Early caps were made of iron, pewter, or copper and contained a small charge covered with a tinfoil seal and waterproofed with shellac. About 1816 copper was finally selected as the best material since it was soft enough to deform readily under the blow of the hammer (thus insuring detonation), yet tough enough to hold together under the force of the explosion.

The cap was placed over the tube—called the

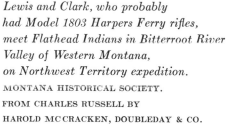

*Lewis and Clark, who probably
had Model 1803 Harpers Ferry rifles,
meet Flathead Indians in Bitterroot River
Valley of Western Montana,
on Northwest Territory expedition.*
MONTANA HISTORICAL SOCIETY.
FROM CHARLES RUSSELL BY
HAROLD MCCRACKEN, DOUBLEDAY & CO.

cone or nipple—that led to the bore. The newly designed hammer, acting like the flintlock's cock, banged down upon it to produce the flash. It was quickly discovered that if the face of the hammer was flat, bits of metal from the exploding cap would fly about dangerously. This was remedied by hollowing a cup in the striking surface.

The percussion cap was a quick success. Best of all, the flintlock could easily be converted to the new system by switching to a few new parts and altering the touch hole.

The military was slow to take advantage of the innovation. Percussion guns were simpler to make and more certain to fire, even in wind and rain. This they could see. On the other hand, they were concerned about the more delicate operation of placing a cap on the cone in the excitement of battle, or on the back of a galloping horse, or with cold-numbed fingers. Also they were concerned about safe methods of carrying the sensitive caps and of assuring the troops an adequate supply at all times. For the long run, exhaustive tests also had to be made to see if the new system actually was faster and more reliable, and if there was an increase or decrease in muzzle velocity and range, and the like.

Thus it is not surprising that it was not until 1833, some seventeen years after the percussion cap was perfected, that the Government placed its first orders for percussion carbines of the Hall pattern for its dragoons, and another eight years before the changeover began in earnest. Even then, the process was excruciatingly slow, and many flintlocks continued to see service throughout the Mexican War.

Another revolution in the history of firearms had taken place. The Scottish minister's invention was accepted everywhere and the whole field of shooting was transformed. Gone forever were the free sparks and the separate priming powder. A new principle had been found which shaped the course of all firearms history to follow.

63

Gun designer William Jenks
joined Remington just before
Mexican War. He created
single-shot, percussion breechloader with "mule-ear"
side-hammer. Later versions had
tape-primer device.

RIFLE vs. MUSKET

Following the experience of the Revolution, the Army decided that both rifles and muskets should be procured as official arms. The relationship remained as it had during the war—the musket as the workhorse with which the bulk of the troops was armed, the rifle for special troops and specific purposes. This arrangement would not change until another example of the inventive genius of the nineteenth century made it possible to combine the best aspects of each into one excellent arm. Ironically, this gun, the rifled musket, appeared just ten years before the end of the muzzle-loading era. Yet those years were a supreme test and achievement, for they included the Civil War in which it was the principal infantry weapon.

There was little change in the design of the musket throughout the years of its service. The Model 1795 was modified in 1808, 1812, 1816, 1822, 1835, and 1840. Dimensions were changed slightly. There were modifications in fastenings and in the shapes of some of the parts, and the pan was changed from iron to brass. Still, it remained a .69-caliber flintlock patterned after the French Charleville. In 1842 there was a radical change with the switch to the percussion system, but the flintlock was produced until 1844, even as the new system was being issued to troops.

Plain and unromantic in appearance though it was, the musket was still the infantryman's closest companion and a maker of history. It was primarily the foot soldier with his musket who occupied the Louisiana Territory, fought the War of 1812 on land, helped General William Henry Harrison defeat the Indians at Tippecanoe, hunted Osceola and the Seminoles in the Florida swamps, chased Chief Black Hawk into the wilds of Wisconsin, and freed the Southwest from Mexican control.

In all, the Government acquired some 850,000 muskets between 1798 and 1848, vastly more than were needed for the wars of that period. Probably most of them were issued to the states for their militia. But whether in Federal or state arsenals, thousands of them would stand, vigilant and obsolescent, until the outbreak of Civil War returned them to the hands of the common soldier, to his sorrow.

The military's fondness for the musket did not mean that it was oblivious to the rifle. It merely viewed rifles as specialized weapons and assigned them limited battlefield functions. The infantryman's target, after all, was the enemy soldier, who generally was engaged *en masse*, normally at short range, and who fell just as surely when hit by musket ball as by rifle shot.

The civilian shooter operated under considerably different conditions and with other objectives. Very often he was alone, without the security of a companion's hit to compensate for his own miss. Frequently he dueled at a distance, without eagerness or compulsion to fight to a finish. And when he hunted for food or pelts, his target either was less than man-size, placing a premium on accuracy, or much greater, requiring more devastating shocking power or additional shots in reserve. Finally, as an individual he was subject neither to collective opinion nor to organizational rigidities. Any crotchets he had were his own. Accordingly, the civilian was free to demand a great deal of his gun and, as a rule, he was more receptive than the military to such innovations as percussion ignition, breech loading, and multiple-shot mechanisms.

The civilian with his rifle often found himself in battle, during the various wars of the period, as a member of a militia unit. In this service he performed well. It is probably too much to say that the rifle won the Battle of New Orleans for General Andrew Jackson, though it did play a very important part. Most historians prefer to make a case for the artillery, and the truth probably lies somewhere in between. The point is that the civilian's Kentucky rifle had come a long way in the military field and New Orleans was probably its finest achievement in war.

The first regulation rifle produced at any United States armory was made at Harpers Ferry. It was the Model 1803, a .54-caliber flintlock with a thirty-three-inch barrel, that saw service along the frontier and in Indian territory until the 1830's. It seems fairly certain that Meriwether Lewis and William Clark took along several 1803's on their epic survey of the Louisiana Purchase. Lieutenant Zebulon Pike probably carried them on his expedition through the Southwest a few years later. And it was definitely used during the War of 1812, where it won new friends among the military.

Following the Model 1803 and the improved version of 1814 came the full-stocked "common rifle" of 1817, officially known as the Model 1819. The term "common rifle" was applied to

distinguish it from the breech-loading Hall, which also was known as the Model 1819.

In 1841, Ordnance adopted a brand-new rifle with a percussion lock, the last to fire the traditional round ball. Still in .54 caliber, it was a sturdy weapon with a handsome brass patch box for tools and spare parts. It was generally known as the "Yager rifle," a misspelling of the German *Jaeger,* or as the "Mississippi Rifle," as a result of its performance in the hands of Jefferson Davis' Mississippi Regiment during the heroic stand at the Battle of Buena Vista.

Even as these historic events were occurring, Ordnance was slowly working on a change that would doom both the round rifle ball and the smoothbore musket to oblivion. Experiments were begun on the use of a new projectile invented by Captain C. E. Minié of the French Army. Minié's bullet was cylindro-conoidal in form, with a hollow base in which an iron plug was inserted. The explosion of the powder charge drove the plug forward, expanding the diameter of the lead projectile so that it would fit the bore tightly and "take" the rifling. James H. Burton, Assistant Master Armorer at Harpers Ferry, made the important discovery that the plug was not necessary and that the same effect could be obtained with a properly designed hollow base alone, thus simplifying manufacture

Eliphalet Remington II, 1793-1861.

considerably and cutting costs. From then on, the experimentation was aimed primarily at determining the most suitable caliber for the guns using the new projectile. In the end the decision was for .58. Thus was born the famous bullet which came ironically to be known as the Minié ball, though it was neither a ball nor Minié's invention. No one ever seems to have called it a "Burton bullet," and Burton's name is largely unknown today, while Minié's is familiar to shooters throughout the world.

This small piece of lead radically altered gun design and helped establish the ground rules under which the Civil War would be fought. As the Minié when loaded was smaller than the bore, it could be dropped in as easily as a musket ball. A rifle could be loaded as rapidly as a musket and there was no longer any reason why all arms should not have the advantage of the rifle's accuracy. The smoothbore was dead.

In 1855, new arms designed for the Minié ball were adopted. There were two, a rifle and a rifled musket, but the terms referred only to the exterior appearance of the guns. Both were, in fact, rifles. Both were .58-caliber and used the same ammunition. In essence, one was long with a thin barrel, the other short with a thick barrel.

The longer rifled musket was the principal infantry weapon of the Civil War. It had a forty-inch barrel (plus an eighteen-inch socket-bayonet) and weighed a mere nine and a quarter pounds. It fired a Minié ball weighing 500 grains and a charge of sixty grains of musket powder. (Rifle powder was found to foul the nipples unduly.) It was good enough to put ten shots

67

into a four-inch bull's-eye at 100 yards, ten shots into a nine-inch bull's-eye at 200 yards, and powerful enough to penetrate four inches of soft pine at 1,000 yards.

A total of 59,273 of these rifled muskets was produced between 1857 and 1861 at both the Springfield and Harpers Ferry armories. All had a special priming device invented by Dr. Edward Maynard, a Washington dentist. Instead of requiring the soldier to place an individual percussion cap on the nipple for each shot, the Maynard tape primer fed a paper strip containing the primers over the nipple much in the manner of the small boy's cap pistol of today.

The final models appeared during the Civil War: the 1861, which was essentially the same as the 1855; the 1863, again only slightly changed, and finally the 1864. Altogether, almost two million of the .58-caliber rifled muskets were made and used during the Civil War, a number far overshadowing any other type of service arm.

The muzzle-loading rifle had reached its apo-

gee. The only improvement could come through breechloaders. And these, after almost fifty years of Army experimentation, were on the way.

THE ADVENT OF THE BREECHLOADER

It is one of the small, pleasant surprises of history that the Army should have relaxed its tedious resistance to change and accepted John Hall's radically different breechloader of 1819. It was not an unqualified success, but the desire of the Army to try something that seemed to offer advantages was encouraging. It was hardly an impulsive action; it took eight years, two exhaustive tests, and an improvement in the breech closure—but accepted it was.

Hall's gun, the Army's first breechloader, was a .52-caliber flintlock with a barrel a fraction less than thirty-three inches long. Over-all, the gun weighed a few ounces more than ten pounds. It had a hinged breechblock containing the lock and chamber. To load, the front end of the

berlain, the incorrigible dragoon and unabashed diarist of the Mexican War, frequently mentions carrying the breech of his Hall carbine in his pocket as he set out on one or another of his romantic escapades in enemy territory.

Hall rifles and carbines were used throughout the Mexican War and, to a limited extent, even in the Civil War. They were never popular, however, because of the gas leakage and difficulties with the breech catch. In the end, the Confederates even converted some back to muzzle-loaders. So ended the Army's first experiment with breech-loading guns.

In one of those interesting associations of history, it remained for a man who had worked at Harpers Ferry under John Hall finally to develop a completely satisfactory breechloader. Christian Sharps left Harpers Ferry after the town's rifle shops closed in 1844 and moved to Cincinnati. There, in 1848, he patented the basic principles of his breechloading system. His was a reliable, single-shot arm that used a linen- or paper-wrapped cartridge. After the breechblock had been lowered by dropping the trigger-guard lever, the cartridge could be inserted. As the breech was closed, the block rose vertically in a mortise and sheared off the end of the cartridge, exposing the powder charge to the action of the percussion primer. The first Sharps had some trouble with gas leakage, but the model of 1859 had a new gas-checking device that effectively sealed off the breech at firing. So good was Sharps' system that it still forms the basis for many single-shot rifles today.

The Sharps had been fully tested by an Army Ordnance Board in 1850 and highly praised. John Brown's abolitionist raiders carried Sharps carbines. And settlers brought them into "Bloody

breechblock was lifted, after releasing a spring catch. The charge was inserted from the front and the action then closed and locked. As with most early breechloaders, however, the seam between the chamber and the barrel was not sufficiently tight. It was inclined to spurt flame from the joint when fired and inevitably lost some velocity because of the gas leakage. This was remedied to some extent before acceptance, but the model never achieved a complete seal.

In 1833, when the First Regiment of Dragoons was formally organized, the Hall was issued as a carbine. In carbine form it was a .64-caliber smoothbore with a twenty-six-inch barrel. It was the first military arm to use percussion ignition and preceded the general adoption of the system by eight years. In 1836, it was also issued in limited quantity with a rifled barrel.

One interesting feature of these percussion Halls is that the entire breechblock could be removed and carried as a handgun, since all the working parts were contained in it. Sam Cham-

Kansas," where they were called "Beecher's Bibles" after Henry Ward Beecher declaimed at a meeting in New Haven that one Sharps would have more moral power and persuasion in the slavery conflict than a hundred Bibles.

The Sharps certainly was the most popular single-shot breechloader used during the war. It consistently outshot the Springfield models in range and, although sighted for a maximum of 1,000 yards, was reasonably accurate to a distance of 1,500 yards. By war's end, more than 80,000 Sharps rifles and carbines had been purchased by the Union Army.

MULTIPLE-SHOT WEAPONS AND METALLIC CARTRIDGES

For centuries, almost since the invention of firearms, shooters had wanted a gun that could fire more than once without reloading. The advantages of such an arm were obvious to all, and inventors throughout the western world turned their attention to it. They tried separate magazines for powder and ball, Roman-candle systems, sliding locks, revolving cylinders, and multiple barrels. All of these and even more ingenious systems had been thought of and tried before the Pilgrims reached America. But it was not until the nineteenth century that really practical repeating arms were developed.

Once again, it was another young Yankee inventor who speeded up the slowly moving treadmill of arms improvement. Samuel Colt, born near Hartford, Connecticut, on July 19, 1814, was a gun crank almost from the first day he could speak his name. In his early years he was kicked around from pillar to post by his father, Christopher, who could ill afford to feed this extra mouth in an already large brood. From the age of eleven he spent little time at home. Successively he was indentured to a farmer in

Glastonbury, then sent off to a textile plant in Ware, Massachusetts, where he had access to chemicals used in processing, and carried on vigorous experiments, with attendant noise, to the great displeasure of the townfolk. From here he was sent off to Amherst—for safekeeping as much as for an education—but his explosive nature kept him in hot water there. Finally, one of his experiments backfired and damaged some school property. Sam left, under cover of darkness, and hitched his way back to Hartford.

In August of 1830, at the age of sixteen, Sam shipped out to sea on the brig *Corvo*, bound for Calcutta and London. He began to whittle pistol models in his spare time almost as soon as the ship was under way. It is fairly certain that he had a look at some samples of Collier's flintlock revolvers during his stopover in London, and perhaps in Calcutta, and got some valuable ideas about gun construction. By the end of his voyage he had fashioned in wood a fair working model of a six-shot revolver, and eagerly sought to have prototypes made by a skilled gunsmith, so that he could apply at once for patents.

The work of building two revolving guns, one

Civil War muzzle-loading percussion weapons included, from left to right: single-shot Model 1841, commonly known as Mississippi rifle; Model 1855 with Maynard tape primer, made at Harpers Ferry; Colt revolving six-shot infantry musket, with triangular bayonet; and Sharps single-shot cavalry carbine. Bugle, blown by Nathaniel Sisson, sounded recall at Appomattox. Union guidon captured by Corporal John R. Keeling, 1st Texas Infantry.
GUNS: WEST POINT MUSEUM.
PHOTO BY ROBERT MOTTAR

a pistol and one a rifle (of similar design except for stock and barrel length), was given to Anson Chase, a noted Hartford gunsmith. After considerable financial difficulty, the sample guns were finished and Sam submitted them to Henry Ellsworth, Commissioner of Patents, in Washington. Ellsworth listened to the eager eighteen-year-old and advised him first to file a *caveat* (an affidavit of claim), then store his samples at the Patent Office while better ones were built.

Almost three years passed before Sam could get the model guns he needed made up. Financially, he was forever insolvent. His sole earnings came from barnstorming tours of the country during which he billed himself as "Dr. Coult, of New York, London and Calcutta" and demonstrated the startling powers and properties of nitrous oxide, the newly discovered laughing gas. At this time he delegated the model-building work on his guns to John Pearson, an expert Baltimore gunsmith, but it progressed slowly.

On December 18, 1835, Sam finally acquired his first firm patent in England—partly because his device gained quick acceptance there, but also because English patent law would have denied him protection in England if he had first secured his patent in the United States. It should be clearly stated that Colt's basic patent was not for a revolving cylinder (which was not new), but for the method of revolving the cylinder and locking it in alignment with the barrel by the action of the hammer as the gun was cocked.

Sam's trials as a manufacturer began with the establishment of his first plant in Paterson, New Jersey. He was convinced that the Government would be a natural and immediate outlet for his new repeating arms, particularly his rifles, on which he placed greater emphasis than on pistols in his early days as an arms maker. But the early Paterson Colts, both rifle and pistol, belched fire consistently from the gap between the face of the cylinder and the bore. This could have been overlooked in an era when guns commonly flared at the breech in one way or another. Colt's guns, however, suffered the added hazard of multiple discharge from the cylinder loads on each side of the one being fired. Colt acknowledged the problem and even went so far as to build an experimental gun with side deflectors, but this was not a definitive answer. In later years he solved the problem by using a tight-fitting ball which was rammed, even swedged, into the front of the cylinder with a loading lever carried under the barrel.

Colt's Paterson pistols were made in fairly small calibers: .28, .31, .34, and .36, all of five-shot capacity. His rifles varied from .34 to .52 caliber, with six-, seven- or eight-shot capacity. He also made some .56- to .70-caliber shotguns, with the .62 (about 20 gauge) the most popular.

Colt's early rifle had unusual firepower. In addition to the number of shots delivered at one loading, extra loaded cylinders could be carried; replacement was a matter of seconds. This doubled its normal firepower and made it a popular gun with hunters. Kit Carson advised General Frémont that "a few men armed with [Colt] repeating rifles were more dangerous than a small army with old-fashioned guns."

Sam Colt agreed enthusiastically with this appraisal and bent all his efforts toward selling guns to Army Ordnance. In February, 1837, his gun was included in a general test of new arms, including the Hall and Hackett breechloaders, the Cochran revolving rifle, Leavitt's rifle, and the United States Standard musket.

But Army Ordnance did not like the Colt. One argument, possibly well-founded, was that the regular-army troops were not bright enough to keep such "complicated" arms in good working order. The more parts, the greater possibility of trouble. Another concern was the ammunition supply. They feared that soldiers armed with repeating arms would fire their charges too rapidly and run out of ammunition. More ammunition meant more weight for the soldier to carry and greater supply problems for the Army on the extended expeditions which were typical of the campaigns at that period. In any event, Ordnance turned down Samuel cold.

He sold a few pieces to General Thomas Sidney Jesup, who was fighting the Seminoles in Florida, and a few more to the Texas Navy, a remarkable but short-lived department of the new Republic of Texas. But discouraged by his inability to get the volume orders from the Government and plagued by financial problems not of his making, Colt closed his Paterson factory in 1842. John Ehlers, his principal creditor, took over and continued to assemble weapons from the factory's stock of parts. He sold fifty pistols and a hundred carbines to the Navy in 1845. The pistols were the first ones ever ordered by the Government under Colt's patent. The carbines saw action with the Pacific Squadron during the Mexican War and were still going strong in 1853 when Commodore Matthew Calbraith Perry included them among the small arms taken on his history-making expedition to Japan.

Perhaps the best test of the Colt repeating arms occurred in 1844, two years after the inventor had closed up shop. Colonel John Coffee Hays and fifteen Texas Rangers, armed with Colt pistols obtained from the Texas Navy, had a gunfight with eighty mounted Comanches and killed forty-two of them. This was an impressive score by any standard and won strong friends for Colt, among them the Rangers' Captain Sam Walker. When General Zachary Taylor wanted

Union soldier holds .58-caliber musket.
PHOTO BY MATTHEW BRADY. LIBRARY OF CONGRESS.

Colts during the Mexican War, it was Walker who went to Washington to get them. Samuel Colt, out of business for four years and seemingly at the end of his string, suddenly found himself on the road back.

Further progress in the field of repeating arms waited upon developments in ammunition. It had long been the practice to wrap the ball and powder necessary for a charge in paper, linen, animal membranes, metal foil, and other coverings. Still, the primer was omitted and a hard case that would hold up in a magazine and help

Confederates give up their arms—probably captured in first place from Union depots.
PAINTING BY WINSLOW HOMER. GIFT OF MRS. FRANK B. PORTER, METROPOLITAN MUSEUM OF ART

serve as a gas check was lacking.

In 1849, just as Sam Colt was well-established in business once more, Walter Hunt, an otherwise little-known inventor, obtained a patent on a repeating arm with a new type of bullet. The primer was still separate, but the powder charge was contained in the hollow base of the bullet itself. The gun, called a "Volitional Repeater," included many good design features; the basic form of the tubular magazine under the barrel, for instance, is still followed in Winchester and Marlin rifles today. But defects of the separate primer and a complex and delicate mechanism marred its performance.

A team of famous names in gun history worked to improve Hunt's gun. Lewis Jennings improved the action and simplified it. Horace Smith and Daniel B. Wesson, who would soon be linked in a far-reaching handgun business, further strengthened the mechanism and improved the cartridge. Under the name of the Volcanic Re-

peating Arms Company (with Oliver Winchester a stockholder), the new repeating rifles and pistols began to appear in 1851. The design featured a hollow-base bullet containing its own primer and fired by a pin passing through the breech.

For several years the Volcanic rifle found the going rough. It needed a better cartridge. Following European developments, Smith and Wesson produced the first practical rim-fire metallic cartridge in 1858. It had a brass case with a cavity all around the rim which held the detonating compound. With this invention the way was cleared for a whole new line of developments in all types of arms. B. Tyler Henry soon adopted the idea and designed a rim-fire cartridge in .44 caliber. Volcanic arms had been of .36 caliber and thus no great shakes for hunting or long-range work. The new cartridge provided the necessary power to make it a real weapon. Henry further perfected the rifle itself, adding a new firing pin and other improvements until it was ready for trial when the Civil War finally began.

The change from the Henry to the Winchester rifle was largely one of name. Oliver Winchester himself had little or no knowledge of firearms. His was a business talent. A sometime carpenter, drygoods merchant, and inventor of an improved way to cut out men's dress shirts, he purchased the corporate assets of the Volcanic Company when it failed. He reopened it in 1857, with Henry as supervisor, and operated as the New Haven Arms Company throughout the Civil War. In 1866 it became the Winchester Repeating Arms Company and its products were known as Winchesters from that time forward.

The practical repeater and a successful, self-contained cartridge had been developed. The cartridge, however, still was subject to misfire if the priming, or detonating compound, was not spread evenly around the rim, inside the case. If the hammer chanced to strike an uncoated spot, nothing would happen. A nice balance also had to be struck between a copper casing strong enough to contain the pressures of a heavy charge and soft enough to crumple easily and cause detonation when the hammer hit.

The answer was found in the center-fire cartridge which was evolving at about the same time as the rim-fire through the efforts of inventors in England, France, and the United States. The trick was to build a striking surface or "anvil" in the bottom of the case to separate the primer from the main charge. The firing pin, striking the base at dead center, crushed it against the anvil, thus exploding the primer by compression and setting off the main charge.

The key contribution from the United States —the basic form of one of the two standard center-fires in use today—was made in 1866 by an extremely capable rifleman, Colonel Hiram Berdan. Berdan's idea was to insert a primer in the base of a solid-head cartridge case of brass, which, once fired, could be replaced. He also invented the method of deep-drawing brass discs to form strong cartridge cases. The combination of the two innovations filled almost every need for fixed center-fire ammunition, and in fact Berdan's ideas are used today in the basic design of all center-fire cartridges.

THE CIVIL WAR

The Civil War was the climactic event toward which all the arms developments of the period had been leading. It provided the crucible in which all ideas would be tested, all theories refined. It was a war on a scale the United States had never faced before and, in proportion to its population, has never faced since. With 4,137,304 men in uniform at one time or another, huge quantities of arms were needed. Before the conflict was over the Union Government alone had recognized as official more than seventy-nine different models of rifles and muskets, twenty-three different models of carbines and musketoons, and nineteen models of handguns.

The Union entered the war with an appallingly inadequate array of weapons. Scattered about in arsenals and depots from coast to coast were quantities of old-fashioned smoothbore muskets, some of them flintlocks. There were not nearly enough of the new rifled muskets, and unfortunately many of these had been in southern arsenals which were captured by the Confederacy. Commenting on the poor arms generally available, Oliver Perry Morton, the capable and intelligent Governor of Indiana, wrote:

"It is the opinion of all military men here that it would be little better than murder to send troops into battle with such arms as are a large majority of these muskets altered from flint to percussion locks."

President Lincoln was well aware of the shortcomings of these old muskets and of the need to acquire more and better guns. He had assumed office, however, at about the same time as the singularly stubborn Chief of Ordnance, James Wolfe Ripley. Ripley, a West Pointer (Class of 1814), was a capable officer in his day but had become set in his ways. He had been superintendent at Springfield Armory when the 1855 rifled musket was developed and he considered it the perfect military arm. It was indeed a fine gun, but Ripley's devotion to it increased a natural prejudice against the newfangled breech-loaders and repeaters. He resisted change implacably, even after the advantages of the new rifles had been conclusively demonstrated to him and despite explicit orders from the President himself. He had an irascible nature and no inclination to moderate it for Lincoln or anyone else. *The New York Times,* commenting on his eventual dismissal in 1863, was exasperated enough to call him "the old fogey."

The desperate scarcity of arms was intensified by complacence among the top brass. Secretary of War Simeon Cameron, a pork-barreling politician from Pennsylvania, announced early in the war that "we have already an army composed of 300,000 men, a number greater than we need for the actual crisis." He gave no indication of being aware that less than half of these invincibles had weapons of any kind in their hands. Even Ripley became alarmed and urged the Secretary to meet the deficiency with arms purchased abroad. The bemused Cameron stalled, however, until the Confederacy virtually had cornered the European market.

Only through the swift, intelligent, and daring work of Marcellus Hartley was the situation retrieved. Hartley, who would later take over Remington Arms and found the Union Metallic Cartridge Company, was then a partner of Schuyler, Hartley and Graham, one of America's finest sporting-arms stores. At President Lincoln's request, he hurried to Europe and brilliantly utilized his vast acquaintance among arms manufacturers to provide the Union with some of the weapons it needed. So shrewd was his maneuvering that he even managed to divert to the Union forces a shipment of guns that had been ticketed for the Confederacy.

As late as the autumn of 1862, more than half the Union regiments carried foreign weapons into battle — an appalling commentary on the Union's self-sufficiency but a tribute to Hartley and his fellow purchasing agents.

The early months of the war went badly for the Union, just how badly becoming frighteningly clear after the disaster at Bull Run. Crackpot inventors by the hundreds besieged Lincoln, offering new designs for rifles, for cannon, and for a number of preposterous devices posing as effective weapons of war. Lincoln listened patiently and passed the men and their models and their plans on to Ripley, who gave them short shrift. It was a confusing and wearing situation, for inevitably among the dross there were ideas of real merit. Relying on instinct or the help of trusted advisers, Lincoln occasionally forced the issue with his crusty Chief of Ordnance.

One bright spot was the performance of Colonel Hiram Berdan's U.S. Sharpshooters, a specially recruited regiment of expert marksmen who wore a distinctive and serviceable green battledress. Volunteers for this select company were given a tryout at Weehawken, New Jersey, and, to qualify, had to prove their marksmanship. None was accepted who could not group ten shots in a target fifty inches square at 200 yards. Many, of course, shot far better.

In assembling his men, Berdan had promised them Sharps breechloading rifles, only to find that Ripley, by now a brigadier general, insisted they use the standard Springfield muzzle-loader.

The marksmen were clamoring for something better and Berdan did his best to convince Ripley, but to no avail. It took a threatened mutiny and great pressure from President Lincoln himself before Ripley finally gave way and ordered the promised Sharps rifles for Berdan's men.

Once they went into action with it, Berdan's troops were an astonishing success, particularly at Gettysburg. Here a hundred Berdan marksmen and two hundred Maine troops with muzzle-loaders fought a fierce, twenty-minute battle with Longstreet's corps as it drove toward Little Round Top. The Sharpshooters reeled off an average of ninety-five shots each. And one of them, who was captured and escorted through the Rebel lines, reported later: "It is impossible for me to describe the slaughter we had made in their ranks. In all my past service, it beat all I had ever seen for the number engaged and for so short a time. They were piled in heaps and across each other. . . ."

The Sharps was the finest breechloader to see action during the war. Soldiers who used it were unqualified in their praise of the gun. There were many other breechloaders also, some privately purchased by soldiers, some bought by states, and some forced down Ripley's throat to be bought by Ordnance. Many of them worked relatively well; some were exceptionally poor. Probably few, if any, would have found a market without the crisis of the war.

President Lincoln himself was also directly responsible for the Army's adoption of Christopher Spencer's fine repeater, a seven-shot, rim-fire rifle. He personally test-fired it on an improvised range, approximately where the Ellipse is now situated, and was so pleased by its

Basic cavalry weapons of Civil War
were Colt Army Model of 1860 and saber.
PISTOL: HERB GLASS.
PHOTO BY ROBERT MOTTAR

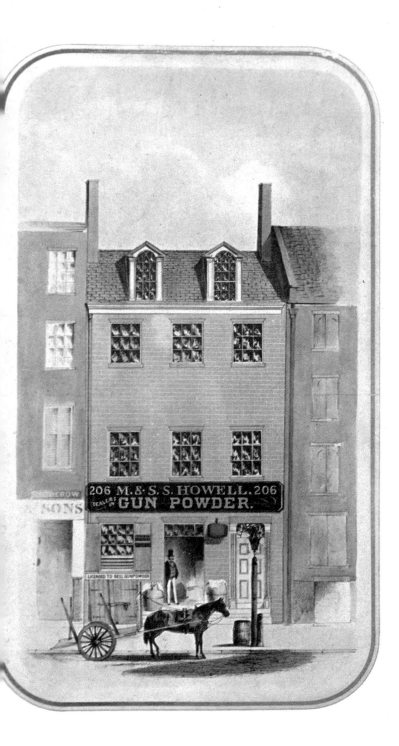

*In 1850's, before the days of
self-contained ammunition, gun
owners bought black powder in shops
like that of M. & S. Howell,
206 Front Street, New York City.*

LITHOGRAPH BY C. EYTINGE.

MUSEUM OF THE CITY OF NEW YORK

performance that he whittled an improved sight for it. His approval and enthusiasm resulted in the mass production of 94,196 Spencers for distribution to Union troops. (A Spencer also was among the arms found with John Wilkes Booth when he was finally trapped in the Garrett barn after assassinating the President.)

The rifle and the carbine that were patented on March 6, 1860, by Christopher Miner Spencer, a South Manchester, Connecticut, machinist, were basically the same except that the rifle had an over-all length of forty-seven inches and weighed ten pounds, while the carbine was thirty-nine inches in length and weighed eight pounds four ounces. Both guns had a blade sight in front, a sliding leaf in the rear.

The Spencer's firepower was impressive, though not beyond improvement. Late in the war a device to increase it was developed. This was the Blakeslee Quickloader, a cartridge box containing ten ready loaded magazines, which was issued to some of the troops. A magazine could be emptied in about eighteen seconds and readily replaced in another five.

Ripley was not impressed by repeaters. In a letter to Cameron in December, 1861, he rejected both the Spencer and B. Tyler Henry's Volcanic repeater out of hand.

"I regard the weight of arms with loaded magazines as objectionable," he said, "and also the requirement of special ammunition rendering it impossible to use the arms with the ordinary cartridges or with powder and ball."

But others were for taking a chance. From the western front in 1863, Spencer received an order for 2,000 repeaters. It was placed by Colonel John Thomas Wilder on behalf of the men of the Lightning Brigade. They had decided, in convention, to damn the Ordnance Department by ordering the Spencers on their own, with their own pay. With them they fought the Battle of Hoover's Gap and the Battle of Chickamauga.

On November 28, 1863, Wilder wrote:

"My brigade of mounted infantry have repeatedly routed and driven off large superior forces of rebels, in some instances five or six times their number, and this result is mainly due to our being armed with the Spencer Repeating Rifle."

In 1863, Lincoln replaced General Ripley with Brigadier General George D. Ramsay. The next year Ramsay was all for the Spencer. He wrote:

"Repeating arms are the greatest favorite in the Army, and could they be supplied in quantities to meet all requisitions, I am sure that no other arms would be used. Colt's and Henry's rifles and the Spencer carbines and rifles are the only arms of this class in the service. Colt's is both expensive and a dangerous weapon to the user. Henry's is expensive and too delicate for service in its present form, while Spencer's is at the same time the cheapest, most durable, and most efficient of any of these arms."

The prices Ramsay had in mind were Spencer, $25; Colt, $44; Henry, $37.

In a postwar trial, when the Army had time to find out what weapon it really should have used, a testing board concluded: "... the Spencer magazine carbine is the best service gun of its kind yet offered."

The Spencer swamped the only other competent repeater that saw service in the war, the Henry rifle manufactured by Oliver Winchester's New Haven Arms Company. Some Henrys were bought by individual states and were used both as infantry and cavalry guns. Only about 2,000 of them ever were issued through regular army channels, but they seem to have performed well. Two regiments that marched to the sea with Sherman had Henrys, and the Confederates who encountered it are said to have called it "that damned Yankee rifle that can be loaded on Sunday and fired all week."

For all its popularity, the Spencer survived only a short time after the Civil War. Then the Henry and the Winchester took over. Why did the Spencer languish? Mainly because it did not have a completely repeating mechanism and fired a cartridge with poor ballistic qualities. Its big .52-caliber rim-fire load fired a heavy 450-grain bullet at low velocities. As a cavalry weapon, for men fighting at close quarters for a few moments, it was fine. As a long-range infantry arm it was deficient.

The postwar civilian, who was thinking in terms of guns for buffalo and other large game, did not want it. The Henry rifle whose popularity skyrocketed after the war was primarily a sportsman's gun—a slender, graceful arm that packed well on a saddle and had more than double the firepower of the Spencer. Though it carried a smaller cartridge, the .44 rim-fire, its velocity was somewhat higher, and this appealed to the hunter. Christopher Spencer's postwar effort, the new Model 1865, went begging. In 1869, the Spencer company was bankrupt and its assets were auctioned off. Biggest buyer was Oliver Winchester, who thus at a single stroke removed his principal rival in the field of repeating arms while acquiring much of his property.

CONFEDERATE ARMS

At the outbreak of the war, the South had on hand a total of about 150,000 shoulder arms, 20,000 of which were rifled muskets of the Harpers Ferry vintage of 1855. The rest were a motley collection of smoothbore flintlocks, percussion conversions, and some Hall rifles and carbines. The South was hard up for arms. At first, a call went out to civilians to turn in any sporting arms which might serve the cause (a situation that was repeated in World War II), but

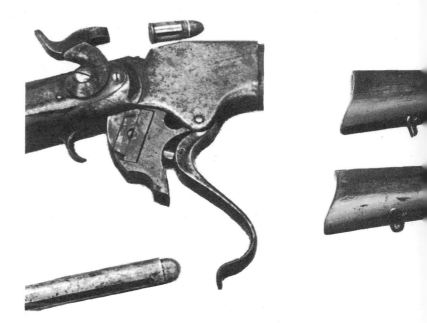

Most popular Civil War repeaters were Spencer rifle and carbine. Rifle was fitted with triangular bayonet. Both models used self-contained, rim-fire cartridges, which were fed from seven-shot magazine in butt stock.
GUNS: WEST POINT MUSEUM

few were offered. Most individuals wisely kept their arms for their own protection in case the Yankees should ever invade Dixie.

The capture of Harpers Ferry gave the South a boost, for gun-making machinery was desperately needed. Most of it was moved to Richmond, and to Fayetteville, North Carolina, where it would be safer from attack. But at best, the machinery turned out only about four hundred rifled muskets per month. Many private contracts were let in a strenuous effort to acquire arms to fire the .58 Minié bullet.

The Rebels captured many arms from the Yankees in the early days of the war. Unfortunately, a number of the newer ones were worthless to Johnny Reb, since he had no cartridges to fit them. Of the total of 323,231 infantry arms issued through the Richmond Arsenal from 1861 to 1865, it is generally conceded that at least half were captured guns.

Basically, the contract arms of the southern manufacturers were imitations of northern weapons: the Springfield, the Sharps, and, of course, the Colt revolver. There also were some copies of the British Enfields. Since the southern army was basically a mounted army, the pair of revolvers was imperative. Curiously, the South did not like the heavy .44 Colt Army model of 1860, but copied instead, in great quantities, the .36-caliber Navy, which was far lighter.

One curious new design of gun, in both handgun and shoulder style, came out of the Confederacy: the LeMat revolving "grape-shot" gun. This two-barreled weapon employed a revolving cylinder firing nine pistol cartridges through its upper, rifled barrel. Its lower barrel, around which the cylinder turned, was a smoothbore, firing a load of small buckshot. This was a formidable cavalry weapon in either handgun or carbine form. About 3,000 were made, and it can be said that this is one of the few examples of a "primary" gun to issue from the Confederacy.

THE AFTERMATH

Despite the experimentation with breechloaders and repeaters, the Civil War was fought basically with the rifled musket of the models described. The wartime experience, however, indicated that a change should be made. An official report of arms collected from the field of Gettysburg, for instance, showed that of 24,000 loaded muskets recovered about half contained two loads each, about a quarter held three to ten

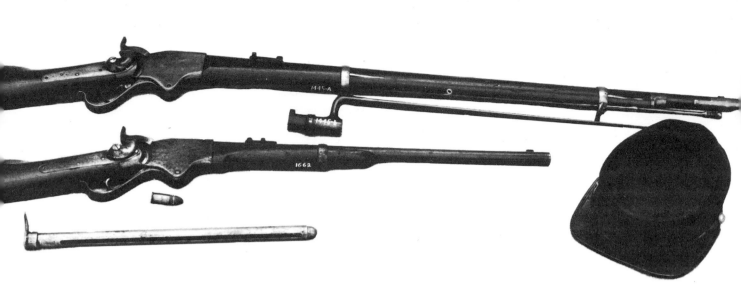

loads, and a great many more held a variety of powder charges, balls, and cartridges inserted upside down. In the heat of battle it was a common occurrence for a soldier to be unaware whether his weapon had fired or not. With the air filled with smoke and the ear-splitting din of roaring guns, the scared soldier would be only dimly conscious of firing his piece. Often, in the excitement, he would forget to prime his piece with a percussion cap, or it would fall off before he snapped the hammer. With the muzzle-loader he had no way of telling whether he had fired by looking at the breech. He had no empty case to extract to prove the gun had, indeed, fired. He then would press home another charge and repeat the process. Not a few of these rifled muskets were found with burst barrels, evidence that several loads had been fired off, disastrously.

This drawback, plus the obvious advantages of a breechloader using a self-contained metallic cartridge, prodded Ordnance into action. In 1863, surveys were made among all troops armed with breechloading and repeating arms to determine their experiences with them in battle. Experiments were conducted at the Springfield Armory, and in 1865 a new cartridge arm was adopted as the official United States infantry weapon. The Springfield Model of 1865, called the Allin conversion, was an expedient permitting use of muzzle-loading arms in stock. The breech end of the barrel was cut off and a rising breechblock was fitted to it. The breech itself opened from the rear like a trap door, a .58-caliber rim fire copper cartridge was dropped in, the gun was cocked and fired. Later models reduced the bore to .50 by reaming out the old rifling and brazing in a new rifled insert. Still later, the action was perfected slightly and the caliber again reduced, to .45. This arm became the standard weapon for American infantrymen until well into the Spanish-American War.

So ended slightly more than half a century of incredibly rapid achievements. It had seen the flintlock give way to the percussion cap, and the cap, in turn, surrender to the new metallic cartridge. The smoothbore musket had disappeared, and all military arms were rifled. Breechloading and repeating arms had become practical after centuries of trying, and mass production was an established fact of life. Few of the gunsmiths who saw the era dawn were around at its climax at the end of the Civil War. Those who did must have felt greatly satisfied—and a little bewildered by it all.

CHAPTER FOUR **GIVE US THE GUNS**

ABOVE: *Backwoodsmen, making use of the best they had, fire Kentucky rifles as Indians charge decoys.* LITHOGRAPH BY CURRIER AND IVES, HARRY T. PETERS COLLECTION, MUSEUM OF THE CITY OF NEW YORK.

PAGES 82 AND 83: *The breech-loading rifle designed by Christian Sharps was most popular single-shot of Civil War and western expansion. Modifications had marked importance for soldier, buffalo hunter, Indian fighter and frontiersman.* GUN: WEST POINT MUSEUM. PHOTO BY ROBERT MOTTAR

A few weeks before the "shot heard 'round the world" was fired at Lexington in 1775, Daniel Boone at the head of a party of eighty axmen hacked out the famous "Wilderness Road" through the Cumberland Gap into Kentucky. Travelers into the "dark and bloody ground" to the west of the Alleghenies were scarce in those days. The discovery of the gap itself, in 1750, had been followed by a series of Indian wars that kept settlers from advancing. Boone's own son had been killed near the gap in 1773. But the urge to move westward was beginning

Stand at Cumberland Gap and watch the

procession of civilization, marching single file—the

buffalo following the trail to the salt

springs, the Indian, the fur trader and hunter,

the cattle raiser, the pioneer farmer—

and the frontier has passed by. Stand at South Pass

in the Rockies a century later and

see the same procession with wider intervals between.

FREDERICK JACKSON TURNER

to stir in a few brave and curious souls, and before Boone died in 1820 he would hear of a million pioneers pouring across the mountains into Kentucky and Tennessee.

Until the end of the War of Independence, the settlers of America hugged the seacoast. The first census of the United States, taken in 1790, turned up small clusters of people in the Kentucky, Tennessee, and Ohio backlands, but not more than five per cent of the new nation's four million inhabitants lived west of the Allegheny watershed. Most Americans were settled within two hundred miles of the Atlantic Ocean.

The impetus to move on came from several sources. Immigration from Europe was increasing the population pressure in the original states. The Continental Army was recruited in part with promises of "a good farm" from a grateful nation when the fighting was over, and whole companies—officers and men—went looking for a better life on the bounty lands of the West. And, finally, during Jefferson's presidency, the Louisiana Purchase was consummated. For a mere $15,000,000, Napoleon Bonaparte ceded to

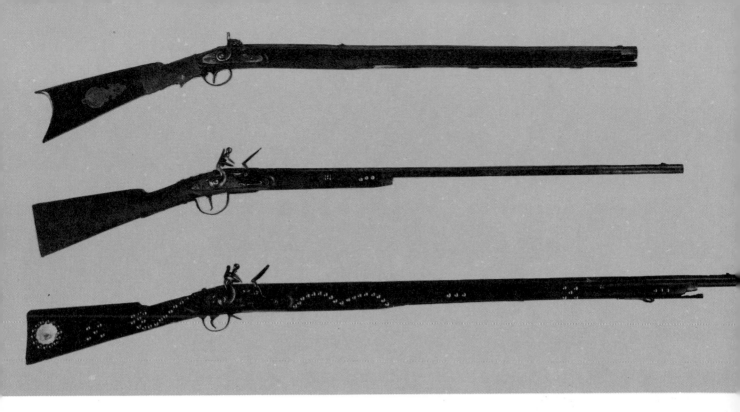

the United States some 827,000 square miles of territory west of the Mississippi and opened the floodgates to expansion. As a dealer in real estate, Bonaparte was not much wiser than the Indians.

Meriwether Lewis and William Clark, surveying the extent of the Purchase, traveled up the Missouri, then overland and down the Columbia, where they gazed upon the Pacific Ocean. They reported game and furs in abundance—and Indians as well, a few hostile, but mostly friendly. Behind them, the Northwest Territory began to fill up. Rivulets of people, uncertain, meandering, but ceaseless, pushed the frontier forward. By 1802, there were enough of them to make a state of Ohio, by 1805 a Michigan, by 1809 an Illinois. By 1820, there was another population belt stretching through Tennessee and western Alabama to Louisiana, although between it and the Carolinas lay the wilderness domain of the savage Creeks, Choctaws, Chickasaws, and Cherokees. "Settlement" frequently meant six people per square mile.

Still, they came. They used four routes, dictated by geography. The so-called northern portage is now, basically, the route of the New York Central Railroad. The Pittsburgh route is followed by the Pennsylvania and the Baltimore & Ohio. The "Wilderness" route is now the roadbed of the Chesapeake & Ohio and the Norfolk & Western. The southern route is used by the east-west systems operating through Birmingham. As someone has said: "People have never abandoned the line of least resistance for travel."

By 1830, the way west was a bulging curve, anchored at Detroit and New Orleans—a line with so many arms reaching up the Wabash, the Missouri, and the Red that it measured fifty-three hundred miles in length. A decade later the anchors had moved only to Green Bay and Corpus Christi, but the flood of settlers had so filled the indentations that the line had shrunk to thirty-three hundred miles. By 1860, it was nearly straight, almost due north and south on the western edge of Iowa and Missouri. The nation was poised for the ultimate dash across the Great Plains.

Wherever they went, the pioneers found a virgin world. It was a world of parching heat and biting cold, of uncertain water, of fever and storms. It was a world of hardship, of unimaginable wonders, and of great beauty. The mountain men, the first to know, had returned from

their lonely excursions in the 1820's, to tell what
it was like—Jim Bridger from Salt Lake and
John Colter from the Yellowstone—and now
the pioneers knew for themselves.

It was not an empty land they entered. Everywhere the Indian stood athwart the trail. It was
the old story. First it was trade: guns for furs.
Then the landgrab, by gift or by guile. Then war.
It was not a calculated pattern. The vitality of
the westward push simply was inexorable and
the Indian was in the way. Treaty after treaty
was written. Move here, the Indian was told. The
white man will not move west of this line and
you will not cross the boundary eastward to
molest him. Now here. Move here. This line is
the limit of the white man's need for land. Everything beyond is yours. And here are guns for your
warriors to seal the bargain.

In 1839, the Indians were given everything
west of the Mississippi, except for Louisiana,
Missouri, and Arkansas. Back, back, moving
westward like his white brother but, unlike him,
in retreat, the Indian went. Sometimes he went
believing the promises made to him, sometimes
he resisted bitterly. But, as we know, he went.

By 1840, there were some sixty thousand
transplanted Indians, most of them armed, living in the country west of Arkansas. Their guns
were trade muskets and rifles. In colonial times,
trade guns were simply those used by the settlers. Low-priced fowling pieces (shotguns) were
the most prized. Muskets of many types were
popular, rifles less so because they required more
care in loading than the Indian was willing to

take. By 1775, however, a particular type of gun
began to emerge as a first choice among the
motley group of trade weapons. This was a light,
smoothbored fowling piece between 24 and 16
gauge (about .58-.66 caliber) which could handle
either shot or ball. About this time, too, the
characteristic "dragon ornament"—a serpent-
shaped side plate like those popular on many
English firearms a century earlier—was added
on the left side. The revival of this design may
have been to suit the Indian's love of ornamen-
tation, to continue a feature of the guns with
which he was familiar, or perhaps to identify
it to the trader as an Indian trade gun.

By 1805, the Hudson's Bay Company, which
was most interested in the Indian trade, had
designed a special gun for this purpose. Sometimes called a fusil, or "fuke," it became best
known as the Northwest Gun or the Mackinaw
Gun. Its basic characteristics were light weight,
a fairly short barrel, and a smooth bore. It was,
of course, a flintlock.

It is possible that no other gun model in
American history had such a widespread use
for so long a time. Hudson's Bay fukes were
actively traded on the western and northern
frontiers, with almost no change in form, for
about a hundred years. They suited the Indian's
needs perfectly: they were just large enough
to kill his game and light enough to carry easily.
Generally, they were of good quality considering their low price—twenty beaver skins—but
the very nature of their light construction often
gave the Indian trouble. Overloads would burst
the barrel, and since the Indian was no ballistics expert, he often was careless in loading.

Yet the Indians were fond of these light guns
and ornamented them heavily with rows of brass
tacks along the stock. The guns usually were
made in England and distributed by the Hudson's Bay Company, the Northwest Company

and, after John Jacob Astor organized it, by the American Fur Company. Many of these guns can be identified by the stamping of a sitting fox enclosed by a circle (Northwest Company) or a tombstone-shaped plaque (Hudson's Bay Company) on lock, stock, or barrel. Belgian and French gunsmiths also produced trade guns, and in later years some American firms, notably George Tryon and Henry Leman of Pennsylvania, turned out trade fusils as well as rifles.

The frontiersman, of course, hankered after the best the gunmaker could offer him. The West —certainly, all territory beyond the Mississippi —confronted him with new problems and only the best would do. The time-honored Kentucky rifle was proving to be too fragile, too long in the barrel to be carried easily on horseback, and, most serious of all, underpowered for long-range, heavy-duty killing. On the plains and in the mountains, the game ran big. Buffalo, elk, and bear—particularly *Ursus horribilis*, the grizzly— gave the hunter plenty of trouble.

Nat Wyeth, the scout who guided Captain William D. Stewart on one of his early trail- blazing expeditions in the Northwest, told how he located a grizzly in a thicket and heaved some stones to bring him out. "Old Ephraim" burst forth, enraged as only a bear can be, and Wyeth shot him—but in the body, "where a grizzly can stand a volley from a company of dragoons." Wyeth, having no time to reload, ran like the wind, with the bear after him. Help was at hand, but it took four more shots to bring the beast down. Prior to 1850, it was almost impossible to take a grizzly with a single- shot rifle unless the bullet found brain or spine.

Frederick Ruxton, early western traveler, describes the difficulty of dropping buffalo. One old bull took eighteen shots, half of them musket balls, through the body at six paces and still remained on his feet. The nineteenth, fired with the muzzle touching the body, finally knocked him down. Even with frontal shots at the head at short range, Ruxton had trouble. "I have fre- quently attempted this," he says, "with a rifle carrying twenty-five balls to the pound [about .58 caliber], but never once succeeded."

Thus the Kentucky gave way to a shorter weapon of larger caliber. One of the finest of these new rifles in the early frontier days was made by Samuel and Jacob Hawken of St. Louis. A typical Hawken of the 1840's was a half- stocked, percussion-lock muzzle-loader. Its thirty-four-inch barrel took a .50-caliber ball and was heavy enough to withstand the stiff charges of black powder required for big game. All the Hawkens were handmade and demand far exceeded the supply. Kit Carson had one, and so did Jim Bridger. It was the favored gun until the advent of the big-bore breechloaders by Sharps, Remington, and Ballard.

The excellence of the Hawken was demon- strated at the mountain men's "Rendezvous," a hurly-burly session of trading, shooting matches, and Homeric drinking that was held each June. In large measure, they simply celebrated the glorious fact of being alive, for each spring famil- iar faces were missing, victims of Indian ambush, accident, or disease. The survivors of those hard seasons had something to shout about. William Hamilton, a veteran of many years in the West, describes a meeting of about sixty mountain men and trappers at Bridger's Fort, on a fork of the Green River in southwestern Wyoming, in the early 1840's. Shooting matches, he says, were held at ranges of twenty to 300 yards for stakes of $5 a shot, and the Hawken was the best rifle he saw. They were accurate up to 350 yards, and the more skillful marksmen could load and fire at the rate of four shots a minute, a creditable performance with a muzzle-loader.

Another favorite competition of the day was

killing buffalo from horseback over a one-mile course, starting with an empty muzzle-loader. Trying to load while pursuing the buff on a hard-running horse was a test even for experts. The common practice was to carry a supply of balls in the mouth and spit them into the muzzle after the powder charge had been poured. The butt was slammed down on the pommel of the saddle to jar powder out through the touch hole into the pan and to seat the ball. It was hoped that the saliva would hold the ball in place until it was time to fire. The trick was to fire the gun as soon as it was pointed downward, for if the ball rolled away from the powder charge before it fired, a burst barrel was almost inevitable. Flintlocks were preferred for this sport. They were easier to use than a percussion gun, which required digging a cap out of a pocket and placing it on the nipple, a difficult task on a galloping horse. Many long-barreled guns were sawed off to make loading and handling easier. Under these conditions, George Catlin, the artist, reports seeing Kenneth McKenzie, an agent for the American Fur Company, kill five buffalo over the run. A decade later, John Audubon, the naturalist, saw another agent, Alex Culbertson, kill eleven. Two runners-up got ten each. (Years of practice apparently had improved the buff hunters' speed.)

Occasionally, the boys tired of targets and started shooting at each other. A rough-hewn pair, made warm and tigerish by liquor, would find their boasts leading to hard words, and soon there was nothing for it but to settle the argument with guns, usually rifles. At the 1835 Rendezvous, Kit Carson had it out with Billy Shunar. They mounted their horses—Kit with a pistol, Billy with his rifle—galloped at each other, and fired at point-blank range. Despite his disadvantage in weapons, Carson disabled Shunar with a shot in the wrist, then got another

pistol with which to finish the job.

For the suicidal, there was a form of amusement known as "shooting the tin cup." The duelers faced each other, about twenty-five yards apart, and took turns trying to shoot a cup full of whiskey off each other's head. A particularly rugged match pitted Mike Fink, the Mississippi keelboater, against his own stepson, a youth named Carpenter. The boy's shot hit the cup low and creased Mike's scalp. Mike's shot, which lacked finesse, hit Carpenter squarely between the eyes. Mike swore it was just plumb bad shooting and an accident, but it smacked of murder to the trappers. A short while later, one of them up and killed Mike with one of Carpenter's pistols.

Aside from the Hawken, there was also a small vogue in double-barreled rifles. Ruxton used one for buffalo. Jim Bridger had an over-and-under rifle made by John Schuler, a Pennsylvania gunsmith. Some of these double guns had one rifled barrel and one smoothbore, thus combining in one weapon all the versatility required for living off the land. Loaded with fine shot, the smoothbore was perfect for small game. With buckshot, it could kill deer—and Indians. The rifle could bring down everything else.

BUFFALO

For forty years (1840-1880), the buffalo was a prime factor in the economic and social history of the American West. He was one of the God-given, seemingly inexhaustible riches of the Great Plains beyond the Mississippi discovered by the pioneering whites. He was food for those passing through. He was money to the hide hunters who stayed. And as the gigantic herds were slaughtered with fearful rapacity, the Indian hungered and the Plains Wars began. As the buffalo died, the Indian went with him. By

the 1880's, neither one was of any consequence to the white man.

The Great Plains, stretching from Canada to Mexico and from the Mississippi to the Rockies, was the world of the bison. It is difficult today to visualize the incredible numbers that literally darkened the prairies a century ago. The most conservative estimates say there were 50,000,-000 animals. Other guesses range as high as 125,000,000. Whatever the exact total, it was without question the greatest concentration of hoofed game animals in the western world. Wagon trains and railroad builders often were forced to halt for several days when migrating herds crossed their trail.

The bison was well adapted to the plains. He needed little water and was never bothered by arid land or dry seasons. His heavy coat withstood the freezing gales of the northern winter. He fattened on the rich grama grass, fought off disease readily, and was seldom harried by natural predators. His size, his muscular forequarters and awesome horns, and his trampling hoofs were more than a match for wolves and coyotes.

For the Plains Indians, the buffalo was the source of life. They never were agriculturists and had no need to be. The buffalo gave them food, hides for shoes, robes, and shelters, bones for tools, sinews and tendons for bowstrings, thongs, and lacings, and manure "chips" to fuel their cooking fires on the treeless prairie.

Before the Spaniards came—and with them the horse, an animal previously unknown to the Indian—the buffalo was stalked on foot, and to kill enough for a steady food supply meant organizing great hunts. Days were spent in preparation, solemn ceremonial days in which tribal gods were exhorted to make the hunters' arrows and lances speed true to the mark.

The stalk was crafty business. The hunters crept up on a section of the herd, screened by clumps of sagebrush or camouflaged with wolfskins, and drove their weapons into as many animals as possible until the rest, sensing dully that trouble was about, lumbered away.

The Spanish horses, and their herds of wild-running descendants, gave the Indian supremacy over the buff. Running the ponderous but fleet-footed giant became not only a food-gathering expedition but keen sport as well. Riding bareback, naked except for a breechclout, and carrying a quiver of arrows for his short, powerful bow, a warrior charged into the edge of the herd and cut out a fat cow. The chase was on. The drum-accents of pounding hoofs rose from the flat prairie and dustclouds choked horse and rider alike. Coming abreast of the stampeding animal's right shoulder, the hunter drew quickly and sent a flint-tipped shaft into the body, just behind the hump. Placed well, one was enough. The rider wheeled and found another victim, again and again, until his quiver was empty and his horse trembling with exhaustion. Multiplied by a hundred warriors, the chase spilled the great bounty of the plains into the laps of the squaws and old men who followed. They hacked the carcasses, skinning out the robes and saving the choice entrails for eating on the spot. The tongue and hump ribs were put aside for the first feasting. The balance was destined to become "jerky" and pemmican.

The running of the buff was also done with firearms, in time, particularly before the herds were spooked almost continually by the hide

Bow and arrows were as good as a trapper's flintlock. Mountain Men later carried Hawken or Sharps rifles.
ILLUSTRATED BY FREDERIC REMINGTON. COURTESY REMINGTON ART MEMORIAL

hunters. Ruxton, an eye-witness to many a hunt, wrote graphically of the powerful lot of killing the beasts took: "Unless shot through the lungs or spine, they invariably escape; and even when thus mortally wounded, or even struck through the very heart, they will frequently run a considerable distance before falling to the ground, particularly if they see the hunter after the wound is given. . . . It is a most painful sight to witness the dying struggles of the huge beast. . . . A bull, shot through the heart or lungs, with blood streaming from his mouth, protruding tongue, his eyes rolling, bloodshot and glazed with death, braces himself on his legs, swaying from side to side, stamps impatiently at his growing weakness, or lifts his rugged and matted head and helplessly bellows out his conscious impotence. . . . Gouts of purple blood spurt from his mouth and nostrils, and gradually the failing limbs refuse longer to support the ponderous carcass. . . . A convulsive tremor seizes it and, with a low, sobbing gasp, the huge animal falls over on his side, the limbs extended stark and stiff, and the mountain of flesh without life or motion."

The early mountain men and trappers, tracking through in the 1820's and 30's, learned to utilize the buffalo, too, although their goal was beaver, fox, and other furs. They killed primarily for food. Still, they were wasters, often slicing off only the choice hump ribs and leaving the carcass—some fifteen hundred pounds—for the wolves and coyotes. They made no inroads on the plains herds, but had pretty well exterminated the smaller, less numerous mountain breed by 1840. Of course, when bison were plentiful the Indian ate high on the hump ribs, too. This, however, was an occasional extra dividend. When the supply was scarce, the kill was consumed down to the last bit of shin meat.

For the big kills to come, a big rifle was needed. This was Christian Sharps' big-bore breechloader which appeared in 1848. Almost at once it became the standard arm of the buffalo hunter. It was a long-range weapon that could be depended on to kill at 200 yards with one shot through the lungs. Furthermore, it had the distinct advantage of being able to accommodate a paper or linen cartridge, or loose powder and ball. Should the supply of made-up loads be fired away during Indian attack or buffalo hunt, the old components would serve as well. The Sharps was the only breechloader that could interchange loads effectively.

The hide hunter, despoiler of the bison, came with the railroads. As soon as bulk transportation was available it became possible—and enormously profitable—to ship hides in quantity to the eastern markets. Here the demand for the warm fur was tremendous. The buffalo robe was almost a necessity for every well-equipped rig or surrey to keep legs warm on wintry drives, and they were almost as popular in the home.

The ready market and the post-Civil War depression brought thousands of hunters west to make their fortunes. Tenderfeet they were, many of them, new to the ways of the West, to the techniques of buff hunting, and to the lawlessness of the frontier. But on they came, riding the Kansas-Pacific Railroad, carrying their new Sharps or Remington, their Ballard or Winchester single-shot, eager to get in on the easy pickings before it was too late. They gave no thought to the destiny of the humpbacked beasts awaiting them. But this was not surprising. No one but the Indian did. If, as some tribes believed, the buffalo burst from the earth each spring to replenish his kind, there would always be plenty for the taking. And if not? Well, who would count the slaughter while big money poured into the pockets of the bold and resourceful hunter? A good hide brought $3 at Dodge City and as much as $50 if it were of the extra-fine quality known as "silk." At these prices an expert hunter could make $10,000 in a season.

There were famous names among the hunters. It was, if you care to look at it that way, a glamorous company. Among the first was William F. Cody, "Buffalo Bill," meat hunter for the Union Pacific gandy-dancers. "Wild Bill" Hickok was a successful hide hunter, as was

Charley Reynolds, General Custer's able scout. The professionals, to be sure, were very good at their business. They had nothing to do with the wild, whooping excitement of a buffalo run, or "surround," as it came to be called. There was too much at stake. They worked carefully, methodically, and purposefully, trying not to alarm the herd so as to keep as many animals as possible within range of their hide wagons.

The hide hunter's investment was considerable. He had to have camping gear, rolling stock, and a dozen mules to haul it. He had to have at least one skinner, sometimes more. And one or two companion hunters. A big outfit would have a man whose only job was to reload the big brass cartridge cases after a day's shooting. With several hunters working, this was no light task. The key weapons were the Sharps, Remington,

Winchester, or Ballard rifles, packing a .40- or .50-caliber bullet of at least 350 grains. A large supply of powder, pig lead for bullets, primers, and reloading equipment completed the armory.

A typical day began with the location of a herd. As the first rays of the sun cut through the chill morning air, the hunter searched the horizon for a low-hanging frost cloud. This would be the condensing vapors of the warm breath of a multitude of bison. It was a sure sign; it always betrayed their presence. With daylight, the herd would break up for the morning feed, scattering in small groups, nosing through the thin covering of soft snow for the rich grass beneath. Winter on the plains was bitter, but this was when the bison's coat was at its thick, glossy best, when the hide would command the top price back East. The hunter

followed the trail on horseback. The buffalo moved slowly, browsing always into the wind. They feared nothing and could go as they willed, at their own pace. It was no trouble getting within range and staying there.

When the hunter picked his group for the morning kill, he dismounted, staked his horse in a draw or behind a bluff, and made the final stalk to his "stand" on foot. The choice was seldom arbitrary. The hunter looked for good natural cover to ease his approach—and a good escape route in the event of Indian attack. Lugging his rifle and a bag of ammunition, the hunter might sneak up a shallow gully or scuttle behind sagebrush, keeping himself downwind, until he was 200 yards from his quarry. Forty or fifty buff, grunting and snuffling, head down, nosing around for feed—that was the ticket. The

Bareback rider lances buffalo—a favorite hunting method before the coming of the white man's firearms.
FROM FREDERIC REMINGTON BY HAROLD MC CRACKEN, COURTESY J. B. LIPPINCOTT CO.

hunter would scan the group and pick out the leader. He estimated the range, set his rear sight, and if he wanted to make extra sure, he rested his rifle barrel on crossed sticks for support. Firing from the kneeling or prone position, he aimed for the vital spot just behind the shoulder and let fly. The rifle banged, white smoke spurted into the clear air, and the first buffalo dropped with a heavy slug in its lungs. Usually, the other animals merely lifted their shaggy heads, stared about with stupid curiosity, and returned to feeding. The hunter, meanwhile, reloaded and selected his next victim.

If all went well, buffalo would stagger and fall after a small expenditure of ammunition. If it did not—if an animal were merely wounded and started to run, or if the others began to register the smell of death—the herd might begin to mill about and scatter in alarm. Then there was nothing for it but to pump as many shots into the confused beasts as could be managed before they thumped out of range. The hunter would high-tail it for his horse and resume the chase, sometimes picking up the same group after it had settled down a few miles beyond, sometimes another section of the herd.

Behind him, awaiting the sound of the big rifle, was the skinner and the hide wagon. As soon as the first fusillade ended and the hunter was on his way to the next stand, the skinner came onto the field to fleece the stricken. In the cracking cold of winter he had to work fast or the stiffening bodies would cool out and lock

the hide rigidly to the carcass. He first unhooked his team and rigged a heavy line to the clevis on the doubletree. Then he ringed the thick hide at the neck of the first buffalo with his sharp, curved knife, passing behind the stubby horns, and rolled it back. The belly was slit from throat to tail. Another quick slash up the inside of each leg joined the body cut. Next, he took a short, heavy iron rod and drove the pointed end through the buff's nose and into the frozen earth with a sledge. The team was brought up, the line looped and knotted around the roll of hide at the top of the neck. The bullwhip snapped and the team hauled. With a rending sound the hide separated from the naked carcass and flapped

over the snow in the wake of the team. The rod was removed. The soggy hide was piled into the wagon. And the skinner moved on.

Thus the team of hunter and skinner worked, day after day, as long as the blizzards and the Indians held off, the powder and lead held out, and the buffalo stayed within reach. In a month, a thousand hides or more would be piled up at the hunters' main camp, awaiting transport to Dodge City or some other nearby shipping point, where the pay-off would be made for reinvestment in more hide-hunting gear or for squandering at the gaming tables.

This was the Great Plains in the 1860's and 70's. Any one hunter's effort could be multiplied

a thousand times, and the "Big Fifties" were fired until their barrels were too hot to touch and had to be cooled in the snow. The hunter blasted and the skinner ripped until the pressure of death was too great to offset. The buffalo multitudes thinned and shrank and disappeared.

The magnificent Republican herd of north Kansas was the first to go, its endless trainloads of hides moving east on the Union Pacific until there proved, in fact, to be an end. Next was the Arkansas herd whose existence created Buffalo City—later Dodge City, to avoid confusion with the western New York community that had priority on the name. The Texas herd came next. And finally the Northern herd, whose few sur-

PAGES 98 AND 99: *If a plainsman, buffalo hunter or cowboy could afford the best, he was likely to own one of these fine guns of the 1880's. Top to bottom: Winchester '73, "One of One Thousand"; Remington Frontier revolver, Model 1875; Remington-Hepburn single-shot rifle; Sharps buffalo rifle, modified by Freund; and the Smith & Wesson Third Model American .44-caliber revolver, with Mexican Eagle grips.*
GUNS: WILLIAM SWEET, WILLIAM FLORENCE, LARRY SHEERIN. PHOTO BY ROBERT MOTTAR

Mountain Men, guns in hand, opened up the West, won a foothold; but pioneer farmers and cattlemen, needed to settle it, migrated in their greatest numbers only after the laying of track.
LITHOGRAPH BY CURRIER AND IVES. HARRY T. PETERS COLLECTION, MUSEUM OF THE CITY OF NEW YORK. COURTESY SHOREWOOD PRESS

vivors escaped into Montana and the Dakotas. By 1883 nothing remained from Canada to Mexico and from the Mississippi to the Rockies but mountains of bleached bones. Dodge City had sunk into lethargy. Even the bone pickers, who had scoured the prairies for skeletons at $8 a ton, were out of business. The buffalo run was over.

THE PLAINS WARS:
"The only good Indians I ever saw were dead."

Guns for the hide hunters were only a fraction of the traffic in arms to the West. Farmers and miners, scouts and trappers, cattlemen and sheepherders, casual travelers and plain citizens —none of them would think of going unarmed in country where firepower settled so many arguments, where guns superseded so many laws. Claim jumping, robbery, and Indian attack were routine occurrences. The homesteader strapped his rifle between the handles of his plow and

wore a cartridge belt and six gun at his waist. Back East, it was a seller's market for gun manufacturers. In addition to the well-known names, there sprang into being a gnat-swarm of small companies producing rifles, shotguns, and handguns of every conceivable model and design. It was one of the greatest booms ever enjoyed by the arms industry in the United States.

Chief among the needs for guns was the mounting hostility of the Indian. The great wave of westward migration trespassed upon his lands and poached on his food supply. His game was going, most importantly the buffalo, but other animals as well: elk, pronghorn antelope, mule deer, whitetails. The wagon trains, rolling ceaselessly over the plains, frightened the game herds away from the Indians' traditional hunting grounds or, worse, outside the boundaries of the treaty lands established by the whites.

The wanton killing was bad enough. The wanton waste was unforgivable. Many of the new-

100

comers were shabby hunters and poor shots. They frequently used military muzzle-loaders, ancient smoothbores loaded with buckshot, or rifles that were underpowered and inadequate. They crippled much more than they killed.

These were the Indian's principal grievances. There were lesser ones, too, wounding to the pride and mortifying to the spirit, which he possibly might have borne had the basic and essential pattern of his days been undisturbed. He was saddened and dismayed by the lies of the land agents, the swindles of the traders who sold wormy flour and rancid bacon at blackmail prices, and the seduction of his women. If for some tribes laxity in sexual matters was condoned, or considered a mark of hospitality, for others, such as the Sioux, it was a grave affront to tribal honor. Yet trouble might still have been averted had the treaty boundaries been respected and the buffalo permitted to flourish.

A few wise chiefs foresaw the approaching dis-

"The Greatest Light Cavalry in the World," *as typified by this Blackfoot, was destroyed by disease, loss of buffalo, and warfare with whites.* PAINTING BY KARL BODMER. SMITHSONIAN INSTITUTE

101

Frederic Remington

aster. As early as 1846, Yellow Wolf of the Cheyennes predicted that the bison was headed for extinction. He urged his people to acquaint themselves with the white settlers' cattle and wanted the herder at Bent's Fort to teach his young people animal husbandry. His efforts were drowned in ridicule. Who needed cattle while the buffalo roamed the plains? He was paid no heed.

Other Cheyenne chiefs, fearful for the continuity of the tribe, proposed at a council with Government agents that a thousand white women be given their people as wives. The notion had a certain grain of sense. By Cheyenne custom, all children belonged to the mother's people; in effect, the Cheyenne were willing to sacrifice their tribal identity to assure that their issue might live in the white man's world. It was tragic and naive and totally disregarded.

All other efforts failing, the Indian next sought to acquire the white man's weapons. Tribes on the various reservations clamored for the new repeating Henrys and Spencers, and traders often made a fast dollar supplying them in defiance of prohibitions. The Indians appreciated the power of the firearms they begged for. General Grenville M. Dodge, returning in 1865 from the expedition which found a pass through the Laramie Mountains for the Union Pacific, reported that Henrys had kept pursuing Cheyennes at such long range that they could never close for a sustained attack.

The redskins got the guns. One of the first, a Henry repeater, Serial Number 2729, was found

"Yellow Boy" was the name given to the Winchester '66 because of its brass receiver. A scout armed with this fast-loading, practical, compact repeater was a match for any Plains Indian.
FROM FREDERIC REMINGTON BY HAROLD MC CRACKEN.
COURTESY J. B. LIPPINCOTT CO.

on the body of High Backed Wolf, a Cheyenne killed at the Platte Bridge on the Oregon Trail, as early as July 25, 1865. Other Henrys fell to the Indians by such astonishing incidents as the encounter of a party traveling up the Missouri to establish a wood yard near Fort Union, North Dakota, for the river steamboats. Going ashore, they were greeted by some Sioux who said they'd admire to have a look at the white men's rifles. Incredibly, the men handed over their guns for inspection and died under a hail of fire that proved beyond doubt the Henry's qualities.

Probably few agents were foolish or treacherous enough to arm warring tribes, but no doubt many allowed themselves to be solicited by friendly tribes who were, accordingly, well armed when conditions changed. The Fort Bridger post trader's journal of November, 1869, lists "20 bxs Henry cartridges and 1008 Spencer cartridges" as charged to the "Wind River Adventure." The consignment also included "ear rings, beads and mirrors." Wind River was Shoshone country. There is little doubt as to the destination of the ammunition. William Henry Jackson, pioneer photographer of the West, took a picture of Ute Indians with Henry repeaters in 1874; also Nez Percés at about the same time. When war broke out, many Indians were more than ready.

Many, it should be emphasized, but not all. The traditional Indian weapons—the bow and the lance—were never completely replaced and often were adequate when the tactical situation was to the war party's liking. The Plains Indian was essentially a cavalryman and adept with his weapons whether in pursuit or retreat. With his fourteen-foot lance he could reach over the bobbing head of his pony to skewer a fleeing white, with flint- or steel-tipped arrows he could sustain a quite-accurate barrage to the rear against charging horsemen. The familiar encirclement of the wagon train was developed to

Cowboys—firing Winchester Model '66 rifles and single-action Colt revolvers—dash for the timber where they will make a stand with their repeating weapons.

FROM FREDERIC REMINGTON BY HAROLD MC CRACKEN.
COURTESY J. B. LIPPINCOTT CO.

force the riflemen to expend ammunition; in the moments spent reloading the Indians sought to break the ring. White men soon learned to fire carefully and in sequence, so that some weapons always were primed for the onslaught.

Even the Indians who got rifles were not, as a rule, very good shots. "Uncle Dick" Wootton, a grizzled mountain man (born Richens Lacy Wootton in Virginia, in 1816), recalled after fifty years of wandering the West and Southwest that, "We could shoot more accurately and handle our guns a great deal quicker. To shoot with any accuracy, the Indian had to have a rest for his gun and he always was slow about taking sight, while the mountain men all shot offhand and lost no time in drawing a bead on an enemy."

The final resistance of the Indian to the excesses and encroachments of the white man was encompassed in the fifteen (1862-1877) bitter years of the Plains Wars. The blow-off came from an unexpected quarter: Chief Little Crow,

the leader of the Santee Sioux of Minnesota. Years back, the Chief had signed a treaty with the United States Government and despite abuse by the whites and the wrath of his tribe he had kept within the hunting grounds that had been granted him. At first he had been friendly to the whites and called them brother. He had accepted gracefully the indignities accompanying the migration through the tribal lands. Ultimately, however, there came an insult too grave to be overlooked. In 1862, a routine request by the Sioux for Government food allotments guaranteed by treaty, was met by Andrew Merrick, trader, with the sneering reply: "If they're hungry, let 'em eat grass, for all I care."

Other incidents followed. Little Crow and the Sioux put on war paint. A force of one hundred and fifty of them descended on the Redwood Agency, a trading station on the Minnesota River, and slaughtered every white settler in sight. The fighting had begun. According to the admittedly incomplete records of the state of

Minnesota, some six hundred and forty-four settlers were killed in the skirmishes which followed. Hundreds more were captured and many of them did not return. About twenty counties were swept bare of settlers.

For a while, the rampaging Indians had things pretty much their own way and the uprising spread into Iowa and Dakota. The Civil War was in progress and garrison troops had been withdrawn from western outposts for service in the Union Army. Several months passed before cavalry and infantry regulars could be detached to suppress Little Crow, with the aid of superior weapons, and force his surrender. Some fifteen hundred Sioux were imprisoned and thirty-seven simultaneously hanged from one scaffold. Little Crow escaped the pursuing troops, but shortly came to a sad and inglorious end. Soon after New Year's Day in 1863, a pair of deer hunters came upon two bedraggled Indians searching the wintry plain for berries. Depredations had continued and all Indians were enemies now. The

hunters fired and killed one. They dragged the body to a nearby village and dumped it unceremoniously into the offal pit of a slaughter house. It was, of course, Little Crow. His son, who had been the other berry picker, confirmed the fact when he was himself captured some time later.

For the next two years, the broken and leaderless Sioux were quiet. But other tribes were on the prod. To the south, in Kansas and Colorado, roving bands of Kiowas, Comanches, and Cheyennes launched repeated attacks against the wagon trains. It was a part of the bitterness and confusion of the Plains Wars that the Indians themselves were divided. Some tribes tried to stay at peace with the whites. Others went on a rampage. Even within tribes, a chief and his followers might abide by the tribal treaty with the settlers, while war parties broke off under the leadership of a hot-blood to live as wandering guerrilla warriors. Among the Comanches, for instance, even before the arrival of the whites, custom permitted any warrior so disposed to or-

ganize and lead an attack or feat of daring in order to acquire "coup," or, roughly, prestige. This was not considered to usurp the power of the chief, but simply to enhance the standing of the brave. It is quite likely that many of the combatants in the Plains Wars fought to remove the stain of humiliation and to retrieve honor by achieving "coup" at the white man's expense.

The niceties of the situation were lost upon the whites, however. Indians were Indians and a cruel and remorseless foe. Torture and savagery were visited upon captives just often enough to convince the whites that when war came no quarter could be asked or given. This feeling frequently worked hardship on non-violent groups such as the friendly Cheyennes of Chiefs Black Kettle and White Antelope, who lived in the area of Sand Creek, Colorado, nominally under the protection of Major Wynkoop, at nearby Fort Lyon. Colonel J. M. Chivington, a Methodist minister when he was not riding at the head of the 2nd Colorado Cavalry, could not see the distinction. Riled by the depredations of the Cheyennes, he cried in a public speech: "Kill and scalp all [Indians] big and little; nits make lice." Then, acting on his own advice, he led the Cavalry on November 29, 1864, in the Sand Creek Massacre of three hundred men, women and children, most of them unarmed. The few Cheyennes who escaped fled north where the Northern Cheyennes and Sioux welcomed them and swore to carry on the fight. The war spread. Sioux, Cheyenne, and Arapahoe, too, campaigned against the border outposts, killing, burning, and looting the devastated settlements

of arms and ammunition. Fighting in the north was brought under control only after two years and the application of the heavy hand of General Phil Sheridan, whose conviction it was that "the only good Indians I ever saw were dead."

On one occasion, a typical incident, Sheridan sent a free-lance company of fifty tough frontiersmen, under Major (Brevet-Colonel) George A. Forsyth, to beat the Indians at their own game. Heavily armed with seven-shot Spencers, Colt revolvers, and a good supply of ammunition, they caught up with the Indian raiders on the banks of the Arickaree Fork of the Republican River, in Kansas. The frontiersmen were outnumbered, but they barricaded themselves

on a sandbar offshore and withstood a series of charges and attacks for seven days.

Like all brush-fire wars, however, the Indian troubles were no sooner extinguished in one place than they blazed up in another. It was at this time that the notorious Fetterman Massacre occurred, near Fort Phil Kearney, in Wyoming. Riding out at the head of a column of eighty officers and men to relieve a wood-gathering party that had come under Cheyenne attack, Captain William Judd Fetterman disobeyed orders at his peril. Relieve the party and no more, Colonel Carrington had said. But when the column dispersed the raiders and the Indians skittered away, Fetterman couldn't resist the temp-

tation to pursue. The Indians led him up a draw where several hundred Cheyennes, under Big Nose, brother of the great Chief Little Wolf, leaped from ambush and slaughtered the column in a matter of minutes.

Of Fetterman's command, only six fell to bullets. The Indians were armed principally with bows and lances. The troopers carried single-shot Springfields. But those who sold their lives most dearly were two scouts, Jim Wheatley and Ike Fischer, who were armed with new sixteen-shot, .44-caliber Henrys. Around their position, somewhat apart from the main body of the cavalry, was a profusion of cartridge cases. J. P. Dunn, in *Massacres of the Mountains*, says: "Within a

107

few hundred feet of this position were found ten ponies and sixty-five great gouts of blood which had flowed from death wounds of as many Indians. No ponies and no death spots were found anywhere else." Years later the Cheyennes admitted that their casualties in this battle, laid side by side, made two long rows—perhaps fifty or sixty men in all. It is fairly clear that the outcome would have been different had all the column been equipped with Henry or Spencer re-

peaters. Colonel Carrington, acknowledging the fact somewhat late, immediately ordered repeating weapons for his remaining troops.

The Wagon Box Fight, which also took place in Wyoming directly after the Fetterman debacle, proved the point again when Captain (Brevet-Major) James Powell and twenty-six soldiers stood off an estimated eight hundred Sioux, later reinforced to two thousand. Caught in the open, Powell and his men hastily rigged a

Hard-riding Indian, following standard tactics, sends arrow into lead horse. Stagecoach guards, who usually carried six guns and double-barreled shotguns, loaded with buckshot, will make a fight of it, without horses.
FROM FREDERIC REMINGTON
BY HAROLD MCCRACKEN. COURTESY
GOLDEN BOOK OF AMERICA

fortification of fourteen upturned wagon bodies, sheathed with boiler iron. The Sioux were led by the statuesque Red Cloud, who stood six-foot-six and was a veteran of some eighty battles. His allies were the famous chiefs Crazy Horse, American Horse, and Big Crow. The Indians were not heavily armed, although some of them had guns. Powell's group was equipped with a new 1865 issue of Springfield-Allin conversions. These were Civil War muzzle-loaders that had been changed to single-shot breechloaders firing a .58-caliber, rim-fire cartridge. While not superlative weapons, their relative power and reloading speed made the Wagon Box defenders more than a match for the horde of Sioux. When the battle ended, Powell estimated that one hundred and eighty Sioux had been killed and wounded. His own casualties were two killed and two wounded.

Eventually, the Government made another treaty with Red Cloud which granted his nation

Geronimo (1829-1909), photographed in last years of his life, holds an extremely rare Dance Brothers revolver, made in Texas. He led an Apache band that fled to Mexico, and launched there brutal raids on Arizona settlements.

PHOTO COURTESY OF HERB GLASS

all of the Powder River region of North Dakota, including the Black Hills, for its hunting grounds. All outposts and forts were removed from the territory, Red Cloud finding particular relish in personally destroying Fort Phil Kearney, long an irritation to the Sioux.

The Sioux now were quiescent and might have remained so but for the arrival of George Armstrong Custer. Fresh from small triumphs over the Cheyennes in the south—notably the massacre at Washita River—Custer undertook to explore possible routes for the Northern Pacific near the borders of the Sioux treaty lands in the summer of 1873. With ten troops of the Seventh Cavalry, Custer made his survey. He had virtually no trouble with the Indians. When he returned, however, the word spread that there was gold in the Black Hills. Treaty or no treaty, a wild, California-style gold rush began.

The Sioux protested. These were the sacred hills of their deities and protected by treaty. The Government equivocated. General Alfred H. Terry, who was Commander, Department of the Dakota, finally received a confidential letter from President Grant, by way of General Phil Sheridan, stating that while miners and prospectors were officially to be forbidden to enter the Black Hills, the Army was to make no further attempt to enforce the provisions of the treaty.

Their treaty violated and meaningless, the Indians fought for survival. From the Black Hills, across the prairie lands of the buffalo, and south to the desert retreat of the Apache, the bloody conflict spread. The loss of life among Indians, civilians, and the military in the area was enormous, higher on a per-capita basis than even the Civil War. The high point was Custer's last stand in the celebrated—and controversial—Battle of the Little Big Horn, in 1876.

Briefly, the familiar story begins with the General and all twelve troops of the Seventh

Cavalry tracking Sitting Bull and his Sioux in the valley of the Little Big Horn River, in southern Montana. He had split his command into three detachments, so that when the onslaught on his personal contingent began, Custer was forced to meet it with only five companies. The overwhelming Indian force—estimated at twenty-five hundred to three thousand warriors —swept Custer to higher ground where, at several points, he made his stand. His horses had been driven off, captured or shot. No relief could be hoped for. At two in the afternoon the fight began. At sunset the last man fell.

Controversy still surrounds the event. On balance, however, it appears that Custer was brave but foolhardy, and he is usually condemned for disobeying explicit orders, evidently in the hope of achieving personal glory—or "coup." That he made a big, fat mistake is incontestable.

Custer was both outnumbered and in a sense "outgunned" by the Sioux and their allies. By June of 1876, the warring Indians had collected many modern rifles, the best of which were Winchester 1866 repeaters. Estimates as to who was armed with what are varied, depending on who tells the story. It is a fair statement, however, that probably no more than twenty-five per cent of the Indians had repeaters, another twenty-five per cent single-shot firearms of many kinds, and the balance the basic bow and lance.

The Seventh Cavalry's issue weapon was the single-shot, breech-loading Springfield of .45/70 caliber. It was rugged and usually dependable as an all-around cavalry arm and had excellent ballistic qualities. On the best day it ever saw, however, it could not match the firepower of a repeater. In fact, after sustained firing (with black powder) the action frequently would foul and fail to close properly. When the gun was fired, the case head would sometimes break off in the extractor and jam the action. Springfields later

recovered from the Sioux in this condition conjured up the tragic picture of some of Custer's hard-pressed men expending the last moments of their lives trying to clear a useless weapon.

The cavalry had no repeaters other than Colt revolvers, which were fine for close work but inadequate for fighting off a full-scale attack. Ammunition was plentiful at the start and lacking at the finish. It is fairly certain that most of it was either with the pack train or carried in the saddlebags of the cavalry's mounts and that the Indians lost little time in stampeding many of these horses away from the scene.

Custer himself disdained to use the Army Springfield. His weapon was a Remington rolling-block sporting rifle with an octagonal barrel, a single-shot arm neither better nor worse than the breechloaders carried by his men. In addition he carried as side arms two English double-action revolvers with white grips and lanyard rings in the butts. The exact model of these revolvers has never been determined, but they were probably Webleys.

The General was an excellent shot by reputation—and by his own account—although Frank North, one of his scouts, thought otherwise. North once told of an expedition into the hills when Custer fired successive shots at three ducks swimming in a river and missed them all. North concluded modestly that he himself then decapitated the ducks with three more shots.

Despite Custer's crashing defeat, it was the Indian who made virtually his last stand at the Little Big Horn. The Plains Wars were nearly over. The military would be occupied until the 1880's in quelling outbreaks by Chief Joseph's Nez Percés, the Apaches of Cochise and Geronimo, and the Utes of New Mexico. But for the most part, the Indian was done. It was a triumph for the superior arms of the white man; for the Springfield as opposed to lance and bow, for the repeater as opposed to the Springfield, and for the Sharps that eradicated the buffalo.

For the wars themselves were perhaps less decisive than the disappearance of the Indian's food supply. When the Texas legislature sounded the first official alarm at the decline of the buff, and proposed a bill to outlaw the hide hunter, "Little Phil" Sheridan hastened to Austin to protest. Restore the buffalo to the plains, he argued, and the Indian will never be defeated. Give the hide hunters medals for outstanding kills, he urged, rather than restrict or prohibit their operations. It was a cruel but valid philosophy. It convinced the Texans, and its echo undoubtedly influenced President Grant, who was considering a similar bill for the Territories, to exercise a pocket veto. The buffalo went and the Indian's resistance broke. The wars ended.

Civilian arms made great strides forward in the period of the Plains Wars. The Henry rifle, which loaded from the front of the magazine grew into the Winchester Model 1866, which loaded more easily and quickly through a gate on the right side of the receiver or, as a single-shot, through the top as well. The Model 66 was the dominant arm for hunters, scouts, and cattlemen for almost twenty years, but Winchester was constantly developing new ideas for improvements and variations.

In 1873, a new Winchester model was designed for sale to the Government as a military arm. The military did not want it, but it was a tremendous success with hunters and adventurers. Before it was discontinued in 1924, a total of 720,610 was sold. Aside from some simplifications of the mechanism and the use of stronger materials, its great advance lay in its ammunition. The powder charge for the .44-caliber bullet was increased from twenty-eight to forty grains, providing greater striking power and a flatter trajectory, and a more reliable center-fire primer

High esteem in which firearms were held initiated custom of presenting fancy models as gifts. Gideon Welles, Secretary of Navy, received a Henry rifle, top. General W. E. Strong gave General P. H. Sheridan a Winchester Model '76, .50-95 caliber Express, center; and Buffalo Bill gave a Winchester Model '73, .30-20 caliber, to a boy, Robbie Campbell Adams. GUNS: WILLIAM SWEET. PHOTO BY ROBERT MOTTAR

replaced the old rim-fire. The Colt revolver was chambered for this same cartridge in 1878, just as the Model '73 was really getting into production, thus giving the plainsman two weapons for one load. Buffalo Bill and Theodore Roosevelt both thought highly of their '73's, and the list of westerners who joined them would read like a "Who's Who" of Indian fighters and rangers.

The disaster at the Little Big Horn might have been expected to convince the military that the day of the single-shot rifle and carbine was ended. There were other considerations, however. None of the repeaters then on the market could match the .45/70 Springfield ballistically. It had a flatter trajectory, less deviation in flight, and greater penetration than any other available arm. Also it had a higher muzzle velocity than most. Finally, it had a simpler action, a most important factor for a military arm. Thus, no repeating rifle of any kind was officially adopted by the Army until 1892, when the Norwegian Krag, adapted to accommodate the new smokeless-powder .30/40 cartridge, became the official shoulder weapon.

The defeat of the Indians and the arrival of smokeless powder began a new era in American firearms. The civilization of the West diminished the need for guns in work and war. At peace and at leisure, the modern rifle and shotgun emerged —sleek and efficient sportsman's weapons, to be fired in anger no more.

BOOK TWO | ROUGH AND READY

CHAPTER FIVE **THE**

PERSONAL COMBAT WEAPON

America is the country where life is

cheaper than anywhere else.

ANDREW STEINMETZ

Mr. Steinmetz, an English visitor who traveled extensively in the United States prior to the Civil War, was speaking of the frequency with which Americans shot each other. In most countries, he went on to say, the duel was an "offhand diversion." But "where men fight in the States they fight in earnest, 'killing is the word.' Revolvers are forever revolving."

A peaceable man, Mr. Steinmetz may have overstated his case, though not by much. His visit came at a time when the tradition of personal combat was well-entrenched and flourishing, particularly in the wisteria-scented South, where satisfaction for honor besmirched was eagerly sought under the *code duello,* and in the short-tempered West, where hasty words were followed by a fast draw.

As always, tactics were sharpened and refined by weapons. The shoulder arm secured the beachhead, repulsed the Indian, filled the cook pot, and fought the wars—and in the pursuit of each task, the weapons became better and the task more easily accomplished. Shooting it out, man to man, was likewise a special technique that came to full flower only with the development, over a period of years, of a purely personal combat weapon—the handgun.

Among the first champions of the personal

PAGES 116 AND 117: *Men who went down to the sea in ships seldom went unarmed. Pirates bombarded merchantmen with cannon balls, leaped aboard swinging cutlasses, and dispatched foe with flintlocks, like Queen Anne pistol, below. Sailors preferred longer naval pistol, top.*
GUNS: HAROLD PETERSON. PHOTO BY ROBERT MOTTAR

RIGHT: *"In time of Action, he (Captain Edward Teach, called 'Blackbeard') wore a Sling over his shoulders with three brace of Pistols, hanging in holsters like Bandoliers; He struck lighted Matches under his Hair...appearing on each side of his Face, and his Eyes, naturally looking fierce and wild...all together such a figure that Imagination cannot form an idea of a Fury from Hell to look more frightful."*
QUOTE AND PAINTING FROM HISTORY OF PIRATES BY CHARLES JOHNSON.
COURTESY RARE BOOK DIVISION, NEW YORK PUBLIC LIBRARY

Heavily armed British buccaneer,
Captain Henry Morgan, stands for portrait
before taking Panama from Spaniards.

weapon were the pirates who followed close on the heels of the explorers and, almost beyond reach of maritime authority, sailed brazenly through the virgin waters of the New World. Heartless and lupine men, they chopped and shot their way through the rich Caribbean empire of Spain, plundered coastal settlements, and preyed upon the ships of all nations. Piracy and buccaneering reached their height off the Atlantic coast in the late years of the seventeenth century and continued at full blast through 1725. Thereafter they gradually slowed down as law enforcement on the seas stiffened. Nonetheless, there still were pirates in the Caribbean as late as 1815, and one of them, Jean Lafitte, joined Andrew Jackson to fight the British in the Battle of New Orleans.

The cutlass, thrust through a wide sash at the waist or hung from a sword belt, was the pirate's principal weapon for boarding or beach-

head assault. But the well-equipped raider also carried one or more pairs of pistols of which he was inordinately proud. There was no time for reloading once a ship had been boarded and hand-to-hand combat had begun. Thus, some pirates carried as many as six pistols when they went into action, and they devised intricate ways of fastening them so they could be drawn quickly. They were hung from both waist belts and shoulder belts, attached to "different coloured ribbands over their shoulders," or thrust under the flaps of coat pockets. The contemporary print on the previous page shows the infamous Blackbeard with two rows of three holsters each hung from shoulder belts, so that the pistol butts point inward across his stomach for quick and easy drawing.

Because they carried so many pistols, the pirates normally favored the smaller sizes to lessen the weight of their loads. The cannon-barreled "Queen Anne" pistol seems to have been a particular favorite after 1700. Many of these had barrels which unscrewed at the breech to permit loading directly into the chamber and so were unencumbered with ramrods or bulky forestocks. All kinds of pistols found use, however, especially those which were well made and showy, and the pirates took good care of them. Speaking of this, Captain Charles Johnson, who quite probably had engaged in piracy himself, states, "In this they were extravagantly nice, endeavoring to outdo one another in the Beauty and Richness of their Arms, giving sometimes at an Auction made at the Mast £30 or 40 a Pair for Pistols."

Many other persons also used pistols throughout the colonial period. Sailors on men-of-war used them much as did their lawless cousins, but they usually carried only one or two instead of six, and they favored longer and bigger weapons with belt hooks for fastening to their waists.

Cavalrymen carried pistols in saddle holsters and officers fancied more elaborate ones as personal arms. As for the civilian, the pistol became an accouterment of wealth, a household defense, and, often, suggested that the bearer was willing to defend his honor on the dueling ground.

The duel, as a means of settling personal differences, did not flourish in the Colonies. New England seems to have regarded it as one of the less desirable imports from the homeland and enacted severe penalties against it prior to the Revolutionary War. In later years the prohibition spread to almost every other area of the United States. The laws, however, were honored more in the breach than in the observance. Subrosa dueling swept the country like a hot flame. Not until the 1870's or 80's was it possible to convict a successful duelist of murder. Senator

Matched pair of Le Faucheux percussion dueling pistols, complete with loading accessories. Made in France, about 1840, they were superbly designed for the job of defending honor.

GUNS: WEST POINT MUSEUM. PHOTO BY ROBERT MOTTAR

Lewis F. Linn of Missouri compared dueling with marriage: "The more barriers erected against it, the surer are the interested parties to come together."

The deep South was the point of origin, beginning shortly after the young nation won its independence. By the middle 1800's, many cities claimed to be the center and focal point of dueling, Charleston, Savannah, New Orleans, Natchez, and Vicksburg among them. The effect of the duel on political and military history was enormous. Many famous and brilliant leaders of the young nation died on the field of honor, often to settle little more than verbal disagreements or fancied insults.

Outstanding among northern duels was the encounter between Alexander Hamilton and Aaron Burr. Political enemies for many years, they were all too ready to give credence to second-hand reports of each other's slanders. The climax came hard upon Burr's failure to gain the Presidency, for which he blamed Hamilton. Their meeting on Weehawken Heights, across the Hudson from Manhattan, on July 11, 1804, is a familiar tragedy. They dueled according to the code of the day: pistols at ten paces. Hamilton, no dueler or even gun handler of any experience, was mortally wounded in the first exchange of shots. His pistol, in fact, was not discharged until he dropped, and it is a matter of record that he was unaware of firing at all.

Burr fled to the seclusion of Major Pierce Butler's estate in Georgia, barely escaping murder indictments brought against him by both New York and New Jersey. In the South he was regarded as something of a hero, if for no other reason than that he had acquitted himself favorably on the field of honor. Within four months, the furor had subsided sufficiently to permit him to take his seat as Vice President and presiding officer of the Senate. In Hamilton the nation

Alexander Hamilton, hit by lead ball from Aaron Burr's flintlock pistol, falls mortally wounded.

lost a brilliant leader and a financial genius, and public indignation at his death led to the further suppression of dueling in the North.

In the South, however, duels continued almost as a way of life for at least another fifty years. Virtually any difference of opinion was an excuse to take the field with pistols: politics, personal grudges, opposing views on slavery, and, quite frequently, the honor of a lady. When duels involved friends, pistols often were aimed to inflict a slight wound on the arm or leg, which satisfied honor without destroying life. But the grudge fight was another matter. Death was the aim. The duel between Andrew Jackson and Charles Dickinson was a classic example.

Dickinson was an aristocratic young blood and reputedly the best shot in Tennessee. He apparently took keen delight in riling Jackson, especially when drunk, which was often. His remarks about Jackson's wife, Rachel, and his caustic comments on Jackson's choice of racehorses were calculated to trigger the General's

notably quick temper. Jackson, however, who was a poor pistol shot for a westerner, believed that his political enemies were prodding young Dickinson into an attempt to assassinate him legally. Twice he faced the younger man and achieved a settlement without bloodshed. Then, Dickinson published a scurrilous article in the local paper calling Jackson a "worthless scoundrel, a poltroon and a coward." There could be no third settlement. General Thomas Overton, acting for Jackson, delivered a challenge.

In deference to Tennessee's anti-dueling laws, the antagonists rode forty miles to Kentucky. There, on May 30, 1806, just before the sun rose over the poplar trees which surrounded their clearing, the two men faced each other at a distance of twenty-four feet, their positions marked by pegs driven into the ground. Jackson's pistols were used, Dickinson having first choice from the case. They were matched .70-caliber weapons with nine-inch barrels.

Because of Dickinson's skill, Jackson and

Overton had planned a neat strategy. They agreed that Dickinson should be allowed to fire first, that Jackson would make no effort to beat him to the shot. Jackson expected to be hit, perhaps badly, but he counted on his iron will to sustain him until he could aim deliberately and shoot to kill—even if it were the last act of his life. This duel was to the death. To further Jackson's chances, Overton insisted he wear a loose-fitting frock coat. Jackson, notably spare, would then offer a less sure target within the hanging folds of the big garment.

Overton won the toss to give the command. He shouted, "Fire!" quickly, hoping that this might force Dickinson into a hurried shot. Dickinson responded with alacrity and, to his dismay, saw only a small puff of dust spurting from the left shoulder of Jackson's coat. "Great God!" he groaned. "Have I missed him?" He recoiled somewhat from his position, perhaps in surprise, perhaps in fear. Overton, raising his own pistol,

ordered him to assume his original stance. Jackson then took deliberate aim and pulled the trigger. The pistol failed to fire. The hammer had stopped at the half-cock notch. Jackson, according to the rules, was given another chance. The wretched Dickinson, standing only eight paces away, was forced to wait as the hammer was pulled back again, as Jackson once more aimed deliberately at the heart, and fired. Dickinson dropped immediately, doubled over from a heavy ball through the body, just below the ribs.

Jackson stalked coolly from the field. He was, in fact, wounded severely; Dickinson's bullet had broken a rib over the heart, then deflected. But he wanted to exact the last measure of revenge. Dickinson, the superb marksman, died that night without the satisfaction of knowing he had, indeed, made a good though not fatal shot.

The duel was commonplace among the military, not only among officers who felt the need to protect the honor of their station and their

Traditionalists, following the code duello, *faced dueling pistols. Westerners, such as these with rifles, used anything that killed.* AMERICAN WEST BY LUCIUS BEEBE & CHARLES CLEGG

branch of the service, but among young midshipmen in the Navy. Commodore Stephen Decatur, for trivial reasons, was killed by another Commodore, James Barron, in a duel at eight paces in 1820. In 1836, Midshipman Key, son of Francis Scott Key, author of the "Star-Spangled Banner," died under the pistol of another Midshipman, Sherburne, in Maryland. The argument was a simple one. Key, a Marylander, was inspired by wine to make a derogatory remark about Sherburne's New Hampshire background. The record suggests that perhaps two-thirds as many officers were killed by dueling as died in action in all naval engagements from the early 1800's to the Civil War.

The formal duel restricted the choice of pistols. For a century the dueling weapon—always made in matched pairs to assure that the contestants were equally armed—conformed to fairly rigid standards. It was, in its post-Revolutionary form, a smoothbore flintlock of about .60-.70 caliber, with a browned or blued barrel up to ten inches long. There were no silver or gold inlays or decorations which might catch the sun and distract the dueler from his objective. These were simple but finely made, functional arms

FIVE SINGLE-SHOT PISTOLS USED
BY AMERICANS FROM
1799 TO 1855: *Top to bottom, Harpers
Ferry flintlock of 1807, one of most graceful
single shots; rare Elgin cutlass pistol, made for
Navy in 1837 (cutlass was used when there
was no time for reloading); North and Cheney Model
of 1799, first pistol contracted for by armed
forces; Johnson Model of 1836, last issue
flintlock. Left: Pistol carbine, made at Springfield
in 1855, has swivel rammer and detachable stock,
permitting use as pistol or shoulder weapon.*
GUNS: WEST POINT MUSEUM.
PHOTO BY ROBERT MOTTAR

which "pointed" naturally with the arm. Unless one wanted to risk taking an opponent's shot, as Jackson did, it was speed that counted. The first shot frequently carried the day.

Most of the duelers used in America were made in England or France, but there were a few Americans who made fine pistols for the murderous custom. Philadelphia seems to have been the center of the industry, with such noted makers as Henry Deringer Jr. and Richard Constable heading the list. Since good duelers were both highly specialized and very expensive, the interesting and macabre business of renting pistols for the purpose developed.

The dueling pistol was a single-shot weapon for a formal engagement in which each man was to have a relatively equal opportunity to slaughter his opponent. For personal or household protection under greatly varied circumstances a man needed more. The pirates had carried a number of pistols to obtain the necessary firepower. The average citizen wanted it in a single gun that could be carried without being obvious in coattail, vest, or hip pocket.

The first pistol meeting these requirements—and popular acceptance—was the multi-barreled pepperbox, particularly the double-action pistols introduced by Ethan Allen, of Grafton, Massachusetts, who was, incidentally, no relation to the Revolutionary War hero. Before the Allen, all guns had been single-action, that is, the hammer had to be cocked manually before the trigger could be pulled. With Allen's pistol, pulling the trigger revolved the barrels and simultaneously cocked and fired the gun. It was a tremendous improvement and Allen, with his various partners, Charles Thurber and Thomas Wheelock, probably made more pepperboxes than most of the other producers put together. Allens outsold Colts for nearly a decade, but then succumbed to Sam's ever-improving revolvers.

MID-NINETEENTH-CENTURY REMINGTON PISTOLS:
*Above, .44-caliber percussion revolver was a popular
cavalry weapon. Right, .50-caliber
rolling-block single-shot pistols.* GUNS: WEST POINT
MUSEUM, ABOVE, AND WILLIAM FLORENCE, RIGHT.
PHOTO, RIGHT, BY ROBERT MOTTAR

*Stephen Decatur kills a Barbary pirate with a flintlock
pistol, during Algerine War of 1815. The Commodore
subsequently lost his life in a duel.* CULVER SERVICE

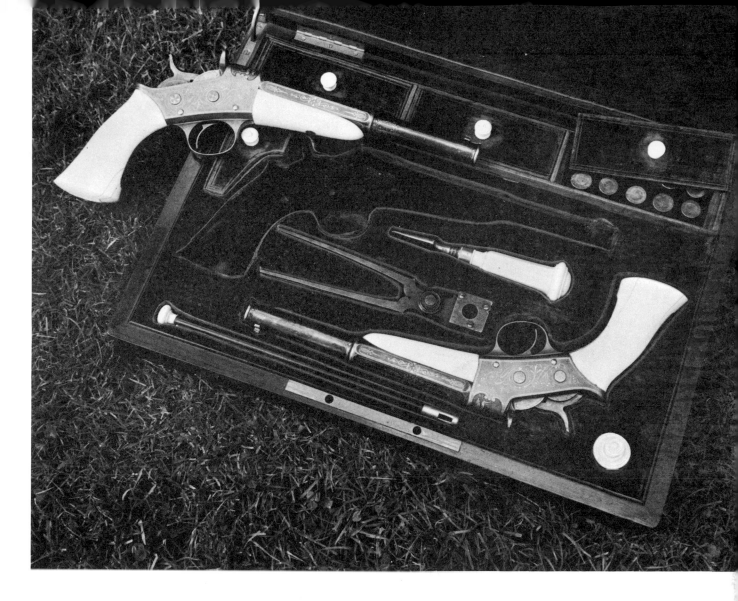

Colt's adventures in the evolution of long arms has already been told. It was the pistol, however, for which he became primarily known. Indeed his name is almost synonymous with it. There was little new in his invention, but circumstances dictated that he should come forward with the first practical and accurate multiple-firing weapons that could easily be carried on the person, at a time on the western frontier when they were most needed by most men. Sam Colt was not always first with the best in the course of his energetic career. He often was mistaken in his judgments. But he had a single-minded devotion to his craft and he scored frequently enough and, over-all, in such prodigious volume that he well deserves his honored place in the history of American firearms.

Anson Chase, who produced Colt's first model guns, made pistols as well as rifles for the young inventor. And when Colt opened his first factory at Paterson, New Jersey, in 1836, both pistols and long arms were put into production. These Paterson Colts were made in a variety of sizes from small pocket models with two-and-a-half-inch, .28-caliber barrels to large holster, or "Texas," models with nine-inch, .36-caliber barrels. Light guns with little stopping power and fragile construction, they were far from the perfect handgun for the developing West. Yet these were the guns with which Colonel Hays and fifteen Texas Rangers drove off eighty Commanches and thereby brought the new arm to the attention of the whole Southwest.

After Colt's business failed in 1842, it was the pistol, not the rifle that got him started again. Captain Samuel Walker, who had seen the Paterson pistol in the West, visualized some improvements and persuaded the Army to order some revolvers made according to specifications he had worked out with the inventor. The result was the famous Walker Colt .44 (actually a .45), a big, sturdy weapon of real stopping power. Because of its bulk, the next efforts were directed at reducing size and weight, and three models of Dragoon pistols followed. These were still big guns, weighing over four pounds, and designed for a mounted soldier. An ideal weapon for personal use both mounted and afoot was still to be developed.

In his search for such a gun, Colt turned to radically smaller pistols. First came his "Baby Dragoons," scaled down versions of the bigger guns; then, in 1849, the .31-caliber pocket pistol, one of the most popular and long-lasting models he ever produced.

Though the easterner, the bank clerk, and the storeowner liked the pocket pistol, it certainly did not suit the ranger, scout, Pony Express rider or other citizens of the West. Their needs were served in turn by the .36-caliber Navy revolver of 1851 and the .44 Army revolver of 1860. Here were man-sized guns, light but effective, and beautifully designed. The early gunfighters took quickly to them, among them Wild Bill Hickok, who was reported at Springfield, Missouri, in 1865 "girthed by a belt which held two Colt's Navy revolvers." The gun and the men had gotten together, and these two pistols remained standard until the development of big-bore cartridge pistols after the Civil War.

Of all the manufacturers who tried to rival Colt, Eliphalet Remington came closest to equalling him. By 1860 his firm had marketed models of small revolvers developed by Fordyce Beals and a peculiar-looking pocket gun designed by Joseph Rider. It was with the big .36 and .44 revolvers that Remington really scored, how-

ever. The principal difference from the Colt revolvers lay in the solid frame over the top of the cylinder. This made them stronger than the Colts and also provided for a fixed sighting groove. Modern black-powder shooters consider the Remingtons at least equal to and possibly superior to comparable Colts. Nevertheless, Remington never seriously challenged Colt's popularity with the military or in the West.

Just as it had with shoulder arms, the team of Smith & Wesson pioneered the breakthrough from percussion cap to metallic cartridge in handguns. Leaving their Volcanic pistol in the hands of Oliver Winchester, these two capable young mechanics formed a partnership in 1856 to develop a new gun even further advanced than the Volcanic—or the Colts. It was to be ready for the market when Colt's basic patent expired in 1857. It was to fire a metallic cartridge Wesson had developed, and it would incorporate, through S. & W.'s purchase of the patents, Rollin White's method for boring the cylinder all the way through, so that cartridges could be inserted from the rear. White originally had offered the patent to Colt, but Sam, not thinking of metallic cartridges, had considered the idea ridiculous. How he must have kicked himself throughout the remaining years of his life when he realized he had rejected one of the most important basic notions in revolver design! As it was, Smith & Wesson had virtually a monopoly on cartridge revolvers until the patent finally expired in 1869.

Smith & Wesson started with small-caliber guns, evidently with an eastern market in mind. They were seven-shot, .22-caliber pistols with spur triggers, only seven inches long over-all. They were fine for pockets, but for little else. Nevertheless, they were an immediate success. In 1861, a heavier, .32-caliber revolver was added to the line and designated Model Number 2.

Young Sam Colt designed his first revolver and later, in
1834, had John Pearson make the experimental model, top.
Paterson Colt, center, an improved version of John Pearson
model, was manufactured by Colt in Paterson, New Jersey. It was
first Colt pistol offered to public, but its sales were
poor, and plant closed. After subletting contracts, he returned
to manufacture with Dragoon Colt, shown at bottom in
presentation Third Model. GUNS: CONNECTICUT STATE LIBRARY.
PHOTOS BY SID LATHAM. COURTESY SPORTS ILLUSTRATED

*Second Model Colt Dragoons,
made in 1850 for millionaire, James
Van Syckel, proved Colt could
produce guns as artistic as any from
Old World.* GUNS: LARRY SHEERIN

*Navy Colt, Model 1861, .36 caliber, six shot,
in case; and Police Colt, Model 1862,
standing, were presented to General James Ripley,
Civil War Chief of Ordnance, by Sam Colt.*
GUNS: GERALD FOX. PHOTOS BY ROBERT MOTTAR

*Army Colt, Model 1860, above, was a gift to Lieutenant
Charles Morton from Territory of Arizona for bravery
against Apaches.* GUN: WEST POINT MUSEUM.
PHOTO BY SID LATHAM. COURTESY SPORTS ILLUSTRATED

*Colt Root, fully-engraved and cased, Model of 1855,
page 131, was a gift from Colt factory to
New York Metropolitan Fair of 1864—held to raise
supplies for Union Soldiers.*
GUN: ARNOLD MARCUS CHERNOFF. PHOTO BY SERGE SEYMOUR

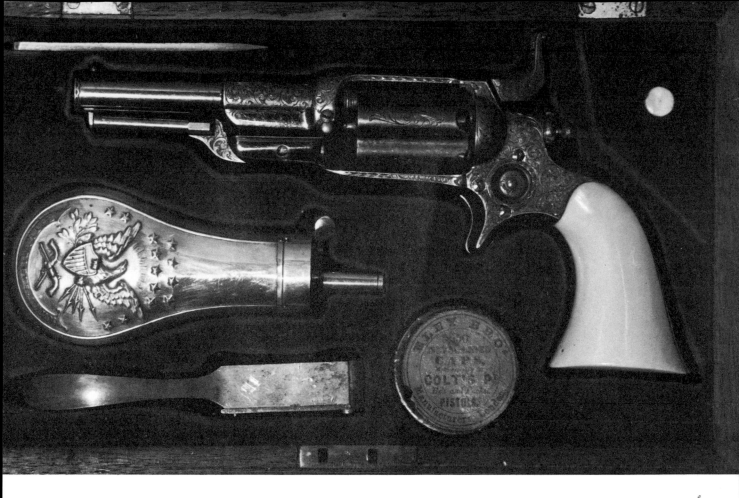

It still had a spur trigger, but it became vastly popular with the soldiers who purchased it privately during the Civil War.

The need for a large-caliber revolver became apparent to Smith & Wesson early in the Civil War, and a .44 gun with a trigger guard was designed. Unfortunately, patent troubles and other difficulties prevented its manufacture in quantity until 1869. The new pistol, known as the Number 3, or "American," also had improvements in the frame and an extractor which would eject all six cartridges at once. It was an immediate success all over the West. Buffalo Bill bought one and had his name engraved upon it. So did "Texas Jack" Omohundro, famous Army scout and frontiersman, who later appeared in many of Buffalo Bill's Wild West shows.

Ballistically, it was an appealing weapon for gun-toting Westerners. It fired a center-fire cartridge loaded with twenty-five grains of powder and a 218-grain lead slug. With a muzzle energy of 316 foot-pounds, it was a potent man-stopper.

Just at the time the Smith & Wesson Num-

ber 3 was beginning to hit the market, the Rollin White patent expired, and the cartridge revolver field was open to all. Colt quickly jumped in. First came the Richards conversion of 1871, which permitted the old percussion Colts to fire metallic cartridges by cutting off the cylinder at the rear and inserting an adaptor ring. Then came an open-top cartridge model, called the 1872, and, finally, the 1873 Peacemaker, also occasionally known as the Single-Action Army and the Frontier Model.

The sturdy .45 Peacemaker soon surpassed the Smith & Wesson as the handgun of the West. In 1878 it was chambered for the same .44-40 cartridge used in the Winchester rifle and this again boosted its popularity, since only one type of ammunition needed to be carried for both arms. Its load had more power than that of the S. & W. and its parts were less complicated.

The simplicity and strength of the Colt especially recommended it in the West because of the regional penchant for an activity known as pistol-whipping. The local peace officer in fron-

tier towns was often much addicted to clubbing a tough hombre over the head when he became drunk and disorderly, rather than shooting him down. Persons on the other side of the law often used it to intimidate their victims. Whatever the objective, the heavy Colt, with its solid frame, could withstand rough treatment with little damage. The S. & W., with its break-open frame, finer fittings, and more delicate parts, might well have to be sent back to the factory for refitting of its hinge joint after such a fracas.

The Peacemaker established the pattern for the six-shooter in the West. Remington turned out a fine model in a similar design in 1875, and Smith & Wesson offered a stronger and simpler Schofield Model in .45 caliber, but neither of these quite matched the Colt performance or really threatened its popularity.

The final step in the development of the revolver during its post-Civil War heyday was the introduction of double-action. The double-action principle was not new. In the 1870's however, the time seemed ripe for its application to a wider market. Colt responded with the .38 Lightning and .41 Thunder models in 1877,

and Smith & Wesson followed in 1880 with a .38. Acceptance was quick and, without displacing the single-action Peacemaker, the new guns found many friends, ranging from peace officers to the famous terror of the Lincoln County cattle wars, Billy the Kid, who used a Thunderer "self-cocker" with deadly effect during his brief and bloody career as an outlaw.

And what of the military through this long period of handgun development? Its record was remarkably progressive and open-minded. The first official U. S. pistol had been made under contract by North & Cheney in 1799, copying the French model of 1777. Thereafter Americans developed their own patterns. Percussion ignition came in 1837, and the last single-shot percussion muzzle-loader, the Springfield pistol-carbine, which had a detachable shoulder stock for greater accuracy at long range, made its appearance in 1855.

One interesting digression during the period of the single-shot pistol was a weapon ordered by the Navy for a South Seas Exploring Expedition in 1838. These were single-shot percussion pistols with cutlass blades attached to the un-

Sam Colt, 1814-1862, created Army Model 1860, shown above with detachable shoulder stock. Frontier Colt, left, is final evolution of single-action design.

GUNS: ARNOLD MARCUS CHERNOFF, ABOVE; AND HERB GLASS, LEFT. PHOTOS: SID LATHAM, LEFT, COURTESY SPORTS ILLUSTRATED; AND SERGE SEYMOUR, ABOVE

derside of the barrel. They had been designed by George Elgin, of Georgia, with the thought that once the single shot had been discharged the user would still have an edged weapon with which to defend himself or carry on his assault. They were a flop, but the Navy showed itself broad minded in being willing to try out a small number—and at the same time acquired the first official percussion pistols.

With regard to the revolver the Army maintained an excellent record. When Sam Colt went out of business, it was an Army order for an improved revolver which got him started again—and kept him going with orders for Dragoons and, later, holster pistols. With the Colts also, the Army was interested in increasing accuracy at long range, so the revolver might replace both the single-shot pistol and carbine. Thus it tried detachable shoulder stocks with the Dragoon revolvers and continued the experiment through the Model 1860 Army.

Only once did the Government seem to retreat from its progressive interest in the revolver. This was when it placed orders for small quantities of a Remington rolling-block single-shot

cartridge pistol between 1866 and 1871, for both Army and Navy use. Experiments soon indicated that though these were beautifully made and wonderfully accurate for shooting targets, they were an anachronism as a weapon and a throw-back to the old horse pistol. They were never widely used. Instead, cartridge revolvers of all makes were carefully tested until the Army, too, expressed its preference for the famous Colt Peacemaker.

The tools with which Americans shot at each other to the horror of Mr. Steinmetz and his fellow European visitors had fully developed. Only the advent of heavier loads through smokeless powder and the invention of the automatic remained for the years between then and now. The revolver has been called one of three basic inventions that permitted the conquest of the West (the others being barbed wire and the sod-breaking plow). From its appearance in 1836, it played a dominant role for over fifty years. During the nation's explosive adolescence, it was the perfect sidearm for cowpuncher and outlaw, for peace officer and soldier, for all who needed it in the moulding of history.

133

\$800 REWARD

CHAPTER SIX

BAD MEN AND PEACE OFFICERS

PAGES 134 AND 135: *Nine notches on its steer-head pearl grip is grim testimony that this single-action Colt .45-caliber Peacemaker was an instrument of society's retribution in the hand of a Ranger in and around Sweetwater, Texas.*
GUN: HERB GLASS. PHOTO BY ROBERT MOTTAR

ABOVE: *Having decided that discretion is the better part of valor, driver throws hands in the air instead of drawing six guns. Guard sits passively, his shotgun still secure in its boot. After robbing the stage, bad men will mount up, gallop over sagebrush, and disappear into foothills.*
PAINTING BY N. EGGENHOFER. COURTESY KENNEDY GALLERIES

A golden October sun beat down upon the main street of an Arizona town. Its slanting afternoon rays picked out four men heading grimly toward a rendezvous that would become one of the shortest and deadliest gun fights in western history. Three were tall, lean, and tough and looked strangely alike in build, their dark, almost funereal garb, and their purposeful stride. The residents of Tombstone who crouched in open doorways of the false-fronted buildings along Allen Street recognized them immediately as the brothers Earp. Their companion, singularly out of key in this stalwart company, was a wizened, cadaverous figure with the sunken chest of the consumptive, dressed in a gray suit

God created men. Colonel Colt made them equal.

OLD FRONTIER SAYING

and overcoat. What he lacked in appearance, however, he made up for in reputation. For this was the Earps' firm friend, Doc Holliday—"the coldest-blooded killer in Tombstone."

Around the corner and still out of sight, the opposition stood near the wall of the O K Corral. Sheriff Johnny Behan was trying to persuade them to give up their arms. Ranged shoulder to shoulder were Ike and Billy Clanton, Tom and Frank McLowery, and Billy Claiborne. Representing one of the rival interests in Cochise County and generally believed to be intimately associated with cattle rustling, horse stealing, stagecoach robbery, and other forms of outlawry, the gang had been feuding with the Earps

for nearly two years, or ever since Wyatt Earp had been brought down from Dodge City in 1879 with a deputy Federal marshal's badge to enforce law and order. The other Earps and Doc Holliday had followed shortly, Virgil eventually becoming town marshal.

Tombstone was too small for two such divergent groups. One of them had to go. All through 1880 and the greater part of 1881 there had been rumblings, threats, incidents. Generally, the Clanton-McLowery group had come off second best, taking assorted pistol whippings and suffering fines, jailings, and other indignities from the Earp faction. By October the feud had built to a climax from which there could be no retreat.

137

Fancy version of single-action Frontier Colt.
PISTOL: HERB GLASS
PHOTO BY SID LATHAM. COURTESY SPORTS ILLUSTRAT[ED]

*Scalp hunters, diversifying their activities
by searching for El Dorado, discover massacre of
emigrant family. Gang member, Mountain Jim,
knowing Indians never left a number of arrows
behind, judged: "This is the work of white men."*
QUOTE AND PAINTING FROM MY CONFESSION
BY SAM CHAMBERLAIN. COURTESY LIFE

Dance, dude, dance.
DRAWING BY FREDERIC REMINGTON.
COURTESY REMINGTON ART MEMORIAL

Thus, four grim men walked down Allen Street, cut over to Fremont, and headed for the group waiting at the Corral. Wyatt Earp clutched a single-action Colt revolver in the pocket of his black overcoat. Virgil and Morgan Earp wore revolvers in holsters under their coats, and Doc Holliday carried a sawed-off double-barreled shotgun suspended by a thong under his coat, as well as a revolver on his hip.

Sheriff Behan made one vain attempt to halt the advancing men, then ducked for cover in the doorway of Fly's Photograph Gallery. The four moved on, drawing their guns as they neared their enemies and stopping finally a scant five feet from them. "Throw up your hands!" ordered Virgil Earp. Wyatt said, "You fellows have been looking for a fight, and now you can have it."

Exactly what happened in the murderous twenty seconds which followed will never be known. Sheriff Behan couldn't see, and the survivors told contradictory stories at the trial which followed. Ike Clanton said that his group complied with Virgil's command and that Wyatt and Morgan opened fire on them as they stood helpless. Wyatt admitted that he and Morgan had fired first, but said that Billy Clanton and Frank McLowery had jerked their guns out with every intention of starting a fight.

However it started, it was a vicious performance. Morgan's first shot dropped Billy Clanton, but the boy propped himself up and continued to shoot. Wyatt's bullet ripped a hole in Frank McLowery's belly and sent him reeling into the street. Tom McLowery turned and started to run for his brother's horse, probably to get the Winchester rifle that hung from the saddle, since he had left his own pistol in a saloon. The two charges from Doc Holliday's shotgun lifted him off his feet and dropped him lifeless under the hind feet of the horse. Ike Clanton and Billy Claiborne took to their heels and escaped without harm. But the desperately wounded Frank McLowery and Billy Clanton continued the fight with their last breaths, putting slugs into Virgil Earp's right leg and Morgan's shoulder before additional bullets finished them off. Wyatt Earp and Doc Holliday were unhurt.

This epic battle by no means established a pattern for the conflict between the badman and the peace officer in the West. It simply confirmed a pattern that had been in existence for many years, dating back to the first gold discoveries and the land rush at mid-century. At no time was crime a novelty in early America, but in the settling of the wide open spaces beyond the Mississippi the law frequently was left far behind. The absence of the curbs and restraints of urban living often worked astonishing transformations in presumably honest men. No period of American history offered better opportunities for profit for the man who was a good shot, a quick shot, and without compunction about "dry-gulching" a victim or shooting him in the back. Depending entirely upon his special

Often badly fed, cowpunchers celebrate as they bring home a new and, hopefully, good cook. Gunfire punctuates fun.
FROM FREDERIC REMINGTON BY HAROLD MC CRACKEN. COURTESY J. B. LIPPINCOTT CO.

talents, a man took what he wanted at the point of a gun, whether it was jumping a gold claim, robbing a Wells Fargo stage, stealing a herd of choice stock, or cracking a bank. For at least half a century, the gun was the basis of western law and lawlessness. The hired gunman, charging sometimes $500 a head for his murders, was a favorite of the unscrupulous cattle baron and other conniving criminals who preferred to hire out their dirty work, rather than stain their own hands with a victim's blood.

There was a curious ambivalence in this behavior. For while the western bad man put few limits on his deviltry, he was not implacably or irrevocably anti-social. In countless frontier towns, outlaws with truly fearsome reputations often were persuaded to embrace respectability

as peace officers. Morality was perhaps contorted by expedience, but to the harried citizens there was attractive logic in retiring the most active, most accurate gun around—or at least, getting it to point in another direction. The recruitment of renowned killers also instilled a little honest caution in less able killers and, for a time, the homicide rate would slacken.

Unfortunately, appointments were often lightly regarded, and law men were known to use their positions of trust to engage in further depredations on the community.

A notorious example was Henry Plummer, who became sheriff of Alder Gulch, near Virginia City, at a time when it was the world's richest, most abundant placer gold field. As sheriff, Plummer knew of all shipments leaving the town

and he arranged for the coaches to be held up by his gang of confederates somewhere along the outgoing trail. After over a hundred murders, and robberies of countless gold shipments, the Vigilantes finally organized and hanged the principal members of the Plummer gang, including its leader, in Virginia City in 1864.

Once the great gold fields were depleted, a new harvest ripened for the desperado—cattle. The great herds coming up from Texas to railheads at Dodge City, Ellsworth, and other railroad towns offered tempting pickings for rustlers. Then, as cattle raising became the great new industry, the experts with the "running iron" began to build herds of mavericks stolen from the big ranchers. As one problem was brought under control, another arose. The fencing of the range,

the coming of the sheep ranchers, the fight over water rights, and other major issues of the times kept the West in a continual state of bloody turmoil, where a man's life was often less valuable than that of a horse. Again the Vigilantes reorganized and went to work, sweeping southward from Montana over the entire cattle range, hanging rustlers as they went, without benefit of trial. In the ten years from 1876 to 1886 it is likely that more men were hanged illegally by the Vigilantes in the West than were legally executed throughout the United States during the next quarter of a century.

Throughout this period, a man's handiness with his gun determined not only his success or failure, but also the length of his life and the health of his friends and supporters. It was no era for the queasy, the hesitant, or the slow of hand. Keen eyes, quick reflexes, and dependable weapons meant life or death, success or failure. Marshals and sheriffs, as well as bad men, often shot first and asked questions afterward. Scores of twenty-thirty men were not unusual.

The successful gunfighter of this era was not a one-weapon man. He selected his guns to fit his needs as a carpenter chooses his tools, and he normally kept a variety handy: the rifle for long range and accuracy, the shotgun for close-range work with the deadliest of results, and the revolver for easy carrying and general all-around service. As has been noted, weapons changed greatly during the fifty years that they dominated the West. All were used, and although a gunman might prefer one model, he normally owned others as well. Even after the cartridge had been well established, it was frequently the practice to keep a cap-and-ball revolver handy in the event of an ammunition shortage. A competent gunslinger had a small, private arsenal.

One of the earliest of the famous gunmen and an all-around all-weapons man was James Butler

Hickok. Born back in Illinois in 1837, "Wild Bill" as he was known, was probably the first of the famous "two-gun" men. Fiction populates the West with many of these ambidextrous wonders, but actually they were rare. Many carried two guns but used the "border shift" in action —firing one gun with the right hand until it was empty, then holstering it while drawing the other with the left hand and tossing it to the right with almost no loss of time in sustained firing. Wild Bill could and did fire his guns with deadly accuracy with both hands at the same time. He was a natural shooter, born to the use of weapons and highly skilled with all of them. He took no chances and was perhaps quicker than most to shoot first and ask afterward. He once killed one of his own deputies by whirling and shooting on reflex when the man ran up behind him during a fight in Abilene.

Illinois was no place for the proper exploitation of Wild Bill's talents, so he soon set off for the West. He hunted buffalo with the heavy rifle on the plains, took part at eighteen in the bitter fighting between pro- and anti-slavery forces in Bloody Kansas, and became a constable before he was twenty. Joining the Overland Stage Company, he drove for a while, then was stationed at Rock Creek, Nebraska.

At Rock Creek occurred one of the most controversial episodes in Hickok's young career. Accounts differ as to whether Bill was attacked by a gang or shot his opponents separately, sometimes from cover; whether he killed three men or

Everywhere Wells Fargo went, a guard was sure to go, in this case armed with a Smith & Wesson Schofield .45-caliber revolver and a double shotgun.
The transcontinental express was organized to serve fortune-seeking Californians, four years after James W. Marshall discovered gold at Sutter's Mill.
GUNS AND CHEST: HERB GLASS. PHOTO BY ROBERT MOTTAR

six. No matter how it happened, at least three and probably more men who opposed the operation of the stage agency were dead in an act of violence that encouraged gaudy stories of Hickok's prowess throughout the West.

The Civil War interrupted Bill's career briefly. He served as a scout and a spy for the Union Army and compiled a list of sixty-six kills, exclusive of Indians, all of them attributable to his devastating skill with his guns.

Following the war, and for most of the remaining years of his life, Wild Bill worked as a peace officer. He was town marshal of Hays City, Kansas, of Abilene, Kansas, and then United States Marshal back in Hays City again. He was killed in 1876 by Jack McCall, a hard gambler, after an argument over a card game. McCall sneaked up behind Bill as he sat playing cards and shot him in the back of the head. Bill was holding aces and eights, a combination since memorialized as a "dead man's hand."

Wild Bill Hickok was a classic example of the "bad" man or tough hombre on the side of the law. He brooked no interference, but shot to kill, quickly and unhesitatingly. Of the numerous weapons he handled and approved, the .36 Navy Colt seems to have been a favorite, and he often wore two of them. When the Number 2 Smith & Wesson appeared during the Civil War he also took a fancy to that despite its light .32 caliber. The model was discontinued in 1865, but Hickok still clung to it in preference to many others. He was wearing one when McCall killed him.

When Hickok died, the Model 1873 Colt Peacemaker had been on the market only three years. Wild Bill, representing an earlier generation, ignored it, but the new one took rapidly to the Colt as the virtually ideal weapon.

The deadly efficiency of the single-action Colt in the hands of a skilled gunman can be partly accounted for by its excellent grip design for the

143

quick draw and repeated rapid firing. Probably no gun, before or since, has had a better grip for gun-fighting. Fingers curl naturally around the butt, placing the thumb in the easiest position to cock the hammer for the first shot. The "hook" of the grip curve clings to the fingers, making it a natural pointer for hip-shooting at close quarters. It is a handgun designed for instinctive shooting by a man in danger.

In spite of the western novel, Hollywood, and TV, the gunfighter was a careful shooter. If he wasn't he didn't last long. Imaginative writers have exaggerated him beyond all reason. They describe him as a marksman capable of picking his man off the back of a hard-running horse with a snap shot from the hip at fifty yards. He fans his six gun at blinding speed, placing five or six shots into a playing card at a hundred feet. From far across a wide street, he bags the villain, with a single shot through the heart—unless he merely wishes to disarm him by creasing his shooting hand. This, of course, is nonsense that ignores the built-in limitations of handguns and violates all rules for handling them effectively.

Wyatt Earp was certainly a famous gunfighter and peace officer. It is true that opinion is still divided as to his moral character, but there is little argument that he was a handy man with a gun. His account of his experiences as a gunfighter, among gunfighters, gives a clue to the methods used by the men who lived to tell the tales. He said, "The most important lesson I learned from those proficient gunfighters was that the winner of a gunplay usually was the man who took his time. The second was that, if I hoped to live long on the frontier, I would shun flashy trick-shooting — grandstand play — as I would poison. . . . When I say that I learned to take my time in a gunfight I do not wish to be misunderstood, for the time to be taken was only that split-fraction of a second that means the

difference between deadly accuracy with a six gun and a miss.

"In all my life as a frontier peace officer, I did not know a really proficient gunfighter who had anything but contempt for the gun-fanner, or the man who literally shot from the hip. . . . From personal experience and from numerous six gun battles which I witnessed, I can only support the opinion advanced by the men who gave me my most valuable instruction in fast and accurate shooting, which was that the gun-fanner and the hip-shooter stood small chance to live against a man who, as old Jack Gallagher always put it, took his time and pulled the trigger once.

"Whenever you see a picture of some two-gun man in action with both weapons held closely against his hips and both spitting smoke together, you can put it down that you are looking at a picture of a fool, or at a fake. I remember quite a few of those so-called two-gun men who tried to operate everything at once, but like the fanners, they didn't last long in proficient company."

It is fairly obvious that at close range, say ten feet or less, a quick gunman could draw and fire his weapon in a fraction of a second and hit his target without actually taking aim. If the distance were widened to fifteen or twenty yards, the smart operator would take time, even if an infinitesimal amount, to raise his six gun, sight it and then, and not until then, pull the trigger. Life hung on mere fractions of seconds, yet the real gunfighter who survived the deadly engagements aimed his weapon. To beat a man to the draw was not necessarily to win the fight. The hastily fired first shot so often missed that the flashy quick-draw artist usually felt the savage punch of death in his vitals before he could cock his single-action for a second shot.

The gunfighter, ever aware of the importance of those split seconds, wore his six gun where he could reach it with the least movement of his shooting hand—about halfway between his elbow and his fingers. With his holster tied down by a thong around his thigh to prevent any "riding-up" as the weapon was drawn, a good one could go into action in about a quarter of a second. The holster itself was designed to do no more than barely hold the gun in place, allowing complete freedom not only to grasp the butt instantly, but to give the thumb access to the hammer and the forefinger to the trigger as the gun was pulled free. (Single-actions, for safety's sake, usually were carried with the hammer down on an empty chamber, thus making them five-shooters.) The act of drawing, cocking the hammer, and pulling the trigger was done in a blended movement at eye-blurring speed.

Ever conscious of the fact that the smallest increment of time could be a life-saving advantage, the gunfighter used various devices to shorten the firing time once he went for his gun. The "slip-hammer" was one of these. To modify the single-action gun, the hammer was re-shaped by grinding to produce a short, straight stub on the spur, or cocking piece. The trigger was tied down with a rawhide string or else completely discarded. The gun was fired by pulling back the stubby hammer with the knuckle joint of the thumb, then releasing it as it came to full cock. Specialists in "slip-hammer" shooting would often grab the barrel of the six gun with the left hand and "slip" with the right thumb until either their man was down or the gun empty.

One of the famous slip-gun experts was John Newman, a noted marshal in both Arizona and Alaska. He used the slip gun, two-hand technique with a holster gun, but was even deadlier with a pair of two-inch-barrel, .45 slip guns that he carried in his pockets. His deception with these concealed weapons was disconcerting to many criminals. On one occasion in Alaska, word

Model 1872 Colt, .44-Henry caliber,
was first Colt revolver designed to use self-contained
cartridges. This fancy pair has "Tiffany" grips.
GUNS: LARRY SHEERIN. PHOTO BY ROBERT MOTTAR

reached him that a tough character had come to town for the express purpose of killing him. Newman went looking for his foe, finding him at last in a saloon, armed with a double shotgun. Before his surprised antagonist could raise and fire the scattergun, Newman killed him with one of his worked-over .45's.

Knuckling the hammer, despite the slip technique, inevitably wasted some time between shots. The pressure was unremitting for an even faster-firing handgun for close work.

The Colt .38 Lightning and .41 Thunderer of 1877 and Smith & Wesson's .38 of 1880, all double-action "self-cockers," provided this speed. They never completely supplanted the sturdy Colt single-actions, but a number of famous badmen and law officers changed over to them.

One of the most notorious of the gunslingers to use a double-action revolver was William E. Bonney, the New Yorker who became known in the West as "Billy the Kid." Born in 1859, Billy began his wild career in 1877 and died four years later at the age of twenty-one. The gun he preferred was one which came out the year his violent spree began, the .41 Colt Thunderer.

While most of the legend of the western bad men and peace officers is linked to their six guns,

145

other weapons also played important roles. The shotgun, whether sawed off like Doc Holliday's or used full length, was the standard arm of the stagecoach guard who could count on the lethal spread of the shot pattern to help compensate for inaccurate aiming as his vehicle lurched over the rutted trails. Wells Fargo had the shotguns for their guards made specially in England with short 10-gauge barrels. Wyatt Earp was known to have had one of these special guns during the latter days of his career. Deadly as he was with the six gun, Earp usually reached for the scattergun when trouble was brewing. It was a basic weapon in the arsenal of every sheriff or marshal, and no weapon was ever feared more at close range. Its appearance was normally a signal for the hold-up man to retire out of range.

The Winchester, and even the big buffalo rifle, played a vital part in the long-range duels between the posses and the outlaw gangs. The revolver remained holstered for all but close-range fighting. Classic western conflicts, with the opponents sniping at each other among hillside boulders, were fought with rifles and carbines; the six-shooter just didn't have the range.

Wyatt Earp sums up the armament of the bad man and peace officer of his day: "When mounted on a horse and 'armed to the teeth,' as the saying goes, a man's rifle was slung in a boot just ahead of his right stirrup, his shotgun carried on the left by a thong looped over the saddle horn. With the adoption of breech-loading weapons, a rider equipped with two pistols, rifle and shotgun customarily had one of the belts to which his pistol holsters were attached filled with pistol ammunition, the other with rifle cartridges, while a heavier, wider belt filled with shotgun shells was looped around the saddle-horn underneath the thong which held that weapon. He was a riding arsenal, but there might well be times when he would need the munitions."

No gun was too big or too small for some use in the bloody warfare of the West. Big six gun or Deringer, Winchester repeater or Sharps buffalo rifle, all were the tools of law and lawlessness on the frontier. Gradually they were supplanted by more modern means of dealing death, but none has ever gripped the imagination of Americans

THE MODERN POLICE WEAPONS

like the "Equalizers" with which men asserted—
and defended—their claims to life.

The West had no monopoly on violence. East
of the Mississippi, the pattern differed, but
gangster and police officer fought each other no
less earnestly. Gunplay was usually the exception, not the rule. For all its reputation, New
York's Tenderloin district, the crime center of
the metropolis in the 1880's and 90's, was partial
to clubs, knives, and brass knuckles, rather than
firearms. The same was true in other cities.

Still, there was some shooting and the policeman always carried a pistol. Since both his life

and his effectiveness as a law officer might de-
pend on it, he wanted the best that was available
for his type of work. The gangster felt the same
way. Certain weapons particularly suited to organized gang warfare came into prominence.

The essential requirement that in matters
bearing on public safety the policeman should
excel—and the stiff opposition of the gangs to law
and order—brought the double-action handgun
to its present high rating as a holster arm for all
police work. Today both Colt and Smith & Wesson have extensive lines of police weapons in all
calibers from the .32 Smith & Wesson to the .357
Magnum; Colt, however, has steadfastly ignored
the .44 and .45 double-actions since discontinu-
ing its New Service line of big-bore police guns

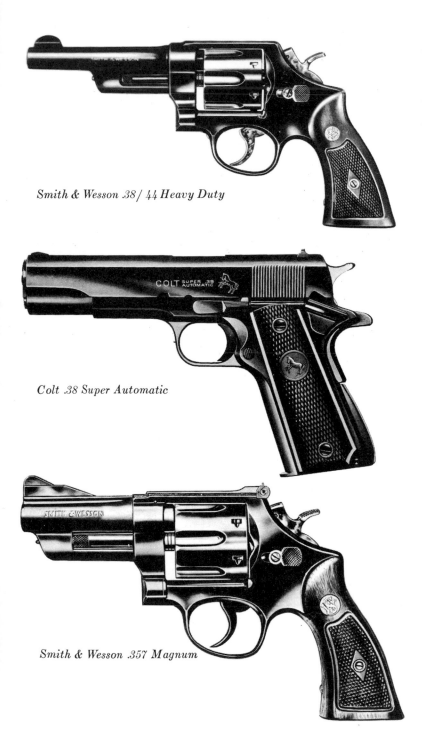

Smith & Wesson .38/44 Heavy Duty

Colt .38 Super Automatic

Smith & Wesson .357 Magnum

during World War II. The present standard police weapon is the .38 Special. Its modern loading with 200-grain bullets makes it a real man-stopping weapon for all normal use other than shooting through cars and bullet-proof windows—gangster-type cars, that is.

During the wildly vicious and bloody days of Prohibition, a special police weapon came into being. The smart gangster and hijacker often went into battle wearing a bullet-proof vest. The regular police weapons, including the .45, simply did not have enough velocity to penetrate this body armor. Colt developed a high-velocity cartridge, the .38 Super Automatic, which drilled a neat hole through them—with power to spare for puncturing the wearer as well.

The automatic never has been a popular police weapon, although it is standard equipment for the modern bad man. Its fairly flat shape adapts nicely to comfortable and inconspicuous carrying in the shoulder holster, in true gangster style. The peace officer, more concerned with quick action and dependability, demands the double-action cylinder weapon. For shoulder holster or pocket holster use the plainclothes man still prefers the revolver, usually the .38 Special in any one of a number of short-barrel models: the Colt Detective Special, Agent, or Cobra; in Smith & Wesson guns, the Chief's Special, .38 Military and Police, or the two hammerless pocket guns, the Bodyguard and Centennial. These are all real hideout guns, designed for fast action at close range. An equation of basic differences in the two handgun types favors the revolver for last-ditch defense. The automatic, to be completely safe, should be carried with the chamber empty and firing pin down. To load the weapon means pulling back the slide to feed a cartridge from the clip and cock the hammer for firing. This, obviously, is a two-hand operation and satisfactory only if the gunfighter has a free hand.

The revolver is a true one-hand gun. It can be carried fully loaded, yanked from holster or pocket and fired, double-action, with one hand and at great speed. The automatic certainly can be carried fully loaded and cocked, with safety on, if the wearer is willing to assume the complete reliability of the safety device under all conditions. Even so, the safety must be snapped off before the gun can be fired, involving some loss of time and an additional loss through hurried fumbling if the mental strain is great.

Of even greater importance to the police officer is the positive functioning of the revolver. Since the automatic depends solely on uniformity of ammunition for proper functioning, a misfire puts the gun out of order until the slide can be yanked back to feed a fresh shell. A misfire with the double-action revolver is not so serious. Another pull of the trigger revolves the cylinder to bring a fresh load under the hammer. Where split seconds count, this feature can mean life or death to the law man.

Recognizing that the Colt .38 Super Automatic had moved a long way forward in police popularity during the Prohibition era, Smith & Wesson set out to produce a more powerful revolver load to retrieve losses among their regular police and F.B.I. customers. Major Doug Wesson himself took over the design problem and, working with the .38 Special case, quickly developed a cartridge that virtually matched the .38 Super Auto ballistics. However, the load had just too much kick for comfort in the heaviest of the Smith & Wesson guns, so a larger-framed, heavier revolver was created. This .38/44 Heavy Duty gun quickly became a standard for peace officers for whom extra size and weight were not disadvantageous or objectionable.

Not content with this extra-powerful police weapon, Wesson went a step further in producing a cartridge which would fire through the rear

Horace Smith
(1808-1893)

Daniel Wesson
(1825-1906)

end of a car, piercing heavy metal and upholstery, yet retaining power enough to kill the driver. This cartridge, the .357 Magnum, was a lengthened version of the .38 Special case and had enough added kick to require a heavier gun for the shooter's comfort. The .44 frame was heavied up here and there, a top rib was added to the barrel, the grip was changed for less recoil effect, and the cylinder lengthened slightly. The result is the present .357 Magnum revolver, a weapon as modern as any peace officer could hope to have. Its wallop is deadly, its effect frightening. In field testing the gun for killing effect, Major Wesson hunted big game with the Magnum in the Rockies, bagging elk, deer, and grizzly bear at ranges comparable to those achieved with the high-powered rifle.

East or West, bad man or sheriff, mobster or policeman—all have lived and worked by their guns. The man with the best gun and the greatest dexterity in using it lived and helped his side prevail, at least momentarily, in the endless conflict between Good and Evil as he understood it. From the Colt cap-and-ball to the Smith & Wesson Magnum, the battle lines have varied little, the skill and courage demanded have been the same. Only the tools have changed.

AND FANCY WOMEN

Frankie went back to the corner.

This time it wasn't for fun.

Sewed up in her yellow kimono

Was a blue-barreled forty-four gun.

For he was her man, and he done her wrong.

THE BALLAD OF FRANKIE AND JOHNNY

PAGES 150 AND 151: *Cards and coins made the play; pocket pistols backed it up. Few river-boat gamblers sat down to draw who were not armed, often with a Remington .41-caliber double derringer, upper right. And a lady of professional pleasure was not fully dressed unless she packed a gun, either in her bosom, or in the case of this Remington Vest Pocket .22, in her stocking.*
GUNS: WILLIAM SWEET. PHOTO BY ROBERT MOTTAR

RIGHT: *Fabulous camp follower of American Army during Mexican War, Sarah Borginnis, refuses, gun in hand, to serve Mexican in her barroom.*
PAINTING BY SAM CHAMBERLAIN. COURTESY LIFE

The year was 1852. The place San Diego, California, in the lush days following the gold rush. Two men, together with their friends, faced each other across a dining room table where the wine had flowed freely for several hours. A lively discussion had turned into a bitter argument between the two principals as to who was the greatest man in the United States. Colonel John Magruder, later of the Confederate Army, nominated Andrew Jackson. Dr. William Osborn, of New York State, dissented violently; he nominated his father. The argument became so heated that Osborn finally challenged Magruder to settle the issue by a duel.

As the challenged party, Magruder had the choice of weapons. "Derringer pistols across the dining room table," he specified, to be fired at the seconds' call of "Ready! Fire!" Dr. Osborn, however, jumped the gun, firing at "Ready!" and when the smoke cleared he found himself looking into the big black bore of his opponent's

pistol. Suddenly sober, he groveled and begged for mercy, which was granted only after he had been thoroughly reviled by the Colonel and had received a few well-placed kicks. No one but Magruder knew that the seconds had loaded the derringers with black powder and bottle corks.

There are two interesting facts about this story. It is the first public mention of the derringer in California and it is probably the least lethal use to which the deadly little pocket pistol was ever put. On many other occasions in the sinful early days of California, it was employed with devastating effect.

The habit of carrying pocket pistols for personal protection was well-established by the time the Colonel thrashed the doctor, but men were still fretting over the lack of an ideal combination of accuracy, power, speed of firing, and ease of handling. Having seen men take a pair of pipsqueak loads from pocket pistols right in the chest, then reach for a big Colt "hog-leg," and

finish the antagonist with a single shot, the non-professional citizen-shooters knew they needed a small pistol of big bore that hit hard.

The first popular handgun that promised adequate personal protection was the pepperbox. Essentially, this was a series of barrels (usually three to six) grouped around a central axis so that they could be revolved and fired singly as they came beneath the hammer. This was not a new idea. It had been tried more or less successfully since the sixteenth century. The percussion ignition system greatly simplified its mechanics, however, and it became a vastly popular weapon for both civilians and soldiers during the 1830's and 40's. The brothers Barton and Benjamin Darling patented the first American pepperbox on April 13, 1836. They based their claim on a means of revolving the cylinder by cocking the hammer. (Sam Colt had obtained a patent on a similar device for the revolver on February 25, and the resultant patent fight did much to put the Darlings out of business.)

The next important advance was made by Ethan Allen of Grafton, Massachusetts—the first American double-action pistol. It found a ready market. Popular pocket models came in .31 and .33 caliber and were percussion fired. To shoot, it was necessary only to pull the ring trigger repeatedly, until the gun was empty. As the fastest firing guns of their day they commanded immediate attention and completely overshadowed the Colt revolver. Sam Walker, writing Colt from Washington in 1847, complained that "nine men of ten in this City do not know what a Colt pistol is and although I have explained the difference between yours & the six barrel 'Pop Gun' [pepperbox] that is in such general use a thousand times they are still ignorant on the subject."

The pepperbox was by no means perfect. There were serious defects which turned the tide toward the revolver. Its caliber usually was small, its range was short, and, worst of all, it could not be aimed properly. The heavy trigger pull and the turning of the barrels disturbed the aim, and the hammer was placed directly in the line of sight. They also had a nasty habit of discharging all their barrels at once. No shooter could be certain he would not get two or three innocent bystanders, as well as his intended victim. Mark Twain commented on their lack of accuracy in telling of the experience of one of his fellow passengers on an early trip to California. The owner of the pepperbox was concerned about the effectiveness of his little weapon against Indians and holdup men and fired for practice out the stage-coach window. "He aimed at the bole of a live-oak tree," wrote Twain, "but fetched the nigh mule."

Twain also commented on another of the pepperbox's failings, the tendency for sparks from the barrel being fired to set off all the other barrels in a multiple discharge. As one of the characters in *Roughing It* complains, "I should have shot that long gangly lubber they called Hank if I could have done it without crippling six or seven other people—but of course I couldn't, the old Allen's so confounded comprehensive."

Meantime, Henry Deringer Jr. of Philadelphia had come along with a handgun that represented a scaled-down version of his dueling pistols, for which he had long been famous.

As fate would have it, the most memorable shot ever fired by a Deringer was the .44-caliber bullet from the hand of John Wilkes Booth that assassinated Abraham Lincoln in 1865. This single act forever established Deringer among the pistol makers of history, even though his name—and the general name for his pistol—have been corrupted in spelling for almost a century: derringer rather than Deringer.

Deringer was a Pennsylvania German and a masterful craftsman. If he lacked some of the inventive flair of Sam Colt, he was nonetheless author of some of the most handsome single-shot weapons ever made in America. His product was notable for simple design, utter reliability, and heavy punch. The awesome blast of his big-bore handguns was acknowledged in a

A man who wanted a gun in the mid-1800's and did not wish to be conspicuous about it carried one or more pocket pistols, which were made either by Henry Deringer, Jr., in Philadelphia, or were copied and modified from his design by others. Three pistols with wooden stocks were made by Deringer, trap-door pistol with ivory grip by James Warner, and all-metal pistol by National Arms.
GUNS: WILLIAM SWEET. PHOTO BY ROBERT MOTTAR

remark by an Alabaman which survives from 1837. As challenger, the southern gentleman asked only "the chance of blowing a hole through his [the opponent's] carcass . . . that a bull-bat could fly through without touching airy wing." The bull-bat was probably the night-hawk, a fairly sizable bird. The blasting, of course, was to be done with a Deringer.

By 1852 his pairs of stalwart little power-houses were on sale in California, where they found eager buyers. In 1855 there were four hundred and five killings in California alone, a fair share of them over the gaming tables. *The Army and Navy Journal* reported: "In the pre-Vigilance Committee era of California, thousands of these pistols found a ready market in their new domain, 'the sharp crack of the Der-ringer' being heard in the land much more frequently than the voice of the turtle."

In writing of the Colorado gold rush of 1859, George F. Wilson remarks: "Liable at any time to challenge, confidence men and the worst class of gamblers adopt a weapon peculiarly their own, the derringer, a light gun of small caliber, so small that it can easily be concealed in a vest pocket or even in the palm of a large hand. As it has the shortest of barrels, its accurate range does not exceed five or six feet. But it is deadly within that range, which is apt to em-brace all at even the largest gaming table."

Deringer seems to have been among the first American pistol makers to use percussion igni-tion. He describes his first pair of pistols of this type as being made in 1825 for Major Arm-strong, who promptly called them "Deringers." All of the early Deringers were muzzle-loaders,

Fancy women invited to English gentlemen's room in sedate Windsor Hotel, in Denver, shoot at insulators on Larimer Street telegraph poles.

DRAWINGS FROM AMERICAN WEST BY LUCIUS BEEBE AND CHARLES CLEGG

Music, cards, women, gun play, but no place for the Word in Bodie City, California, gambling hall.

of course, and no two pair seem to have had identical bores. The pistols were sold with their own bullet molds; if the molds were lost, the owner took himself off to the nearest gunsmith to have his weapons loaded.

The heyday of the Deringer—and the pistols of his numerous imitators—was spanned by the ten years from about 1846 to 1856. During the Civil War the little muzzle-loader declined in favor with the arrival of breech-loading pistols firing metallic cartridges. Yet it was at the end of the Civil War that Deringer's name became a part of the language.

CARTRIDGE DERRINGERS

After Deringer's death in 1868, gunmakers started to turn out the cartridge "derringer," which soon replaced the original weapon. Double-barreled and repeating types also began to appear in great numbers because Rollin White's patents, owned by Smith & Wesson, did not apply to multi-barreled weapons.

The little pistols, many chambered for a .41 rim-fire cartridge, were favorite "hold-out" guns for good men and bad. Captain John G. Bourke, writing in 1891 of his experiences with General George Crook, Civil War hero and conqueror of Geronimo, mentions one peace officer in Arizona who carried eleven of the little guns concealed on his person. Bourke says, "He drew them from the arm holes of his waistcoat, from his boot legs, from his hip pockets, from the back of his neck, and there they all were, eleven lethal weapons, mostly small derringers, with one knife." Yet to the casual observer this walking arsenal was apparently unarmed.

The first of the breech-loading small pistols of heavy caliber was the Moore, which had a .41-caliber barrel that turned down to load and eject. This was first advertised in 1864. Colt soon bought out Moore's National Arms Company and marketed the pistol under the Colt name in 1870. The same year Colt added a side-swinging single-shot pistol, under Thuer's patent, to its line of pocket guns. Colt was also making the Root Sidehammer model of 1855, a cap-and-ball revolver in .28 and .31 caliber.

The four-barreled Sharps became a popular pocket weapon in the early 1860's. These were small calibers, .22 and .30, and the four barrels were fired in turn by a revolving firing pin which struck the rim-fire cartridges one at a time.

The gun which really established itself as the deadly pocket weapon of the era, the one known as the "river-boat gambler's favorite," was the .41 double over-under derringer by Remington. This tiny gun, with its two three-inch barrels, was a powerful package. Its flat shape made it ideal for concealment in a vest or coat pocket and its twin tubes fired as quickly as the hammer could be cocked and the trigger pulled. This arm became the model for powerful pocket weapons until the automatic pocket pistol appeared in the early 1900's. Remington, in fact, continued to manufacture it until 1935, making well over 150,000 of them.

THE LADIES' GUN

The gun knew no limits. It even had its place in the world of brawling entertainment and profane love. No fancy woman of the middle 1800's would ply her trade in the dance halls, saloons, and bordellos unarmed. For her a very small weapon was desirable, even if it lacked real punch. No man, in the code of the day, would shoot at a woman even though she might pot at him with her little .22. Thus the tiny single-shot guns became popular "stocking" and "bosom" weapons—the smaller the better. The tiny three-and-seven-eighths-ounce Remington Vest Pocket model in .22 caliber, single shot, made from 1865 to 1888, became a standard stocking gun for ladies of the evening throughout the West and South. Over 25,000 were made and there is little doubt as to the ultimate destination of most of them.

Many of the early Smith & Wesson revolver models in .22 caliber were ideally suited to ladies' use. The little guns had short barrels, fired .22 rim-fire cartridges (so there was no loading problem) and they were tiny enough to be readily concealed. The first model S. & W., marketed in 1857, was barely five-and-a-half inches long and a seven-shooter. Subsequent changes in models did not materially alter the size and deadliness of the little revolver in female hands.

The rugged individual felt at home in the 1800's. He—or she—relied on inbred courage and acquired armament in the event of trouble, or to get him what he wanted. He didn't call for the cops when things were going wrong. He reached for his "thumb-buster" in his open top, quick-draw holster, or he dived into his vest pocket for his lethal little derringer. Probably at no time in history did firearms become so personal and so vital to everyday living.

In the West during the last century, it was only in moments of secure leisure that a man dared separate himself from Bowie knife or pistol—in this case a Colt's Root 1855, .31-caliber sidehammer pocket revolver; or a woman from her bosom pistol—here a French-made .22-caliber revolver, which hung from her neck. GUNS AND KNIFE: HERB GLASS. PHOTO BY ROBERT MOTTAR

CHAPTER EIGHT WHITETAILS

PAGES 162 AND 163: *Against background of whitetail's favorite cover is Winchester Model 88, .308 caliber, with Leupold 4X scope in Leupold De-tacho mounts—fast-handling combination for timber hunting.* PHOTO BY ROBERT MOTTAR

ABOVE: *Shooting whitetail deer in the northern Adirondack region of New York, along banks of the Shattegee (today spelled Chateaugay) River, where deer come to water.* LITHOGRAPH BY CURRIER AND IVES, HARRY T. PETERS COLLECTION, MUSEUM OF THE CITY OF NEW YORK

Deer have always been important to hunters in America. Before the introduction of the gun to the New World, Indians killed whitetails with bow and arrow; after it, they joined the white man in loading muskets and rifles to bring down the animal that meant food and clothing.

Daniel Boone, armed with a Kentucky long rifle, struck out for the country west of the Alleghenies as much from the desire to locate a new source of deerskins—the game was becom-

His magnificent bounds, in which strength,

speed, ease and lightness are combined, his gallant

carriage, the flaunting defiance of

his white flag of a tail elevated high in

the air . . . together with his natural

capacity for taking care of himself . . . make him an

object of the keenest interest

and desire to every lover of the chase.

RICHARD IRVING DODGE

ing relatively scarce in the East—as from the urge to satisfy his wanderlust. Although sheep's wool provided homespun clothing for eastern settlers, it was deerskin that men and women wore on the fast-growing frontier.

At that time, deer were found only in lowlands and river valleys and along the edges of heavy forests, for the great stands of heavy timber discouraged the small undergrowth on which they fed. Although they were numerous in their chosen habitat, there was not much of it. Not until vast tracts of land were cleared for farming and lumbering were the feeding grounds extended sufficiently for whitetails to flourish.

As the forests fell, opening new second-growth clearings, the herds increased. This situation continued even though the crack of the market hunter's rifle filled the air. But by 1880, the slaughter for hides and venison had become too much for even the fertile whitetail. The drain

on the herds was terrible and unremitting. The carnage was stopped only by conservation laws and growing public sentiment. Starting in the 1890's, states began enacting legislation protecting the does and severely limiting the take of bucks. Market hunting was outlawed. By a narrow margin, the whitetail missed going the way of the buffalo.

With careful supervision, the whitetail has come back in amazing numbers. In many areas, in fact, the deer are far too numerous for the available range. Legislation in some states now permits thinning out the does as well as the bucks, in order to achieve a better balance between the herd and its environment.

Today all deer shooting is for sport. The whitetail can be maddeningly hard to find in its favorite cover, and even harder to hit with a well-placed rifle bullet, but it is not a difficult animal to kill. As a rule, its frame is rather slight — seldom as heavy as that of the average man. To make a clean kill, the hunter must place a bullet within an eight-inch circle directly behind the shoulder, well down in the chest. Any 100-grain bullet driven through this area will penetrate the lungs and result in quick death from a combination of shock and hemorrhage.

This ability to achieve quick, humane killing of deer—and other game—at the longest possible range has been the objective of all rifle and shotgun development for the past fifty or sixty years. For in this time the character and purposes of firearms have subtly changed. The day of the gun as an essential, all-purpose instrument of everyday life has vanished. The firearm is now an exquisitely precise mechanism tailored to the individual requirements of sport, law enforcement, and war.

Today sporting and military arms travel divergent paths, each category pursuing its own dream of perfection and each probably within a few degrees of the ultimate, as far as present ballistic principles are concerned. And at this point their stories diverge as well. In the remaining chapters, the focus will be on the development of sporting weapons and on their efficient use by the citizen hunter and marksman.

The story of military arms since 1900 is quickly told, for it has gone in a single, straight-line direction toward greater firepower, which means autoloading. The automatic pistol came first and, as usual in America, it was John Browning who had the notion and acted on it. Reputedly, it was the blast from his shotgun that started him thinking about ways to utilize powder gases in a semi-automatic action. In any event, he obtained his first patent in 1897 and three years later the Colt-Browning automatic pistol, in .38 caliber, appeared. The Philippine Insurrection of 1902 demonstrated the need for a more rugged man-stopper in combat and by 1905 the solution was at hand: the big .45, firing a fat slug that would bowl a man over with a single hit almost anywhere in the body. With refinement, this became the world-famous 1911 Colt that is still in service.

The hefty Browning Automatic Rifle and .30-caliber machine gun advanced the trend toward autoloading in World War I and led subsequently to a search for an automatic shoulder arm as well. Experiments at Springfield under the direction of John C. Garand culminated in 1936 in the adoption of the M-1, the "Garand."

Finally, just prior to World War II, Winchester developed the neat little .30-caliber rifle which was adopted as the M-1 carbine. It was

Fine specimen of mature eight-point whitetail buck in fall coat, with thickened neck of rutting season. Antler points bear little relationship to age; many bucks never achieve more than the eight shown.
MICHIGAN CONSERVATION DEPARTMENT

intended to replace the .45 automatic, a difficult weapon to fire with accuracy, but actually found its niche as an infantryman's arm for jungle fighting in Asia and the Pacific.

Now the heavy, somewhat clumsy Garand is itself about to be replaced by the new M-14, a lighter (8.7 pounds) semi-automatic whose magazine holds twenty 7.62-mm NATO cartridges (identical to the .308 Winchester). It is scheduled to be issued in 1960.

Military weapons in use are prohibited to the civilian, except for presentation arms, but it is unlikely that the bulky Garand or the little carbine, underpowered as it is for deer or larger game, would appeal to the hunter, anyway.

They may in time be released for civilian sale, as were the superseded Krags and Springfields of another era, but they will probably be neglected, save as curiosities, as was the Spencer after the Civil War.

For sporting arms, meanwhile, the invention of smokeless powder opened the doors to a golden era of gun technology. It lasted for several decades and conferred on today's shooters a legacy of fine guns for every purpose and every taste.

Very little has happened since to make sporting arms more efficient. Hunters are still using, with considerable pleasure and success, rifle and shotgun actions designed around 1900.

Frightened whitetails get away in great burst of speed from standing start, making them difficult timber target.
TEXAS GAME AND FISH COMMISSION

The point is that in view of present game laws —not to mention the present game supply—further arms development is not really necessary. We have the guns we need.

BLACK-POWDER RIFLES

Before protective legislation ended the threat of the whitetail's extinction, any firearm that could kill was used. Daniel Boone's gun was the first weapon (excepting the old wheel lock) that could be called a deer rifle, although to the modern hunter, accustomed to the high-powered firearms of the twentieth century, the Kentucky is quite unimpressive.

From Daniel Boone's rifle to the Civil War repeater, no significant improvement in firearms for the deer hunter occurred. The Kentucky rifle went through the percussion-cap period with little increase in its ability to kill. Breechloaders were something of an improvement, but they still limited the hunter to one good shot.

The single-shots of 1865 to 1890 performed well for the careful shooter. The Remington rolling block, modified from the Rider falling block, for example, was a completely safe and strong action capable of handling the most powerful cartridges then in use. In fact, Remington in 1872 brought out a rolling-block model called the Deer Rifle, a gun that had a twenty-four-inch barrel and was chambered for the .46 long rim-fire cartridge, which was thought to be the last word as an arm for whitetails.

The first American repeating rifle that can be legitimately classified as a deer-hunting weapon was the Winchester Model 1873, chambered for the .44/40 cartridge. This was an improvement on the Winchester Model 1866 in several ways. Most important, the '73 used a more powerful cartridge. Although the Model '66 repeater became the preferred arm of the scout and Indian fighter, its .44 rim-fire did not have sufficient

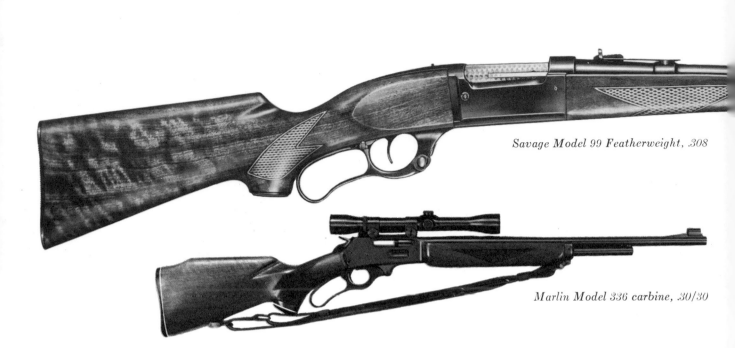

Savage Model 99 Featherweight, .308

Marlin Model 336 carbine, .30/30

impact for deer. (The resistance of the Indian apparently was much lower than that of the whitetail.) The Model '73 loaded forty grains of powder, against a maximum of twenty-eight in the .44 rim-fire, which gave it much greater velocity and shocking effect. Moreover, the center-fire cartridge could be reloaded. The '73 also had a more dependable action than other repeaters—an important factor in a wilderness where gunsmiths were scarce.

The deer hunter was given a still more powerful weapon with the introduction of the Winchester Model 1876, called the Centennial. It was chambered for a new series of bigger-bore calibers carrying heavier charges: .45/75, .45/60, .40/61, and .50/95. These larger calibers were possible because the '76 had a longer and stronger action than the '73. However, the Centennial's series of cartridges was shorter and, therefore, less powerful than the single-shot big-bores in vogue at that time.

Until the 1890's, big-bore rifles with short cartridges also were made by Marlin, Bullard, Evans, and Burgess. Winchester brought out its Hotchkiss repeating bolt action and Remington its Keene bolt action. They were chambered in the .44/40, as well as in more powerful loads.

SMOKELESS-POWDER RIFLES

Designers were still trying to get greater killing power, but the point of diminishing returns had set in. Bigger cartridges—using heavy bullets of larger bore and pushed by huge charges of black powder—were designed. The .50/115 Express, for example, was a fearsome load with an enormous kick. But only a skilled rifleman willing to endure a terrific pounding could make practical and consistent use of it.

To achieve the modern weapon, a basic innovation was necessary. It came in the form of smokeless powder. By the 1870's, Alfred Nobel's experiments had made dynamite (nitroglycerin mixed with *kieselguhr*) safe to handle. And by 1885, a French chemist, Paul Vielle, had brought nitrocellulose to the point where it could be loaded. This was single-base smokeless powder. Nobel, in 1888, produced a double-base smokeless powder by combining guncotton and nitroglycerin. With some modification, it has been used ever since. It burns at a far slower rate throughout the length of the bore than black powder, and it is not so likely to develop high-pressure peaks. With smokeless powder, a much higher velocity was attained without adding

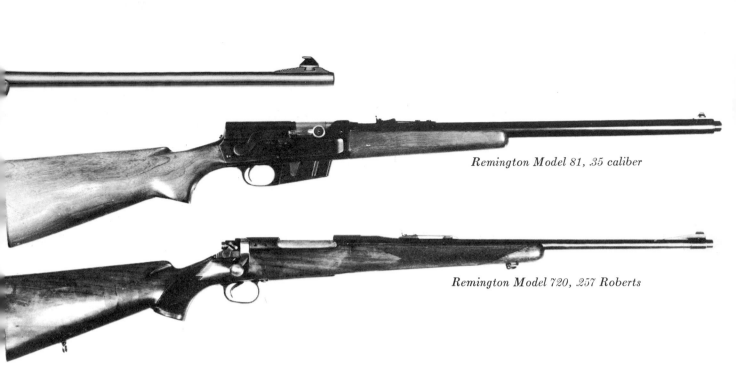

Remington Model 81, .35 caliber

Remington Model 720, .257 Roberts

more weight to the barrel. In fact, all American sporting rifles designed after Francis I. and Pierre duPont produced the first American smokeless powder in 1893 became lighter than their black-powder predecessors.

In the 1880's, another notable event in the history of firearms occurred: John Moses Browning (1855-1926), the man who was to become America's most influential gun designer, joined the Winchester Repeating Arms Company. Born in Ogden, Utah, Browning had designed his first gun at thirteen in the gun shop of his father, Jonathan Browning. In 1879, at twenty-four, Browning obtained his first patent on a rifle which became, in time, the famous Winchester Single-Shot. He also designed many guns for Colt and Remington, and eventually organized the Browning Arms Company, with his brother Matthew. When he died, at the age of seventy-one, this incredibly creative man was the holder of one hundred and twenty-five firearms patents and his name was synonymous with fine guns throughout the world.

His first efforts at developing a repeater for Winchester gave birth to the Model 1886. Its lever action was so strong that it easily handled the most powerful loads of the time, including

the .45/70 (then the official military load) and the .33 Winchester. This rifle was manufactured until 1935.

With the breakthrough in gun design made possible by the development of smokeless powder, Browning created the action of the Model 1894 rifle and carbine for use with the .30/30, the first smokeless-powder hunting cartridge. With this high-velocity, flat-trajectory cartridge, the Model '94 at once became the standard whitetail rifle. In carbine form it still outsells every other deer-hunting weapon.

From the lever-action, tubular-magazine, .30/30-caliber Model '94, with its external hammer, low-comb stock and deeply curved butt plate, the deer rifle has progressed to the latest Winchester, the Model '88, which has a short lever throw, hammerless action, one-piece stock, and detachable, box-type magazine. The entire arm is streamlined, points naturally for the quickest snap-shooting, and has a push-button safety in the front of the trigger guard—pushed "off" by the trigger finger as the gun is thrown up. It is chambered for the .308 Winchester. Loaded with a 180-grain bullet, this cartridge develops slightly more than 2,700 foot pounds of striking energy, only slightly less than the

171

WHITETAIL PHOTOS BY LEONARD RUE,
U.S. FISH AND WILDLIFE SERVICE,
AND FLORIDA NEWS BUREAU

.30/06 Springfield, long a reliable killer of American big game. The '88 is light in weight (about six and a half pounds) and comes with a twenty-two-inch barrel. All in all, it is about as handy a woods rifle as could be imagined. The detachable magazine can be replaced with a loaded extra in seconds. Its capacity is five shots, quite enough for the hunter under most conditions.

The long line of Marlin lever actions closely followed the pattern of the Winchester Model '94. The company's first smokeless-powder design was the Model 1893. It was followed by the '94 and '95, both basic lever actions but with the side-ejection system that made Marlin famous in the field of repeating rifles. These arms could also be had in half-magazine style and in take-down models. The current Marlin Model 336, in both rifle and carbine style, has a round bolt (for greater strength and smoother operation) rather than the conventional flat type of the older lever designs. It is a hammer gun with a tubular magazine and a comfortable stock. The carbine weighs less than seven pounds, has a twenty-inch barrel, and, like the '94, balances nicely and is a natural pointer. It tops the '94 in two respects: it is a side-ejector, making it practical to mount a scope sight low and directly over the bore; it is chambered not only for the .30/30 and the .32 Special, but for the .35 Remington, a more efficient cartridge on deer.

At the turn of the century the Savage Model 99 appeared. It is substantially the same gun today: hammerless action, short lever throw, rotary rather than tubular magazine. The Featherweight Model 99F, chambered either for .308 Winchester or the .300 Savage cartridge, is one of the better deer rifles. It weighs six and a half pounds and has a twenty-two-inch barrel. The design of the stock makes it fast to mount and comfortable to shoot.

Remington developed the first successful high-powered slide-action, or pump repeater, in America—the Model 14—in 1912. This fast-action, lightweight rifle was offered to the hunter in a variety of special rimless Remington cartridges: the .25, .30, .32, and .35. In 1936, it was replaced by the Model 141, which had an improved stock and forearm design. The most recent addition to the Remington line is the Model 760, a gun whose only resemblance to the old Model 14 is its pump action. The Model 760 has a multiple-locking breechblock that is capable of handling powerful modern cartridges, a detachable four-shot box magazine, a large forearm, and a well-designed stock with full comb and close pistol grip. In the deluxe version a high-comb stock, exclusively for use with a scope, can be had as optional equipment. The rifle is furnished in several deer calibers: .270 Winchester, .280 Remington, .308 and .30/06 Springfield, and .35 Remington. Next to the autoloading rifle, the slide-action Model 760 is generally conceded to be the fastest of all the repeating actions.

The next major development in deer rifles was Thomas C. Johnson's autoloading Winchester Model 1905. It was produced in two rimless and relatively low-powered calibers: the .32 and the .35 Self-Loading, today regarded as overgrown pistol cartridges. This rifle was followed, in 1907, by an almost identical design that handled the .351 Self-Loading, and in 1910 by the .401 Self-Loading. The principle of the autoloading action was the same as that of the modern automatic pistol. It was a "blow-back" that depended on the inertia of the breechblock and the pressure of a recoil spring to hold the breech tightly closed until the cartridge had been fired. Because of the limitations of this design, fairly low-pressure cartridges were used. Since no lockup of the breech took place, the final models of this action employed a heavy steel block, concealed in the forearm and attached to the breech mechanism, to increase inertia and hold the action closed against more powerful cartridges.

Browning's outstanding autoloader design, the Remington Model 8, was marketed after he left Winchester. It was modern in every respect, with a cam-operated locking breech capable of withstanding the pressure of the much more powerful .30 and .35 Remington loads. Despite its weight and the bulk of its covered-barrel assembly, it went through one modification in 1936 (Model 81) and remained in production until 1950. Remington's current autoloader, the Model 740, eliminates all the basic objections to the Model 8. It takes several cartridges (.280 Remington, .308 Winchester, .30/06 Springfield), weighs seven and a half pounds, is gas-operated and fires five shots as rapidly as the trigger can be pulled. One more point: it is an excellent weapon provided the user does not get trigger-happy and dump the whole gunload in a quick burst of unaimed fire.

The most recent deer rifle to enter the field in America is the bolt action. While its relatively slow rate of fire and excessive weight have prevented it from winning immediate acceptance, time has proved its worth. It works in rain or snow, and even if filled with mud, sand, or dead leaves. Its parts are simple. It is easy to take apart, and is the strongest type of rifle action yet conceived. Its trigger pull is matchless, its accuracy unsurpassed.

These qualities did not escape an army of returning doughboys familiar with the World War I Springfield. Their demand for modified Springfields led Savage to believe there was a market for another bolt-action rifle. The company brought out its Model 1920, a short action of a modified Mauser type; chambered for the .250 and the .300 Savage cartridge. It did not sell as expected, however, and its life was short. Its successor, the Model 40, suffered from a weak bolt-locking system and survived an even shorter time. In 1957, Savage produced the Model 110, a lightweight, high-powered bolt action with an excellent locking system, trigger pull, and stock. It has a twenty-two-inch barrel and its most effective deer calibers are the .308 and .30/06. Its tang safety—like that of a double shotgun—appeals to all snap-shooters.

Remington's post-World War I bolt action was the Model 30, a sporting modification of the Enfield that Remington built for Great Britain as a military weapon. This was marketed in the popular rimless series of special Remington cartridges and in the .30/06. Its special feature was a side-action safety. In addition, the low upturn of the bolt permitted low scope mounting. The Model 30, after getting an improved stock and being renamed the Model 720, was discontinued in 1942. Six years passed before Remington brought out another high-powered bolt action. This was the Model 721, chambered for the .270 and the .30/06. Concurrently, a shorter action, the Model 722, chambered for the .308 and the .300 Savage, was released. Both of these lightweights are now on the market. They feature a handy side safety, a strong breech lockup, and an adjustable trigger pull.

In 1925, Winchester produced its first sporting bolt action, the Model 54. It was a rifle unique at the time for two reasons: it was not a copy of a military weapon, and was built not only in .30/06 but in the .270, a new high-velocity caliber. In 1937, it was slightly modified and has since been chambered for a range of calibers from the .22 Hornet to the .458 African. Now called the Model 70, it is the leading American bolt-action rifle for all big game. In the Featherweight Model, .308 caliber, it makes a top-grade deer-hunting arm.

As a result of almost a century of progress in design, the modern deer rifle is now able to

MODERN REMINGTON RIFLES: *Top to bottom, Model 740 F autoloader in Premier grade with gold inlays, scroll engraving, choice stock wood, and hand-finished action; Model 760 F, also in Premier grade, a slide-action rifle in similar finish; Model 725 deluxe bolt action, with high-comb Monte Carlo stock; Standard Model 721 bolt action. They are made in wide range of calibers from .222 Remington to .300 Magnum.*

PHOTO BY ALEX HENDERSON

do an effective job. It is as quick to get into action as a gunfighter's six-shooter. That is, it is light and short, so that it swings easily in brush and small timber, and is stocked for quick mounting to the shoulder—almost for snap-shooting. The trigger pull is not over six pounds and is without noticeable creep. The safety is easy to snap off to the firing position.

It is capable of delivering repeated, powerful blows with bullets that expand quickly. This is most important because there is no point in driving a bullet clean through the deer to waste most of its striking force on trees and rocks beyond, and there is every point in rapid follow-up shots. For the game, once down at the first shot, should be kept down for good. The quick kill is not only humane and sportsmanlike, but also the best way to make sure of the trophy; some hunters have no scruples about claiming and tagging crippled or dying deer.

But even if impact and speed of fire leave nothing to be desired, it must always be remembered that the only shot that counts is the one that hits its target—and in a vital spot.

CHAPTER NINE **AMERICAN BIG GAME**

These bears being so hard to die

rather intimidates us all; I must confess I do not like

the gentleman and had rather fight

two Indians than one bear.

MERIWETHER LEWIS

PAGES 176 AND 177: *Rugged mountain country is home for big game. To bag a trophy, hunters need weapons like this Remington Model 740 autoloader, .30/06 caliber, equipped with Bausch & Lomb Balvar 8X scope.*
PHOTO BY ROBERT MOTTAR

RIGHT: *Grizzly bear (Ursus horribilis) on rampage was dreaded by early big-game hunters, whose low-powered, single-shot rifles usually failed to stop charging beast unless a bullet struck brain or spine. Rifles of today, however, have great power at long range.*
LITHOGRAPH BY CURRIER AND IVES. HARRY T. PETERS COLLECTION, MUSEUM OF THE CITY OF NEW YORK

Hunting big game is a sport that is second to none in the excitement it generates and the expenditure of energy it requires. For more than half a century, the seasoned outdoorsman has seldom been willing to settle for a trophy less imposing than the bull elk or moose, the mountain sheep and goat, the great grizzly and brown bear. The challenge is to find game in its chosen terrain—always the last of the wilderness areas, where the hunter can recapture some of the frontiersman's urge to explore, where craggy peaks scrape the lower clouds, and rivers, still uncon-

taminated, rush headlong to the sea.

The hunting and killing of big-game trophies are always tinged with risk. In high mountain country the slip of a foot or the stumble of a saddle horse can bring disaster. Danger from game is not great, except for a tough old boar grizzly or an Alaskan brownie. A wounded bull elk or a rutting bull moose has been known to charge and rough up a hunter, but these incidents are rare. While the threat of harm on big-game hunts actually comes less from the animal hunted than from the land where it lives, the

possibility is ever present to add its peculiar and exhilarating spice to the experience.

Hunting big game for food occurred even before the arrival of the white man. Indians took the larger animals with bow and arrow, lances, and even by driving them into ravines. Later, the Indian used guns, but not so effectively as the whites, in whom familiarity with firearms, a talent and understanding for things mechanical, and constant practice made expert marksmanship an almost routine accomplishment.

The contemporary account by "Uncle Dick"

Wootton indicates the difference in the two cultures' approach to the gun and suggests that the red man was a mediocre rifleman, indeed.

"At hunting game with a rifle the Indians were no match for the white hunter. They were experts at finding the game, it is true, but anybody could do that in this country [Great Plains] twenty years ago [*circa* 1870]. When the game was discovered, however, such as deer or bears for instance, the hunter had not, as a rule, much time to hunt up a tree or a rock to rest his gun on before shooting. The game usually saw the hunter about as soon as the hunter saw the game, and was up and away if he was not quick in his movements.

"It was the habit of the Indian hunter, when using the rifle, to carry a couple of gun rods in his hand and when he got ready to shoot at anything, down would go the rod on the ground in the form of the letter X. With one hand the hunter held the rod together while with the other he managed his gun, resting it between the two rods. Sometimes he would make a single rod answer the purpose, holding it with his hand in the same manner, but he never had sufficient confidence in himself as a marksman to risk a shot at game without some sort of a rest. That was done when the Indian first commenced using rifles. Of late years they have learned to better advantage."

Big-game hunting as sport began with the raids on the buffalo herds. In large part this was the province of the professional hunter, but before long the plains—and forests—were invaded by European nobility on safari, elaborate hunt-

Black bear, although ferocious in appearance, takes little more killing than average deer. Species is on increase in East. PHOTO BY NATIONAL PARK SERVICE

ing parties seeking bison, elk, and moose, trophies available only in the United States.

Until the advent of the sportsman, America's large game animals had been slaughtered wholesale for food and hides—even, in the case of the elk, for its teeth. Countless thousands of these greatest of round-horned deer were killed so that a pair of incisors could be pried out and made into watch fobs for the members of a fraternal organization. Under the leadership of national figures like Teddy Roosevelt and Bob Marshall, the carnage eventually was stopped by state legislation passed in the period from about 1890 to the beginning of World War I. Present game laws ensure the conservation of elk and moose, and mountain goat are in no danger of extinction. But the future of bighorn sheep and grizzly in the United States is uncertain.

Canada will continue to provide the bighorns, the moose, the thin-horned species of sheep, and the grizzly. The new state of Alaska should now take additional measures to protect the giant northern moose and the huge brown bear—the largest animals on the North American continent. At present, the supply of all these big-game species is sufficient to permit limited harvesting each year. Even so, it is no wonder sportsmen contrast the present situation with the days of the western frontier, when a hunter's major problem was not locating game, but finding a gun big and powerful enough to kill it.

EARLY REPEATING RIFLES

The first repeating rifles, whether made by Colt, Spencer, Henry, or Remington, were ridiculously lacking in the power that a big-game firearm must have. The metallic cartridges for which most of these rifles were chambered were relatively weak rim-fires, lacking both in penetration and shock power against large animals.

And until the center-fire brass cartridge came along, it was impossible to build a repeating rifle that was effective on big game.

Invention of the center-fire cartridge design in America has been credited to Colonel Hiram Berdan, the Civil War commander. Official records are less than positive, but it seems certain that he was a key contributor to center-fire development.

Legend says that the Sioux Indians, whose squaws made a practice of picking up empty rim-fire cartridge cases after engagements with the United States Cavalry, made the first center-fire cartridge. Since the red man was always short of ammunition and showed considerable ingenuity in finding ways to survive, it was only a short step to the insertion of a common percussion cap in the base of the empty case prior to reloading it. Unfortunately, legend does not say how the Sioux converted the rim-fire action of the rifle to discharge the new center-fire case.

Center-fire ignition permitted the use of cartridge cases with thick, solid heads and thicker walls than the rim-fire, enabling them to take a more powerful load. The Sharps rifles used center-fire cartridges, as did the single-shot Springfield and other rifles of the 1860's and 1870's. The introduction of Winchester's lever-action Model 1876, the big-game hunter felt, was a step in the right direction. But even this gun did not satisfy him completely. He wanted a repeater that would give him as much power as the bigger loads of the single-shot rifles.

Winchester's next attempt at a more powerful repeater was the Hotchkiss rifle and carbine, a bolt-action design firing the powerful .45/70, the contemporary military load and a cartridge for big game. But the suitable six-shot Hotchkiss Model 1879—incidentally, the first bolt-action arm produced in America—did not find favor with the sporting public. Chapter 8 de-

scribes how John Browning developed a new lever-action, the Model 1886, chambering it for the .45/70. He then adapted it to take the .50/110, the most powerful game cartridge of the day and one of the heaviest black-powder loads ever made. Here was a rifle that could deliver a crushing blow to a big grizzly. In the .45/70 caliber, the hunter had at almost instant command a tubular magazine of eight reserve cartridges. No other rifle of the black-powder era surpassed this dependable Winchester in firepower and ability to knock down the biggest game within the limit of its range. This key phrase, "limit of range," became the gunmaker's incentive to produce even more efficient rifles.

SMOKELESS-POWDER CARTRIDGES

To hit the mark before the invention of smokeless powder, a rifleman had to estimate range accurately and know precisely how much the bullet would drop at any given distance. He could then calculate the amount of "hold-over" needed to compensate for the drop. Needless to say, few hunters ever attained this sort of precise shooting skill at long range.

Almost at once, smokeless powder stepped up bullet speeds considerably beyond those given by black powder. Trajectories flattened out with new cartridge designs, enormously increasing the long-range hitting ability of the rifle. With higher bullet speeds there also came a great increase in shocking power. Smaller bores and

FAMOUS OLD WINCHESTER RIFLES: *Left to right, Model '07 autoloader, .351 self-loading caliber; Model '94 rifle, .30/30 with twenty-six-inch barrel; Model '95, .405 caliber, with box-type magazine (Teddy Roosevelt's favorite); discontinued Model '71, a modern version, in .348 caliber, of popular Model '86 big-game rifle.*
PHOTO BY JOSEPH BURNS

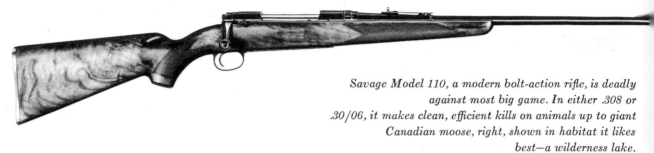

*Savage Model 110, a modern bolt-action rifle, is deadly
against most big game. In either .308 or
.30/06, it makes clean, efficient kills on animals up to giant
Canadian moose, right, shown in habitat it likes
best—a wilderness lake.*

CANADIAN GOVERNMENT TRAVEL BUREAU

lighter bullets could then be used to flatten trajectories without losing killing effect.

By the 1890's, big game had become extremely wary because of the heavy hunting pressure. It was more and more difficult to approach for a close shot, which placed a higher premium on long-range marksmanship.

Although the .30/30—the first smokeless-powder cartridge for sporting use—was deadly on deer, it was not very effective against big game. More powerful loads, and rifles to handle them, were needed for elk, moose, and bear. Meanwhile, the .30/40 had been developed by the Ordnance Department for the new Norwegian Krag (originally the Krag-Jorgensen), which was adopted as the standard Army rifle in 1892.

Again, Browning was called on, this time to design a rifle with an action long enough to handle more powerful loads. Another problem was the newly designed pointed bullet, which could not be safely loaded into the tubular magazine of the existing lever-actions because it might discharge there and injure the shooter. Since the sharp point of the bullet would rest on the primer of the cartridge ahead of it, there was always the possibility, at the least jar in the magazine, that the cartridge would discharge, blowing up the gun. Browning solved the problem with the Model 95 lever-action box-magazine rifle, which eventually was chambered for some of the world's best big-game loads.

The final development of the .30/06 cartridge

practically completed the evolution of the modern sporting rifle. The Ordnance Department abandoned the Krag shortly after the Spanish-American War for two reasons: it could not be clip-loaded and it fired a cartridge with a rimmed case, a load already outclassed by Germany's new Mauser, which clip-loaded and fired a rimless cartridge with a solid head. It could withstand far greater pressures than the Krag, which had only a single locking lug on the bolt.

On a royalty basis, Ordnance got the rights from the German inventor, Karl Mauser, to build a new Springfield rifle based on his action, which would have double locking lugs and a staggered box magazine that fed the rimless cartridge smoothly. A more powerful cartridge, loading the old 220-grain bullet used in the Krag, was designed. This was the short-lived .30/1903 —doomed when the Germans brought out the lighter, sharp-pointed "Spitzer" bullet which was more efficient at long range, particularly in machine guns. Challenged by this advance, Ordnance modified the .30/1903 by changing to a 150-grain, sharp-point bullet and by shortening the neck of the case to accommodate the shorter bullet. The result was the .30 Model of 1906, long known simply as the .30/06—the famous and deadly military and sporting cartridge.

After developing the '06 cartridge, Ordnance immediately called back all existing '03 rifles for conversion to the new load. Barrels were removed, faced off on the breech end, and then

184

WINCHESTER RIFLES FOR LARGEST GAME:
Model 70 Supergrade in .357 Magnum, top,
most powerful weapon required for North American hunting;
standard-grade Model 70, made in many big-game calibers, with .30/06
preferred by hunting experts as ideal all-around big-game rifle.
Rocky Mountain bull elk, below—largest of the round-horned animals—is
choice big-game trophy and one of wariest of deer family.
PHOTO BY U.S. FISH AND WILDLIFE SERVICE

Sioux warriors, using white man's weapons, chase a whitetail buck on St. Peter's River, in eastern Dakota.
PAINTING BY GEORGE CATLIN, FROM SMITHSONIAN INSTITUTE. COURTESY TIME MAGAZINE

rechambered to the shorter, over-all cartridge length. This is why the barrels of the pre-World War I Springfields were just short of the standard twenty-four-inch length. After World War I, when the Springfield was converted to big-game use, its .30/06 cartridge became the standard for almost all new designs, including the .270, .308, .358 Winchester, and the .280 Remington.

The English went a step further in developing a still more powerful .30-caliber cartridge, the .300 and .375 Holland & Holland Magnum, both of which soon were adopted by American hunters seeking accuracy and power at long range.

The latest step in the evolution of the .30/06 came out of South Gate, California, in 1943, when Roy Weatherby, an insurance man who turned to ballistics and riflemaking, rechambered a Winchester .270 to take magnum loads. Weatherby's idea was to pack the maximum amount of modern, slow-burning powder into a case shaped to the powder's burning characteristics. To obtain the greatest possible speed, he sacrificed bullet weight. Big game met quick death from the shock of a disintegrating bullet.

These powerful cartridges and the rifles that fire them are now used for both timber and long-range hunting. Elk and moose are the only American big game that is now hunted primarily in timber. Elk were formerly open-country animals, seeking the edges of prairies and plains and the open "park" areas of the hills. Heavy hunting has forced them into the big stands of coniferous timber in the national forests. Moose have always been lovers of thick, evergreen forests and deep swamps or bogs. Close-cover shooting is the rule for moose over most of their range, except on the tundra of the Yukon and Alaska.

Timber rifles for both elk and moose include the .348 Winchester, formerly made in the Model 71 (an improved version of the old 1886); the newer .358 Winchester; the .30/06 with 220-grain bullet, and the older .35 Winchester (not the .35 self-loading) and the .405. In some sections hunters prefer the .300 Savage and the .308 Savage in several models light enough for woods hunting. The experience of top-notch hunters suggests that the two Savage models may be rather light for dependable kills, although here the skill of the hunter makes a big difference.

All the rifles recommended in Chapter 8 make fine woods weapons for elk and moose, if the heavier calibers in each are selected. The Winchester Model 88 in .358 caliber, for example, is the best possible choice for a big-game woods rifle. Loaded with the 250-grain bullet, this fast repeater is deadly up to at least 200 yards. The same is true of the Savage Model 99, which also comes in .358 caliber. The two fast Remingtons, Models 760 and 740, are best in .30/06, loaded with 220-grain Core-Lokt or Silver Tip bullets.

LONG-RANGE RIFLES

The mountain hunter who finds his game under a wide variety of conditions looks for more power and longer-range accuracy than the timber rifle affords. Late in the year, when the elk herds come down from the high country toward the winter feeding grounds, the hunter will be able to take some long shots. Moose in the tundra are often long-range game; caribou, sheep, and goat as well. And today most grizzly and black-bear hunting in the West and North is done over open slides where the animals are spotted with binoculars and stalked. Much of this shooting is at more than 200 yards.

In this terrain the .300 Magnum, in either the Remington Model 721, the Winchester Model 70, or the new Coltsman, are among the best choices the hunter can make. The .300 Magnums, using the same bullets as the .30/06, give noticeably more velocity and killing power. What the '06 does at 200 yards, the .300 Magnum will do at 300. The ultimate in range and killing power from a .30-caliber rifle is furnished by the .300 Weatherby Magnum—a souped-up version of the regular Magnum — which will do the job reliably and well at 400 yards or more.

Winchester's newest load in the long-range big-game group is the .338, a powerful cartridge that sends a 200-grain bullet at 3,050 feet per second. This is one of the finest all-purpose big-game cartridges. It can be had in the Model 70 Winchester, which weighs only seven and a half pounds. The recoil, while strong, should not disturb an experienced big-game hunter. The cartridge outperforms the regular .300 Magnum, and loaded with the 250-grain bullet is an ideal killer of the biggest game, including Alaska's formidable brown bear and giant moose.

The big-game hunter of the Rockies can seldom limit himself to one rifle. On most hunts he will encounter elk, mountain goat, bighorn sheep, and perhaps grizzly and black bear. For sheep and goat, the lighter .270 Winchester and .280 Remington are splendid long-range weapons, but they are less than ideal for grizzly, elk, or moose. Many of these species, of course, have been killed with the light calibers when the bullets were placed just right. For the best results, however, two rifles are practically a must. One should be a real big-game rifle in one of the calibers previously mentioned, the other a goat, sheep, or deer rifle for long ranges in high country.

THE ALASKAN RIFLE

For targets the size of Alaska's brown bear and giant moose, an exceptionally good caliber is the .375 Magnum, made in the Winchester Model 70. Weatherby's .375 Magnum rifle, in its special caliber, is a shade better. It is a more expensive gun on a foreign-made action and one of the finest rifles in the world. Either of the big

.375 Magnums is a good 300-yard cartridge for the biggest animals and has the virtue of extra stopping power in the event of a charge from the big bruins. Its 300-grain bullet slams out of the muzzle with 4,330 foot pounds of energy, giving the hunter a greater feeling of security when the big brownie turns his way with blood in its eye. Certainly this is the most powerful weapon needed on the North American conti-

Dizzy heights at which Rocky Mountain white goat lives makes hunting it a hazardous adventure.

PHOTO BY JOHN O. SUMNER, MONKMEYER

nent, an excellent weapon for all-purpose use on elk, moose, and grizzly if the added weight does not unduly tire the hunter. The .375 weighs nine pounds-plus; it is no woods rifle by any means. Most sportsmen would feel a bit foolish firing such a fearsome weapon at sheep, goat, or deer.

CHOOSING THE RIFLE

There is no one ideal firearm. The final choice of a rifle should be governed by the terrain, as well as the type of game to be hunted. The sportsman who prefers a high rate of fire for repeated shots must stay with the big-game rifles and calibers. To obtain maximum range and power, he is forced to choose a bolt-action of some type, for none of the magnums is currently built any other way. Such a gun will give him a total capacity of five or six shots, and only the older, tubular-magazine rifles furnish more.

In long-range work, the fast follow-up shots are generally unimportant; the hunter usually has time to get set in either the prone or sitting position, using a rolled-up jacket for a soft rest, like the old-time buffalo hunter. His bolt-action rifle is best suited to the scope sight he will inevitably use. His first shot will be carefully planned to do the job, taking into account the range, the exact drop of the bullet over the range, and the effect of wind drift, If his first shot misses, he is not likely to get a fast second one with the game still motionless. However, if he downs the animal but does not kill it, he still has time to throw the bolt and place a careful finishing shot. Since most long-range chances at big game occur in open country, the animals, unlike the whitetail, will not disappear in a few seconds.

190

CHAPTER TEN **SAFARI**

There is delight in the hardy life of the open, in long rides rifle in hand, in the thrill of the fight with dangerous game.

THEODORE ROOSEVELT

PAGES 192 AND 193: *Tools of the safari hunter: Model 70 Winchester, .458 African; four-wheel-drive vehicle; and wide-brimmed safari hat. The .458 can be depended on to stop the biggest of dangerous game.* PHOTO BY ROBERT MOTTAR

ABOVE: *Safari to Africa offers scenery as magnificent as its hunting. Here party, above East Africa's game-filled plains, trudges through dry grass at base of Mount Kilimanjaro's Kibo peak, highest spot (19,565 feet) on continent.* PHOTO COURTESY ELLEN GATTI

Every year more and more American sportsmen are crossing the oceans in search of big-game trophies. In its dense jungles and on its vast plains Africa affords the greatest variety of game to be found anywhere on the globe, from the elephant to the gazelle—not to mention a wide range of birds. India is in no way comparable as a hunting ground. The American sportsman generally tries India only after he has exhausted the trophies of Africa, and he usually seeks only the huge gaur, or Indo-Chinese buffalo, and the Bengal tiger—counterparts of the African Cape buffalo and the lordly lion.

Outside of the trophies and the thrill of the hunt, there are two main reasons for these jaunts: the fact that an American can reach

Africa and India by air in less than forty-eight hours, and that a well-organized safari or shikar (Hindi for hunt) now costs no more than a first-rate automobile. A trip can even be financed like a car—on the monthly installment plan.

That hunting in Africa is a well-established trend is confirmed by the appearance of American weapons developed basically for taking large, dangerous beasts. Until quite recently, no American rifles—despite Teddy Roosevelt's stout claims for the heavier Winchesters—were designed for African hunting. Roosevelt's armament, although basically American, included heavy double-express English rifles for use on elephant. His .405 Winchester, then the most powerful American-made caliber, could not be

trusted to stop the charge of this great beast.

Roosevelt was the first American to popularize African big-game hunting, but several other United States citizens left their mark on the Dark Continent with American arms. Charles Cottar, a Texan who hunted big game from Mexico to Canada, killing many grizzlies and moose as well as lesser animals, made his first safari in Africa in 1912 carrying the same rifle he had used throughout his American hunts, the Winchester Model '94 in .32 Special. With this pipsqueak weapon—by modern standards strictly a woods rifle for deer—Cottar killed every species of African big game, including rhino, buffalo, hippo, and lion. Using remarkably good judgment, he did not attempt to kill elephant

on these hunts. The real surprise of his first trip, which lasted almost a year, is not that he killed such dangerous game with an undersized rifle, but that he lived to make other safaris.

Cottar returned to Africa with his family and set up residence in Nairobi, where he lived for the rest of his life, making brief visits to the United States to show movies of African game. On the first of these visits, in 1913, he had added two American rifles to his battery, the then brand-new .250 Savage and a .405 Winchester Model '95. The little Savage Model 99 in .250 he used for taking all the smaller game, from the many species of antelope up to and including lion. Today this Savage is disdained by most hunters for game larger than whitetails, and few will trust its light bullet even for them.

Ben Burbridge, an American explorer and writer, made four trips to Africa between 1915 and 1929, killing many of the largest game animals with the .30/40 and the .405. He preferred the .30/40 even for elephant because of its greater penetration in brain shots. D. W. M. ("Karamojo") Bell, one of the most famous ivory hunters of all time, a Scotsman who spent thirty years at his destructive trade, killed well over a thousand of the big beasts with a 7-mm and a .303 British, although both loads are rated well down the list by experts.

However, the hunter of the early part of the twentieth century found conditions in Africa vastly different from what they are today. Bell discovered this when he returned some years after his three decades of successful ivory hunting, again carrying his little 7-mm. He found the elephant far more wary and prone to charge almost without provocation, even when barely catching the scent of the hunter. His last hunt was a dismal experience, fraught with hair-raising escapes from enraged animals. As far as big African game was concerned, the day of the small-caliber weapon had ended.

Heavy hunting over the past two decades has made the close approach to game far more difficult than before. To kill big game with the small rifle, the bullet must be carefully placed in just the right spot, at just the right angle, and at close range. This is no longer possible except by chance. What is more likely is that the hunter, in making such a close approach, will face a determined charge by a maddened beast of great bulk and power and almost at spitting distance. The heavy rifle is essential for such hunting.

Two of the old-time African hunters who are still active confirm this. John A. Hunter, an outstanding Government hunter, sticks to his .450 double for all "last-ditch" protection and prefers the .375 Magnum for all intermediate species and for longer-range shooting at the big animals. John ("Pondoro") Taylor, an admitted ivory poacher, will settle for nothing less than the .400 double in a sticky situation with a charging rhino or buffalo. Lighter calibers are for lesser game, and are used on the big stuff only when a comfortable distance separates the hunter from the hunted.

African Government officials recognize the need for powerful rifles on dangerous game, both for the protection of the hunter and to conserve the game itself. Moreover, animals wounded by

World's most powerful sporting rifle is Weatherby's new
460 Magnum, firing a 500-grain bullet with muzzle energy of more
than 8,000 foot pounds. It has a German-built action,
weighs only twelve pounds, and is designed to stop African
elephant, the biggest quarry of them all,
and one of the most dangerous in a determined charge.
PHOTO OF ELEPHANT BY YLLA, RAPHO GUILLUMETTE

careless shooting with inadequate rifles often become vengeful killers of human beings. Recent legislation in Kenya forbids the use of any caliber smaller than .375 on elephant, rhino, and buffalo. Tanganyika likewise outlaws any caliber smaller than this for its biggest game and in some areas the .400 is fixed as the minimum.

The big, powerful double rifles are expensive and can be bought in the United States only through a few importers in the East. Actually, there is no need to have foreign guns for African hunting unless the hunter insists on using a a double rifle, as the African "white hunter" usually does. The two fast shots obtainable with the double are of great value, yet the extra two or three shells in the bolt-action's magazine are also to be recommended. Using the bolt-action, an experienced shooter will have little difficulty getting off a fast second or third shot with almost as much speed as the "right and left" of the big double. Then, if he needs extra cartridges, he has the firepower at his command.

THE HEAVIEST RIFLES

A cartridge long popular in both Africa and India for big game is the .375 Magnum, made in the Model 70 Winchester since 1937. The Eng-

Two important trophy animals of the Big Five in African hunting:
Rhino, left, male lion, below. Rhino is near-sighted, stupid beast
that charges at sounds and scent of hunter and his vehicle,
but is readily stopped or turned by a frontal shoulder shot. Lion, unless
lightly wounded, is down-rated by experts in the list of dangerous
game, since an unprovoked charge is a rarity. Lion is readily
bagged with lighter African rifles, including the .375 Magnum, the
.300 Magnums and, on many occasions, the .30/06.
PHOTOS BY ELIOT ELISOFON. COURTESY LIFE

lish firm of Holland & Holland created the load for heavy game and it is today one of the best safari calibers in existence. Winchester loadings give the 300-grain bullet a striking energy at the muzzle of 4,330 foot pounds, the 270-grain load 4,500 foot pounds. Short of attacks from the biggest African game, the .375 is the nearest thing to an all-around African rifle. It will certainly drop easily all of the larger antelope up to eland, and will smash a charging lion or leopard in its tracks. "Pondoro" Taylor calls this "one of the deadliest weapons in existence" and admits to having fired more than five thousand rounds of .375 ammunition at game with highly satisfactory results.

Roy Weatherby, with his .375 Weatherby Magnum, has redesigned the cartridge case to hold more powder, thus giving greater energy to its standard bullet. While this load has a slight edge on the regular .375 Magnum, it does not put the rifle in the class of those used against the charge of a buffalo or elephant. Another Weatherby design is the .378 Magnum, built on a larger case than the .375. The extra powder it holds makes it a real high-velocity load with a 300-grain bullet. This is by far the most powerful .38-caliber rifle; the 300-grain bullet has a velocity of 3,022 fps and a muzzle energy of

6,075 foot pounds. The earliest of these Weatherby rifles were built on the F. N. Mauser and the Schultz and Larsen bolt actions. More recent ones are built in Sweden on the Weatherby-designed Mark V action and are the most modern high-powered bolt-action rifles in the world.

Winchester created for its Model 70 a heavier load built on the .375 Magnum case: the .458 African Magnum. In this design Winchester made no attempt to follow Weatherby's lead in stepping up velocity. Instead, it concentrated on a cartridge that would deliver a far heavier

bullet at normal speeds while utilizing the Model 70's regular-length magazine and bolt action. The cartridge is loaded with a 500-grain, full metal-jacketed bullet, the English "solid," that penetrates seasoned oak more than thirty inches. It also loads a 510-grain soft-pointed bullet.

The big .458 takes up where the .375 Magnum leaves off. It is a sure stopper of any charging animal, no matter what its size. A frontal head shot on an elephant drops the huge beast in its tracks. Experience with side-of-the-head shots on elephants shows that the bullet frequently plows right through to emerge on the far side. Aside from its stopping power, the .458 in the Model 70 has a short bolt throw, no longer than that of the same model in .30/06 caliber. This makes it easy to reload, with little possibility that the shooter will fail to draw back the bolt far enough to pick up a cartridge from the magazine. Such failure has been a major complaint with large-caliber British magazine rifles and has resulted in an occasional death from charging game. The .458 is not excessively heavy—considering its power—weighing just over nine pounds. It does, however, have a heavy recoil of about seventy foot pounds.

A lighter, less powerful Winchester rifle, fine for all but the biggest beasts, is the .338 Magnum, a cartridge designed on the .458 case but firing 200- or 250-grain bullets. This load gives

Big double rifle is still favored for close-quarters shooting of dangerous game, such as this Bengal tiger in tall reeds of India. White hunter approaches wounded animal, which rises from its bed to charge. Tiger in the middle of full charge is caught by right-and-left .50-caliber slugs, dropping it in mid-air. PHOTOS BY PETER THROCKMORTON, COURTESY ARGOSY MAGAZINE

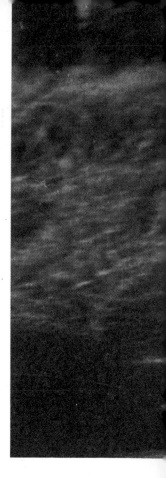

*Fleeing waterbuck in Tanganyika bush is one of
more difficult African-trophy targets. Dozens of antelope
species are available to trophy hunters, and can
readily be taken with lighter-calibered units of African
battery. Below are two of the heavy rifles for the
safari. Weatherby .378 Magnum, mounted with 4X Weatherby
scope, is most powerful of .38-caliber arms. It
is deadly enough for any African game, but restricted in
some areas because of bore size. Griffin and Howe
rifle, right, is English caliber, .416 Rigby, built on Magnum
Mauser action to customer's order by the New York firm.*

PHOTO OF WATERBUCK BY GEORGE RODGER, MAGNUM

the 250-grain bullet a muzzle speed of 2,750 fps
and an energy of 4,200 foot pounds.

What appears to be the ultimate powerhouse
in big-game weapons is Weatherby's .460 Magnum—almost eligible to be classified as a field-
piece. It is likely that no future load will top its
500-grain bullet driven at the fantastic muzzle
energy of 8,245 foot pounds at a speed of 2,725
fps. It weighs twelve pounds, somewhat less than
the .600 Double Express, which has long been
touted as the world's most powerful shoulder
weapon—until the advent of the .460 Magnum.

MEDIUM-GAME RIFLES

Big-game species afford the hunter relatively
few chances—probably not more than a dozen
shots in all. The great bulk of African hunting
and shooting pleasure, therefore, comes from
the small-to-medium game in which the veldt
abounds. In addition to sport, the hunter shoots
many head of game for camp meat and some for
bait. In any case, the hunter usually wants as
medium-game trophies many of the beautiful
antelope: the giant eland, kudu, impala, gere-

nuk, waterbuck, and okapi. Much of this larger game compares with the caribou and elk of the United States and can well be taken with the rifles hunters use on such animals in America, bearing in mind that fairly long shots are the rule.

The .30/06 has long been a standard for Africa's medium game. It has been used with great success on lion also, loaded with the 220-grain, delayed-expansion bullet. Many other of our longer-range calibers lend themselves well to such meat and trophy hunting, among them the .300 Magnum and .300 Weatherby Magnum.

H. W. Klein, world-famous big-game hunter, swears by the .300 Weatherby for such shooting and has even taken all of the "Big Four" with this caliber. It must be remembered, however, that Klein is a dead shot and can place his bullets where they have the greatest effect. For all but the very smallest game—and the ferocious chargers—the .300 Magnum is an ideal choice. It has great accuracy and a flat trajectory over 400 yards and carries a killing punch all the way. The .308, the .270 Winchester, and .280 Remington also are good loads, topped only by the

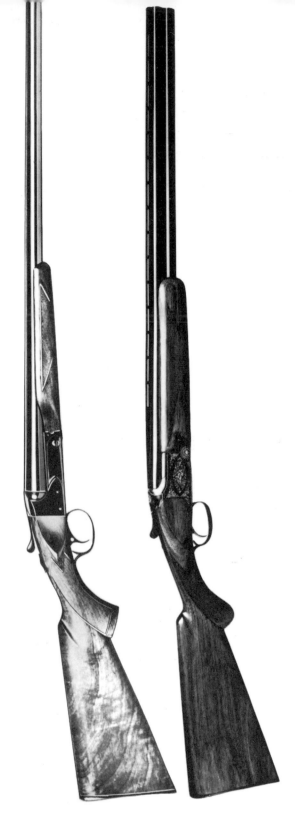

7-mm and the .270 Weatherby Magnums.

The rifles generally classed as woods weapons in America are not a good choice for either African or Indian hunting. For close-range work on the dangerous animals, the .458's are by all odds the best. Rifles such as the .358 Winchester, the .35 Remington, and the .300 Savage, among others, lack the close-range power for big animals and long-range punch for smaller ones.

To take the smallest antelope, a high-powered varmint load is good. Rifles of .22 caliber are, of course, outlawed, but this does not rule out the Winchester .243, the Remington .244, and the .257 Weatherby Magnum. These are flat-shooting rifles which have great shock effect.

THE AFRICAN BATTERY

In making an extended trip into Africa the temptation is to take too many guns, thereby creating difficulties for the outfitter, the white

Shotguns for African hunting are limited to a total of two shots. Two good models are Winchester Model 21 in 12 gauge, left, with single trigger and automatic ejectors, and Browning Superposed, right, a fine over/under in 12 gauge. Impala, opposite, are among the speediest antelope, have graceful trophy horns.
PHOTO OF IMPALA BY YLLA, RAPHO GUILLUMETTE

hunter, and the gun bearers. The number of guns should be kept to the minimum in order to limit the sizes of ammunition that will be needed, which in turn reduces the chances of carrying the wrong loads for the day's hunt.

A typical battery should include the charge-stopper; a .458 Winchester fills this need nicely. The intermediate rifle might be the .300 Magnum or .300 Weatherby Magnum. The .300 Magnum caliber offers several choices—the Winchester 70, the Remington 721, and the Colt Coltsman. The smallest-caliber rifle should be on the order of a .243 Winchester in either the Winchester Model 88 or the Savage Model 99, in lever-actions; the Winchester Model 70, the Savage Model 110, and the Coltsman if bolt actions are preferred.

No hunter should visit Africa without giving thought to the bird shooting. The continent is literally crammed with sand grouse, guinea fowl, wild waterfowl of many kinds, and the great bustards. A shotgun is an essential for this sport, often practiced under conditions much like those experienced by the early American bird hunters. African law prohibits the use of a shotgun carrying more than two shells, restricting the gunner to the Winchester Model 21, the Fox Model B (made by Savage), or the Browning Superposed, among American weapons. (The Browning, although of Belgian make, is assembled and stocked in the United States.)

The 12 gauge is the best choice simply because it has a wider variety of uses and the ammunition for it is available locally. Since African import restrictions limit the hunter to two hundred and fifty rounds of shotgun ammunition, it is probable that he will want to buy more shells on the spot. Once a man gets a taste of African bird shooting, he is almost sure to become a devotee. It is sport of such fabulous proportions that to find its equal one must look back to the early eighteenth century in the United States.

CHAPTER ELEVEN **PLAINS GAME**

After an hour or two's steady tramping I came into

a long, narrow valley, bare of trees and brushwood, and strolled

along it following a cattle trail that led up the middle.

The hills rose steeply into a ridge crest on each side, sheer clay

boulders breaking the mat of buffalo grass which elsewhere

covered the side of the valley as well as the bottom. It was very

hot and still, and I was paying but little attention

to my surroundings, when my eye caught a sudden movement on the

ridge crest to my right, and, dropping on one knee

as I wheeled around, I saw the head and neck of a prongbuck rising

above the crest. The animal was not above a hundred yards

off, and stood motionless as it stared at me. At the crack of the

rifle the head disappeared; but as I sprang clear

of the smoke I saw a cloud of dust rise on the other side

of the ridge crest, and I felt convinced that

the quarry had fallen. I was right.

THEODORE ROOSEVELT

The buffalo, elk, pronghorn antelope, and mule deer that once roamed the thousand miles of Great Plains between the Mississippi and the foothills of the Rockies gave this area a quantity, if not a variety, of game that rivaled the African veldt. The buffalo and elk roam no more, but mule deer are still plentiful and antelope, threatened with extinction only a quarter of a century ago, are staging an amazing comeback since they were systematically trapped and transported from their primitive range to new territory in Texas, New Mexico, and Montana. The mule deer also have extended their range into the mountains and mesas along the deserts and the broad valleys.

Because antelope are capable of running sixty miles an hour, some hunters shoot them from cars and jeeps, while others wait on top of knolls for the fleeing game to rush by. Most sportsmen, however, take them after stalking on foot.

The problem of the antelope and deer hunter on the plains is to place his bullet in the animal's chest cavity at anywhere from 150 to 400 yards. Since most hunters find it difficult to judge distance in the wide expanses of open territory, the best rifles are those that have speed enough to minimize the drop of the bullet. Even with a miscalculation of as much as 100 yards, a flat-shooting rifle still will place its bullet in the vital spot. A hunter using a .257 Weatherby Magnum, sighted at 250 yards, for example, need not worry about misjudging distance, for the bullet will not drop more than a couple of inches in 400 yards.

Because antelope and mule deer are easy to locate, the greatest satisfaction in hunting them comes from bagging a trophy head. To find a proper target, hunters carry binoculars and spotting scopes. Once sighted, the hunter stalks the game to within about 400 yards, sets himself in a firm prone position, aligns the rifle's cross hairs on the chest cavity, and squeezes the trigger. This is precise shooting and the rifle used (generally a bolt-action) should have every possible aid: a high-quality telescopic sight of at least four power, a Monte Carlo stock with a high comb, a cheekpiece, and a light, clean trigger pull. It should have the essential features of a target shooter's rifle, but not its weight.

The refinements, the precision techniques—these are modern innovations. Up to the end of

PAGES 206 AND 207: *Trophy pronghorns are best taken with a special long-range rifle like this Mark V Weatherby Magnum, .270 Weatherby caliber. Rifle has high-comb cheek-piece stock and is fitted with a Weatherby 4X hunting scope.*
PHOTO BY ROBERT MOTTAR

LEFT: *Shunning cover, the pronghorn travels in herds with a keen-eyed scout always on guard. Because it is a difficult animal to approach, it is often killed at ranges up to 400 yards.*
PHOTO BY U.S. FISH AND WILDLIFE SERVICE

*Fleeing band of antelope is herded by a buck.
A successful hunt, right, begins with
spotting animal at long range, judging head
and approach. Firing .257 Weatherby
Magnum, from sitting position, drops trophy.*
PHOTO OF ANTELOPE: OREGON GAME COMMISSION.
SEQUENCE: BILL BROWNING,
MONTANA CHAMBER OF COMMERCE

the Civil War, plains hunting was done mainly with muzzle-loading cap-lock rifles. These guns were slow to reload and their firepower was of low velocity, with the ball dropping sharply at ranges of more than 100 yards. Hitting a deer or an antelope at a greater distance was far more a matter of luck than of shooting skill, except for the expert marksman. In fact, the odds against correctly estimating range, ball drop, and wind drift were so great that most hunters never even attempted a long-range shot. A miss meant wasting valuable cap, powder, and ball. In the mid-nineteenth century, game was far less wary than it is today and a hunter could wait until his target moved into acceptable range. By the turn of the century, however, hunting pressure had put the quarry on its guard. As soon as a man approached nearer than 200 yards, plains game would take off at top speed, making it almost impossible to score readily until higher bullet speeds were obtained with the development of smokeless powder.·

By the late 1890's, shooting for sport trophies had pretty well replaced shooting for food, and, as a result, the rifleman needed even higher bul-

let speeds than were offered by the .30/40 and the .30/06—the popular smokeless-powder cartridges for big game. The earlier Winchester '73 in .44/40 caliber, although functional as a saddle weapon and deadly on deer at short range, was completely ineffective for long-range shooting.

General George Custer was one of the first plains hunters to recognize the need for a rifle with a greater range than Winchester's '73. In 1872, he received Remington's rolling block—a heavy, .50/70-caliber single-shot sporting model with octagonal barrel and adjustable rear sight. In a letter to the Remington Company he praised the way in which the rolling block performed during a hunting expedition to Yellowstone. Custer wrote:

"The number of animals killed is not so remarkable as the distance at which the shots were executed. The average distance at which the forty-one antelope were brought down exceeded 250 yards by actual measurements. I rarely obtained a shot at an antelope under 150 yards, while the range extended from that distance up to 630 yards."

This was amazingly good shooting for such a

low-velocity rifle and reflected Custer's long practice in plains hunting. He studied the trajectory of the weapon and learned the proper sight settings for each range. It would be interesting to know the number of misses he made during this hunt, for comments of on-the-spot observers were not so flattering to his marksmanship as his own accounts. In any case, the shooting of antelope was never a short-range sport, even in 1872.

The development of high-velocity cartridges, beginning with the .30 caliber, was carried on by Charles Newton, an independent ballistics engineer of New Haven, Connecticut, who was ahead of his time in engineering techniques. His idea, later taken up by Roy Weatherby, was to reduce the diameter of the bullet, shorten and lighten it, and thus produce cartridges of velocities never before achieved. His first commercial cartridge, produced in 1906, was the .22 "Imp." It was loaded with a 70-grain bullet that attained a speed of 2,800 fps.

Newton's Imp, which he really designed as a varmint or chuck cartridge, was supplied to the sportsman in the hammerless lever-action Model 99 by Savage Arms in 1911. The company at once capitalized on the fact that it was a high-speed load and advertised it as a big-game cartridge, which it never was, or could be, because of its light bullet. The .22 Hi-Power, as Savage renamed it, did become a good varmint load and was effective against deer and smaller animals at 100 yards range. Newton recognized the Imp's limitations and set about developing a cartridge with greater long-range potential on medium-sized game, such as antelope and deer.

Using the existing .30/06 case as a basic design, he first came up with the .22 Newton, which fired a 90-grain bullet at 3,100 fps. The load, however, was too long to function in the Savage 99, although it was a fine cartridge for the bolt-action rifle. He also turned out two fine .25-caliber cartridges: the .250/3000 (still in production), which would work in the 99 Savage, and the .256 Newton, which he intended to use in a bolt-action rifle as soon as he entered the gun-manufacturing field.

The .256 Newton can rightly be called the prototype of our modern long-range game rifle cartridges. The modern hand loader, familiar

DEADLY PLAINS RIFLES:
*Remington Model 722 deluxe, top,
and Marlin Model 455.*

with the intricacies of resizing, shortening, and generally remodeling existing cartridges, might think it was a simple step for Newton to take the .30/06 case, "neck" it down to .25 caliber, and load it with a properly designed bullet. In Newton's day, however, it was a revolutionary idea which produced a load that drove a 129-grain bullet at the amazing speed of 3,100 fps. This cartridge actually developed more striking energy than the popular .30/06. It also had a much flatter trajectory and lighter recoil. It dropped only two inches below the 100-yard sight setting at the 200-yard range. Its bullet was long enough to carry well at long range, bucked the wind better than any existing cartridge, and in the hands of a good rifleman was a deadly killer of all the larger game animals.

But Newton encountered trouble as soon as he began to manufacture the bolt-action rifle designed to handle his new cartridge. He was barely under way when World War I cut off his supply of German-made actions. He had the greatest difficulty in obtaining good barrels and, still worse, his employees were not skilled enough to produce high-quality rifles. Some of the Newtons were good, but many others were very poor and, in fact, considerably more dangerous to the shooter than to his target.

Despite his failure as a gunmaker, Newton, in

addition to the .256 cartridge, did create some powerful long-range loads that compare well with the best modern cartridges. His .280, .30, .33, and .35 Newtons are not exceeded in performance by the ultra-modern .270 and 7-mm Weatherby Magnums, the .300 Magnum, the .338 Winchester, and the .375 Magnum. He also designed the first bullets with paper-insulated cores, to prevent the lead from melting inside the jacket under the heat generated by friction in the barrel at high velocities. Early experimenters had found that bullets would occasionally disintegrate in flight soon after leaving the muzzle of the rifle, simply evaporating in a cloud of blue vapor. Newton's paper cores effectively prevented this rather alarming by-product of firing high-velocity rifles.

The bad name acquired by Newton's rifles made all his products taboo for gunmakers. His excellent cartridge designs died with the collapse of his last manufacturing effort in 1918. His rifles also had some fine features, demonstrating a grasp of the hunter's needs. His bolt-actions were the first to permit the low mounting of a scope sight without altering the bolt handle. The safety was conveniently located and could be operated by the thumb as the rifle was raised to the shoulder. Other bolt-actions used the military-style safety on the rear end of the bolt, a

*Magnificent trophy mule deer buck, in
the prairie foothills of Montana,
a state noted for long-range game. Mule
deer average more weight than
eastern whitetail, have higher, wider
racks, but are generally less wary.*
PHOTO BY BILL BROWNING

device that was not only slow but awkward to
let off in a hurry. His were the first American-
made rifles to use the multiple interrupted-screw
locking system—a feature that is taken for
granted today. In brief, Newton failed because,
too often, the parts of his rifles did not fit.

MODERN HIGH-VELOCITY
CARTRIDGES

Among arms producers, Winchester actually
made the first contribution to the cause of the
antelope and deer hunter of the plains with its
.270 Winchester, which fired the 130-grain bullet
at a speed of 3,140 fps—almost duplicating the
performance of the old .256 Newton. This cartridge was brought out in 1925 in a new bolt-
action design, the Model 54 rifle.

Because of the great demand for a rifle that
was better adapted for use with the scope sight
—a must in long-range game shooting—Winchester soon modified the design of the Model 54
by lowering the angle of the bolt handle to permit low scope mounting. A safety that could
be operated with the scope in place was added
and a separate bolt stop was incorporated in the
receiver. This rifle, the Model 70, has become
one of the world's finest sporting arms.

Remington, in addition to chambering several

models for the .270 Winchester, created in 1957
the .280 Remington, a cartridge that almost
duplicates the ballistics of the .270. In addition,
both firms make rifles in the .257 Roberts caliber,
somewhat less powerful than the .270 and .280
but well regarded as a good load for antelope
and deer. Both make rifles in the 6-mm field:
the .243 Winchester and the .244 Remington.
These are top-flight varmint loads, shooting 100-
and 90-grain bullets, respectively, at velocities
higher than 3,000 fps. Either cartridge is a good
antelope killer up to 300 yards or more.

Deadliest of the modern plains-rifle cartridges
are the Weatherby Magnum series: .257 Magnum and 7-mm Magnum. These all are reliable
400-yard cartridges and effective at greater
ranges if the bullets are well placed. The .257,
driving a 100-grain bullet at 3,700 fps, is by far
the most powerful .25 caliber on the market.

Killing the far-off muley and antelope buck
on the wide plains and open prairie country is a
highly specialized type of hunting. No sportsman without a background of long-range target
or varmint shooting, or both, using the best in a
modern rifle, cartridge, and telescope, will gather
these trophies with consistent success. In shooting skill, the hunter of plains game is on a par
with the hand-loading woodchuck shooter. He
simply needs more power to anchor his game.

CHAPTER TWELVE WILDFOWL

"No," said the aged man, "it's not a

very dark Mallard hen. It's a species of its own.

It's a Blackduck drake and quite a prize

hereabouts. Notice his very red legs. He has just

come down here from Canada, where this

variety breeds. Better mount him. You will

not get too many of his kind."

LYNN BOGUE HUNT

Shooting geese and the bigger species of ducks in full winter plumage takes a gun with plenty of power to deliver clean kills. Because wildfowl shooting is a deliberate business, the shotgun also must point like a rifle, have enough weight to swing easily and to absorb the recoil of heavy loads. The importance of easy handling and of power, and the fact that these qualities can be economically built into pump and autoloading guns, have made these types the favorites of wildfowlers for more than fifty years.

The availability, economy, and efficiency of these weapons, plus an abundance of birds to shoot at (the result of conservation laws), has put this sport within the reach of most gunners.

It was not always so. Before wildfowling became a mass pastime legal restrictions had to be overcome, leisure—and money—had to be provided, and the proper weapons had to be developed.

The sport of wildfowling—as against "shooting for the pot"—reached its zenith in England at the end of the seventeenth century, although in France it was considered the mark of a gentleman as early as 1650.

Demands for fine fowling pieces of English make—to rival those imported from France and Spain—created some of the world's most beautiful firearms. High prices were no deterrent in building these guns, which were not only fitted with supreme skill but embellished with the most lavish engravings and precious inlays. The great tradition of late eighteenth-century English gunmaking persists in the fine, expensive English guns of today, which for sheer beauty of hand labor are equaled by few gunmakers anywhere in the world.

EARLY SHOTGUNS

In colonial America, fowling pieces were long (up to seven feet) and heavy (up to twelve pounds) and the slow flintlock ignition system made shooting at birds in flight almost as much a matter of chance as a game of skill. Many of these thin-barreled, smoothbore flintlocks fired the charge almost as they pleased, with delays anywhere from a split second to a full second or more. Knowing that a canvasback duck, in high gear and perhaps with a helpful tail wind, can attain a speed of eighty feet per second, the modern gunner, always painfully conscious of the need for a precise lead to hit his moving target, can well stand in awe of the old-time gunner armed with the flintlock.

Actually, the use of shotguns strictly for killing flying or running game played no notable role in early American history. The colonial and the pioneer (with the exception of the few British-born gentry) shot small game for food alone, taking it as expeditiously as possible, while it either crouched on the ground or sat in a tree. The big-bore shotguns used too much precious powder and shot on each discharge to risk missing, and letting the game escape.

Only with the invention of the percussion-cap system of ignition did the fowling piece begin to assume major importance. Not only did it make the gun a practical device for shooting moving game, but the growing scarcity of deer in the East increased the emphasis on small game —ducks and geese in particular—for the hunter's family and for the market. Shotgun bores became bigger and bigger in an effort to kill game at longer ranges. The 8 gauge was common with the run-of-the-mill hunter. Professional gunners used 6 gauge, 4 gauge, and even 2 gauge, although these Big Berthas, charged with large shot that would kill up to 100 yards, were used primarily on massed flocks in the water.

Double guns, created by European makers

Alarmed flock of shallow-water mallards rises almost vertically in take-off. Diving species, such as canvasback and redhead, cannot jump from surface; they need open water to get under way.
PHOTO BY HERB SCHWARTZ, FPG

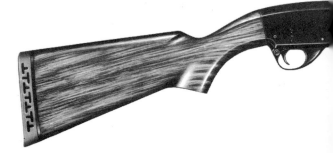

and still the standard sporting smoothbore practically everywhere in the world except the United States, were certainly in existence in America prior to the Revolution and were brought to virtual perfection in design by the English gunsmiths, among them Joseph Manton. His guns, built early in the 1800's, are outstanding examples of design and craftsmanship. Yet the American wildfowler, counting his suc-

cess only in the number of birds killed, wanted more than he could get with the fine European doubles. As birds became more wary he pressed for greater killing range and firepower.

The shotgun, always a straight tube from breech to muzzle until the invention of choke-boring, was a gun of limited range. In 12 gauge it could not reach more than forty yards. The wide scattering of the shot made a pattern that

Modern shooter in duck blind, left, waits for his targets. Old-timer, above, jumped birds from reeds and shot them as they rose. Shotgun is 12-gauge Stevens Model 77 repeater with adjustable choke, large fore-end grip, and rubber recoil pad.

thinned out rapidly, creating open areas through which smaller birds could escape unharmed or, at most, lightly wounded. Effective shooting at long range was a job for the bigger bores, in which more shot could be loaded to increase the needed density. The limit in guns that could be fired from the shoulder probably was reached in the 6 gauge and this was barely a fifty-yard killer of wildfowl.

CHOKE BORING

The system of constricting the muzzle end of a smoothbore gun to control the shot pattern made a wildfowl gun out of the so-so scattergun. The English can claim priority on the idea with a patent ascribed to W. R. Pape of Newcastle in 1866. Yet as far as the American gunner is concerned, it was Fred Kimble who perfected

Large size, great speed, and fact that it must be hit hard to kill, makes Canadian goose a difficult target for most wildfowlers. Guns are Marlin Model 90 deluxe, top, with non-selective single trigger and fitted recoil pad, and, bottom, Savage Model 775 five-shot automatic.

PHOTO BY DON WOOLDRIDGE, MONKMEYER

the system that is largely used today. Kimble was an obscure market hunter in Illinois who shot ducks for a living just after the Civil War. His records for long-run kills have rarely been equalled. In fifteen days, shooting a single-barreled muzzle-loader, Kimble killed 1,365 ducks. In many wild-duck shooting matches over several years, he never killed fewer than a hundred ducks per day, regardless of conditions. He made runs of fifty-four straight kills, one on mallards, one on bluebills (lesser scaup), taking them as they came. His kills probably averaged around ninety per cent of all the shots he fired during a season. From the beginning Kimble favored the big bores, but he was never satisfied with the long-range performance of even his heaviest shoulder guns. He regularly used the 6-gauge double gun, a muzzle-loader carrying an ounce and a half of #3 shot backed up with coarse black powder. He experimented with this fearsome weapon by enlarging the entire bore, except for a short section of the muzzle end, to give constriction to the charge somewhat like a nozzle on a garden hose.

At first, Kimble found that he had too much choke; the shot sprayed out even more widely than in the straight barrel. Gradually, by painstaking hand work, he removed some of the constriction at the muzzle, testing the shooting performance as he worked. His final result was a choke-bored barrel that would keep all of its shot load within a thirty-inch circle at forty yards and that, in the 6 gauge, would provide a reliable killing pattern for wildfowl at about seventy yards. For Kimble to achieve such killing distance in a shoulder arm was incredible. The choke won instant acceptance. The big-bored gun was done. The 10 gauge was settled on as the standard arm for the market hunter, with the 12 gauge reaching top rank as an all-around small-game weapon.

EARLY REPEATERS

Although Kimble's choke went a long way toward aiding the gunner, an increase in firepower was still a crying need. The development of a successful repeating shotgun awaited the

invention of a self-contained cartridge — even though Christopher Spencer had produced a pump-action shotgun with a tubular magazine operated by a slide handle enclosing the tube, an operation still utilized today.

Self-contained cartridges began when paper shot shells were substituted for the brass variety in England. (The brass shells were sold empty, to be loaded by the gunner as he saw fit.) Marcellus Hartley's Union Metallic Cartridge Company saw possibilities in this low-cost shell and bought English paper-shell machinery to turn out cheap cases for American hunters. In the late 1870's, it took the unprecedented step of marketing loaded shells as well.

The U.M.C. anticipated a certain degree of risk in opening this new market. It had brought cost within the range of the average man and installed new machinery to guarantee uniform loads. But it also knew full well that shooters are notoriously reluctant to accept unproved ammunition. Conservatively, the U.M.C. built up a stockpile of ten million shells—estimated as a year's supply—before announcing the new loads to the shooting public. The response was immediate and overwhelming. Within a week the "year's supply" of shells disappeared and the loaded, paper shot shell was firmly entrenched in America.

With fixed ammunition in the hunter's hands, the demand for faster repeating guns forced the issue with the gun companies. The Winchester Model 1887, a lever-action, five-shot gun designed by John Browning, was taken up at once by the market gunners; more than thirty thousand were sold in the first four years of manufacture. A good pump gun was a must for the wildfowler, however, and Browning once more rose to the occasion with the Model 1893, a hammer gun. It was almost immediately redesigned and renamed the Model 1897, and dominated its competitors for many years on bays and marshes. This gun, in both 12 and 16 gauge, remained in the active Winchester list until 1956. Shortly after the first appearance of the Winchester pump-action gun, Marlin Firearms followed with a similar design, although it never achieved the popularity of the Model '97. It

was doomed when heavy duck loads appeared in the early 1920's. Its action could not handle these with safety, although the Winchester '97 could and did.

MODERN REPEATERS

Browning was not permitted to rest long on his shotgun laurels. The ultimate in fast firing—the autoloader, or self-loader—had to come. By 1900 he had conceived such a gun, the first autoloader in the world. It is notable not only for this fact, but for the influence it had on Browning's relationship with Oliver Winchester. For many years Browning had designed almost exclusively for Winchester under a gentleman's agreement to turn over his new models. The firm would redesign them, if necessary, for production, take out the patents in Browning's name, and make a stipulated cash settlement. Aside from minor irritations arising from the distance between Browning's shop in Ogden, Utah, and the Winchester plant in New Haven, this arrangement proved highly satisfactory.

But with the invention of the new autoloader Browning felt he had something special, as indeed he did. He declined to turn it over on the existing basis and asked for a royalty contract. Winchester refused, for reasons unknown, but most likely for fear of setting a precedent. Browning then took the gun to Remington, which grabbed it like a trout rising to a fly. Marketed in 1905 as the Model 11, it has been world-famous for half a century and, almost

REMINGTON REPEATING SHOTGUNS:
Left to right, Browning-designed Model 11,
an autoloader famous for a half century,
but which is no longer made; Model 58 three-shot
deluxe, also an autoloader; and Model 870
deluxe, a pump action.
PHOTO BY ALEX HENDERSON

unchanged except for some modern streamlining, has been a favorite with wildfowl gunners. The five shots fired as fast as the trigger could be pulled—a duck shooter's dream—although Federal law has since prohibited the use of more than three shells for wildfowling in any gun.

Winchester countered Browning's move by bringing out an autoloader called the Model 1911, but it was not quite the gun that Remington's proved to be. It did not sell up to Winchester standards and was dropped in 1925.

New pump guns, in the more modern hammerless design, but basically the same as the older Winchester Model '97, appeared in the lines of many makers after Remington brought out the Model 10, unique in that it ejected its empty shells through the bottom of the receiver. Savage, Marlin, Stevens, and Winchester all produced hammerless guns in the first quarter of the twentieth century. Few important changes have been made in these basic designs since.

As to shotgun gauge, the 12 is best for all-around use. In magnum loadings with the standard two-and-three-quarter-inch shell it is a sure killer at sixty yards with #6 shot for small-to-medium-sized ducks, #4 shot for the larger sea ducks and brant, #2 for geese. For average ranges, up to fifty yards, the regular duck load of one-and-a-quarter ounces does the same job. For decoy shooting, where ranges are likely to be forty yards or less, the field load of one-and-an-eighth ounces will give a wider pattern, yet quite dense enough to accomplish clean kills with very few cripples.

Smaller gauges—the 16 and 20—unnecessarily handicap the wildfowler, although many fine gunners repeatedly take their daily limits with the lighter loads. The 16 gauge in its heavy one-and-an-eighth-ounce loading is a killer up to fifty yards, and the magnum loads in 20 gauge are not far behind. However, the wildfowler will hesitate to take a long-range chance with these guns—and he is right. When shooting over decoys, such gauges have a place, but they can hardly be classified as all-around duck guns. Nor do they throw such uniform patterns with the larger shot required for big birds.

For long-range shooting, full-choke guns are preferred. If birds do happen to ride in close on set wings, there's no law that says they must be shot immediately. If the gunner feels that the full choke will mangle his duck, he can give it a second or two to get under way, stretching out the range a little to open the pattern. It's that simple. But if the shooting is almost entirely over decoys, a modified choke will deliver a deadly, somewhat wider pattern to give the shooter a bit of help in making a difficult shot. Actually, the problem is often best solved by adding a variable-choke device to the single-barreled type of gun. This gadget lets the gun-

Model 12 shotguns in final stages of assembly at Winchester plant, New Haven, Connecticut. Fitting actions by hand demands highest skill. PHOTO BY HANK AUBIN

WINCHESTER REPEATING SHOTGUNS: *Left, Model 12, a basic pump-action design in a 12-gauge Magnum duck gun using three-inch shells. Right, Model 50, 12-gauge, gas-operated autoloader with non-recoiling barrel.* PHOTO BY JOSEPH BURNS

ner, in a matter of seconds, pick the choke that best suits conditions.

For pass shooting—a highly specialized form of wildfowling—no shotgun on the market is too big. Ducks and geese trading back and forth, high above a hunter stationed on a point jutting into a bay, or along a river bank, offer the longest-range targets in any shotgun sport. The Magnum 12-gauge pump guns, firing a one-and-seven-eighths-ounce load, will work up to seventy or eighty yards. The problem is to place the pattern on the bird at these extreme ranges. The calculations of lead, wind drift, and drop of the charge involved make this a fascinating sport and the most difficult shotgunning of all. Winchester, Remington, and Savage all make a Magnum pump gun for pass shooting, although most wildfowlers will stick to the regular 12-gauge model and shoot the standard magnum load rather than the three-inch variety. The shooter's skill is a factor in the choice.

In regular-size pump guns there are the Winchester Model 12, Remington Model 870, and the Stevens Model 77, which also come in Magnum sizes and are equipped with recoil pads. The J. C. Higgins Model 20 pump, for the standard two-and-three-quarter-inch load, built by High Standard, is another pump-action that can be recommended.

The autoloaders include the Remington Model 11-48, the Sportsman-48, and Sportsman-58 (Sportsman models are three-shot), the Winchester Model 50, Savage Model 755, the Browning Standard Automatic, and the Browning two-shot Double Automatic.

For the shooter who prefers a double-barreled shotgun the choice among guns of American make is limited. The superb Winchester Model 21 is made in both standard and three-inch Magnum models; this is a side-by-side double with selective single trigger and automatic ejectors. The only other quality double is the Fox Model B, made by Savage, which can be had with either double triggers or non-selective single trigger. Last on this list but by no means least is the fine

Belgian-made, American-stocked-and-assembled Browning Superposed over/under, made in both standard 12 gauge and three-inch Magnum.

Most of these guns are made in smaller gauges for the wildfowler who is willing to accept the challenge posed by the lighter loads. Few hunters on marsh, bay, and river, however, will get more sport by using shotguns that are too light for the job. They result in too many lost cripples and too few birds killed in the air.

CHAPTER THIRTEEN **UPLAND BIRDS**

. . . the gunner must select a bird from

the thundering mass of rocketing fowl, because the man

who shoots into the brown takes home no meat.

ROBERT C. RUARK

In the days of the muzzle-loading scattergunner, upland game birds filled the fields and covers of America in heart-warming numbers. Passenger pigeons darkened the skies in migration, the whistle of bob-white quail was heard along every rail fence, the pulsing drum of the ruffed grouse filled the hardwood forests as the buds burst in the spring. But little has been recorded of early American bird shooting, other than the fact that the wild turkey was a prime target from the beginning and almost never shot on the wing.

PAGES 228 AND 229: *Brace of ringneck pheasants and Winchester Model 21 double gun are pictured in front of ideal upland-game country. Elaborately engraved and custom made, the gun has single trigger and automatic ejectors.* PHOTO BY ROBERT MOTTAR

RIGHT: *Upland shooting has a long tradition in American sport.* PAINTING BY GABRIEL ALEXANDRE DE CAMPS, COURTESY STERLING AND FRANCINE CLARK ART INSTITUTE

The economy of the times dictated shooting at a flock of birds on the ground or in a tree because it produced a greater amount of meat for each ounce of precious powder and shot.

Almost from the birth of the concept of killing birds in flight, upland-game shooting has been for sport. It is true that the market hunter dimmed its glamor during the late 1880's, but such slaughter only emphasized the sportsmanship involved in shooting game birds on the wing.

These birds—the quail, the grouse, and the woodcock—which stirred the pulse and tickled the palate of the early American upland shooter are still with us, though in far fewer numbers. But the gaudy oriental newcomer, the ringneck pheasant, has helped enormously to fill the great gaps torn in our native bird population by overshooting. To some, it fails to fill the breach, but no present-day sportsman can deny that the beauty, strength, and enduring character of this longtailed foreigner make him a welcome addition to the upland bird family.

In view of the bloody harvest reaped by pro-

fessional gunners during the late 1800's, it is a wonder that any birds are left for sport shooting. Most of the hunters for profit shipped an average of one barrel of grouse, woodcock, or some other species to market each week. They earned their pay, however, by the simple expenditure of energy that was required to reload their muzzle-loading double guns after each discharge.

THE DOUBLE GUN

This market hunter's double gun was never really replaced in upland shooting by the early repeater. For one thing, there was little advantage in having a multi-shot weapon—two clean shots was about all a good gunner could get at a single bird, and if he dropped two from a flock he was reasonably satisfied and happy.

Physically, the double gun was shorter, lighter, better balanced, and easier to handle than early repeaters. Even today, only the most modern repeaters, fashioned with light alloy receivers, can compete in weight with doubles of the same gauge. And there simply is no way to make a repeating gun as short in over-all length as a double. To the length of the barrel must be added the length of the receiver that encloses the repeating breechblock mechanism. The clinching argument is that the double offers two choices of choke borings for different ranges: the right barrel, of open bore, for a close shot; the left of choke bore, for a long shot—as the bird moves off. An adjustable choke device recently has been designed for repeaters that allows a first shot through an open bore, then closes down automatically for succeeding shots. Although the theory is logical, the device is not yet widely used in the field.

From the beginnings of the factory-loaded shot shell, the big names in gun manufacturing turned out doubles. Remington marketed a graceful double hammer-gun in 1873, the Whittmore, made in 10, 12, and 16 gauge. Winchester countered with an English hammer double in 1879. Remington's first hammerless double appeared in 1894, inaugurating the large-scale pro-

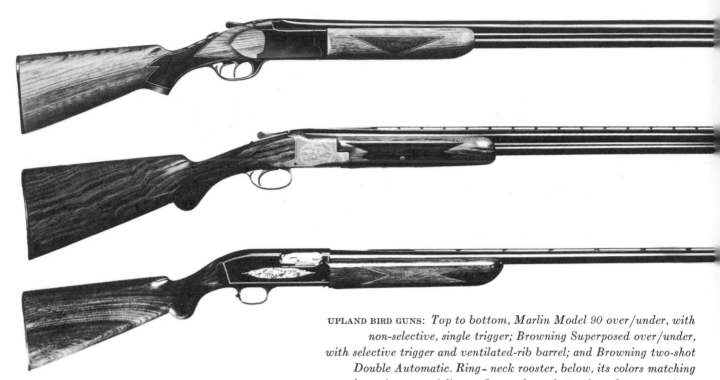

UPLAND BIRD GUNS: *Top to bottom, Marlin Model 90 over/under, with non-selective, single trigger; Browning Superposed over/under, with selective trigger and ventilated-rib barrel; and Browning two-shot Double Automatic. Ring-neck rooster, below, its colors matching glory of autumn foliage, offers a clean shot as it rockets away from gunners and dog.* PHOTO BY JOE COUDERT, COURTESY SPORTS ILLUSTRATED

duction of fine double guns at popular prices, under such famous names as Parker, Fox, Ithaca, L. C. Smith, and Baker. But the double gun was consigned to oblivion by American makers because of the high cost of skilled guncrafting. Of the many familiar names in double guns over the past half-century only two survive: Winchester, with its Model 21, and the Fox, made by Savage Arms. (Another Savage product, the Stevens Model 311 double, makes no pretensions to being in the fine-gun field, although it is a sturdy and reliable arm.)

The double gun is, in effect, two guns joined side by side and attached to one stock. Costs of producing this arm are necessarily high since it has two barrels and two complete locking systems. Fitting barrels, fore ends, and other parts to frames is also a problem of skilled hand labor that does not face the maker of a modern repeating weapon whose parts are accurately machined to close tolerances.

Many sportsmen regret the passing of the double gun from the field of American firearms. In the words of straight-talking Elmer Keith, one of the great hunters and all-around good shots of our time, ". . . the fine double appears as a beautiful, streamlined chorus gal compared to the usual repeating shotgun, which more nearly resembles a fat, misshapen squaw." The trim lines and beautiful balance and "feel" of a well-made double can never be duplicated in a repeating arm. The need for a magazine and long breech mechanism defeats artistry in design.

But enough of mourning for this gun of the past. Modern pumps and autoloaders do a fine job afield. Stock designs for quick, accurate pointing are now a special feature of new models, unlike the old-time "corn-shellers." For the man who insists on the double there's still the Winchester 21, and exceptionally fine doubles from England, Spain, Italy, and Belgium can also be bought in this country.

Coturnix quail, an Asiatic import that spirals up toward tree tops before leveling off, much like woodcock, below, a more-traditional upland-game bird. Guns are Savage-made Fox Model B, with single trigger and wide fore end, top, and Winchester Model 42, .410 gauge.
PHOTOS: LEONARD RUE, QUAIL; N. Y. STATE
CONSERVATION DEPARTMENT, WOODCOCK

CHOOSING A GUN

A quick-handling shotgun is a must. Birds rise at speeds of from thirty to fifty miles an hour, often in cover so heavy that the gunner gets only the merest glimpse for his shot. For the most part, the shooting is at fairly close range, usually within thirty yards. Long-range guns, heavy loads, and tight chokes are as foreign to this sport as the .458 African would be in hunting whitetail deer. The gunner who kills the birds is the one who gets on them the quickest, and a fast-handling gun will usually save the split-second delay that leads to a miss (or no shot at all) as the bird rockets or twists and darts in its frantic flight toward screening cover.

A gun handling a one-ounce load of shot is almost ideal for all purposes. For half a century this was the standard load in the 12 gauge. It is now merely a heavy load for a standard 20 gauge, a field load in the 16 gauge. The trend in present upland guns is, therefore, toward the smaller gauges, which throw a heavy enough pattern at all normal ranges and are markedly lighter for the hunter to handle.

Differences in regional terrain have considerable influence on the choice. In the heavy covers of New England grouse and woodcock country, where shots are seldom made at more than thirty yards, the open-bored 20 is deadly. In the more open country of the West, longer shots with 16 and 12 gauges are the rule in hunting sharptail grouse, prairie chicken, chukar and Hungarian partridge, several species of quail, and pheasant.

The choice of a shotgun is also influenced by whether the gunner hunts with a dog, and, if so, its breed. Well-trained pointing dogs give the hunter a chance to get well up to the bird before it is flushed, and the quick shot will get the game well within a thirty-yard range. If springer span-iels are used, the flushing range will usually be longer—often twenty-five yards or more—and shots will be taken up to forty yards. When no dogs are used, as in the midwestern cornfield shooting of pheasants, any sort of shot can reasonably be expected. Birds will often flush right underfoot, or will run to the end of a corn row before taking off at thirty or forty yards. Therefore, the shooter who is not using a dog is probably best suited with a 12 gauge. Also, without a dog, crippled birds are far more difficult to recover, so the bigger gauge, because of its heavier load of shot, executes more cleanly.

Of the pump guns, the Ithaca Model 37 heads the list for lightness in an all-steel action. In 20 gauge with twenty-six-inch barrel, it is one of the best-handling upland guns made. Following closely are the Remington Model 870 pump, just a shade heavier and with an action only slightly less smooth, and the Winchester Model 12 with alloy receiver. Good, though weighing somewhat more, are the regular Winchester Model 12, the Stevens Model 77, and the J. C. Higgins Model 20 made by High Standard.

In 20 gauge, with a twenty-six-inch barrel, the weight of these guns ranges from five and three quarter pounds for the Ithaca to six and a half pounds for the heavier models; in 12 gauge they weigh from seven to seven and a half pounds. The reduction in weight of a single pound may seem fairly trivial, but it separates the ideal upland gun from the so-so class. It gives the fast gun handler an important fraction of a second longer to get on his bird.

Autoloading guns are usually considered less than perfect for upland work, although modern designs have drastically reduced their weight. The two Remington Sportsman models, the 11-48 and the 58, for example, weigh six and a half pounds in 20 gauge. But even at their lightest, the slightly faster rate of fire doesn't

Remington Model 11-48 28-gauge autoloader.

Chukar partridge, recent import from India, does well in west and on public shooting preserves.
PHOTO: OREGON STATE GAME COMMISSION

compensate for their comparative clumsiness—a pump gun, in experienced hands, is fully as fast for repeated good shots as the autoloader.

The over/under double gun has many attractive features. It offers the single-sighting effect of a pump gun, is somewhat lighter, always shorter in over-all length, and has two different borings. The only over/under still made in America is the Marlin Model 90, which is plain in appearance but reliable. In 1932, Remington marketed a fine 12-gauge over/under, but dropped it early in World War II. The old Savage over/under was a crude specimen that never achieved much popularity during its short life. Finest of the over/unders is the Browning Superposed, which, in 20 gauge, is a dream gun for all upland shooting. This gun is made in Belgium—as are all Brownings—but it is stocked and assembled in the United States. It has a selective single trigger, automatic ejectors, and weighs about six pounds in 20 gauge.

Since lightness is such an important factor in a shotgun, few gunners care to add equipment.

A matted rib, although desirable from the viewpoint of flat-plane sighting and elimination of glare, adds a quarter of a pound to the average pump or autoloader. An adjustable choke device such as Polychoke, however, adds nothing to the weight of the gun, because a section of the barrel is removed before it is attached.

RANGE AND GAUGE

In regular field loads there is roughly a difference of five yards in the killing range of the three different basic upland gauges. The one-and-an-eighth-ounce load of the 12 gauge is a certain killer at forty-five yards; the one-ounce of the 16 gauge at forty; the seven-eighths-ounce of the 20 gauge at thirty-five. In heavier express loads the killing range is increased by about five yards for the 20 gauge, eight yards for the 16, ten yards for the 12. Magnum loads in these gauges improve the killing pattern in direct proportion to the added amount of shot. But the basic difference between the small gauge and the big

Mossberg Model 200 12-gauge pump gun.

Ithaca Model 37 Featherlite pump gun.

Savage-made Stevens Model 311 double-barreled gun.

Ruffed grouse are always difficult to find, and when flushed, flight is unpredictable.

PHOTO BY U.S. FISH AND WILDLIFE SERVICE

one is that the 12 makes a better pattern with larger shot sizes, such as #2 or #4, which the 20 gauge does not handle with equal uniformity. Therefore, trying to stretch the killing range of a 20-gauge gun by loading it with #4 shot is drastically unsuccessful. Small gauges are meant to be used with small shot—nothing larger than #6—but in the 20 gauge the deadliest shot size for upland birds is probably #7½ or #8. Large shot, such as #4, shows its superiority only at the longer ranges (over forty yards), where the smaller shot begins to lose velocity rapidly. But the forty-yard pattern of #4 shot in a 20 gauge becomes too thin for positive kills on small birds.

The ideal 20-gauge shot size for the larger birds—ringnecks, sage hens, ducks—is #6. These hold a fairly dense pattern up to the limit of the little gun's killing range, and will have enough velocity to get through the heavy feathers and larger bodies of these birds. For smaller birds such as woodcock, quail, snipe, and doves, #8 shot performs well in the 20 gauge.

With the exception of wild turkey, no upland game bird needs to be hunted with shot larger than #6. The turkey is of course a big, tough customer and is a special case in upland gunning. Shot of #2 and BB size, fired in a 12 gauge or, better still, a 10-gauge gun, is none too large. The Magnum 12-gauge pump gun, used in wild-fowl pass shooting, is a reliable turkey killer.

BORINGS

Choice of the best boring for upland shooting is directly governed by two things: the kind of cover to be hunted and the presence (or absence) of dogs. The open bore, either cylinder or improved cylinder, is deadly up to thirty yards. At so close a range the shotgun, if tightly choked, must be pointed almost as accurately as a rifle in order to hit the bird. And if the shot is made with a 12 gauge, full choke, very little will be left for the dinner table. The best all-around choke in a single-barreled gun for upland shooting is modified, so that about half the shot go into a thirty-inch circle at forty yards.

One of the best arguments in favor of the 20 gauge in close-cover shooting is that patterns are not likely to be so dense as to mangle the game. Making clean kills without blowing the bird to bits is the aim of the upland shooter, and a nice balance between gauge, choke, shot size, and load must be achieved to obtain the best results. Probably a 16-gauge gun, modified hoke, loaded with the one-ounce field load in #7½ shot, comes the closest to the nebulous ideal of an all-around package.

The tiny 28 gauge and .410 bore are in a class by themselves. Both handle a three-quarter-ounce load of shot, in itself limited in killing range to not over thirty-five yards. Of the two gauges the 28 is noticeably superior in uniform pattern, which is highly important when such light loads are used. They both require a fast, expert gunner, but within the limits of their range they will kill game as quickly as the big 12. These are guns for small shot only—nothing larger than #7½—and perform best on the smaller birds up to and including grouse. Except under ideal conditions, neither is a reliable pheasant gun. The sportsman using either of these gauges must not only be able to shoot accurately in a big hurry, but must know when to hold his fire because of the danger of losing crippled birds. Neither gauge can be recommended as an all-purpose upland gun.

English setter with retrieved ringneck. Dog is great aid, not only in locating birds but in tracking down and recovering cripples. PHOTO BY GEORGE SILK, COURTESY SPORTS ILLUSTRATED

The modern upland gunner is forced to evaluate his shooting skill—or his potential—in order to choose the gun that will suit him best. The commonly held but erroneous belief that 16- and 20-gauge guns are more difficult to shoot than the 12 often influences a beginner to go with a heavy 12 gauge, handicapping his efforts from the start. The three standard field gauges—12, 16, and 20—perform substantially the same in pattern area with comparable loads in the same degree of choke. The 12 gauge does not throw wider patterns than the 20 gauge, provided the same choke and shot size are used. They differ only in *density* of pattern. All three gauges are bored to give the same percentage of pattern with each different degree of choke. Patterns are made at forty yards, using a thirty-inch circle as the standard. Enough is as good as a feast. There's no need to throw a hatful of shot at a bird when a handful will do the job.

Bye, Baby Bunting,
Daddy's gone a-hunting
To get a little rabbit skin
To wrap the Baby Bunting in.

NURSERY RHYME

PAGES 240 AND 241: GUNS FOR SMALL-GAME HUNTER AND BEGINNING SHOOTER: *Top, Savage Model 24 over/under combination gun, in .22 caliber and .410 gauge, and Marlin Model 39 Mountie, .22 caliber.* PHOTO BY ROBERT MOTTAR

RIGHT: *Dogs tree squirrels, hunter drops them with flintlock.* LITHOGRAPH BY CURRIER AND IVES, FROM HARRY T. PETERS COLLECTION, MUSEUM OF THE CITY OF NEW YORK

The greatest difference between the contemporary young hunter and his early American counterpart lies in their training for the field. Today, a boy getting ready for his first hunt is given a .22 rifle or a small-gauge shotgun, a neat package of brightly colored shells or shiny cartridges, and some instructions on the range. The pioneer boy needed painstaking lessons in how to load the small-bore Kentucky rifle or the family musket, how to cast his bullets, cut his patches, and take good care of his loose powder and spare flints.

An idea of what this amounted to can be gained from an account by John Audubon. The famous ornithologist lived in Kentucky from 1808 to 1820, and on one occasion went out barking squirrels (driving them from their hide-

aways) with Daniel Boone. He reported:

"We walked out together and followed the rocky margin of the Kentucky River until we reached a piece of flat land thickly covered with black walnuts, oaks, and hickories. As the mast was a good one that year, squirrels were seen gamboling on every tree around us. My companion, a stout, hale, and athletic man, dressed in a homespun hunting shirt, bare-legged and moccasined, carried a long and heavy rifle, which as he was loading it, he said had proved efficient in all his former undertakings, and which he hoped would not fail on this occasion, as he felt proud to show me his skill. The gun was wiped, the powder measured, the ball patched with six-hundred thread linen, and the charge sent home with a hickory rod. . . . Boone pointed to one of these animals which . . . was crouched on a branch about fifty paces distant, and bade me mark well the spot where the ball should hit. He raised his piece gradually, until the bead (that being the name given by the Kentuckians to the sight) of the barrel was brought to a line with the spot which he intended to hit, and fired. I was astounded to find that the ball had hit the piece of the bark immediately beneath the squirrel, and shivered it to splinters; the concussion produced by which had killed the animal, and sent it whirling through the air, as if it had been blown up."

The Kentucky "squirrel rifle" Boone used probably was a .30-caliber (large by present standards), but its round ball was light—about forty-two grains, which is only slightly heavier

243

than the bullet weight of forty grains fired by the modern .22 Long Rifle cartridge. The family musket of the time, when loaded with fine shot for birds or small animals, was often of about .60 caliber, comparable to the modern 20-gauge usually chosen for the young shooter.

The novice's first live target today is likely to be a gray squirrel or a fox squirrel, and his first moving game taken with a shotgun is almost sure to be a rabbit. Unfortunately, squirrels and rabbits are set apart from other classes of game because some sportsmen seem to feel that they are unworthy of being seriously hunted. But the ubiquitous squirrel and rabbit have a special place in the shooting scene under the heading of small game. This shooting is for kids —and for grown-ups who aren't ashamed to admit enjoying it. Under small game can be added, in some sections of America, the foolish grouse who roosts in a tree and allows a careful rifleman to pick off his head with a .22 hollow-point bullet, plus the little family of pest animals: the wood-

LIGHTWEIGHT AND COLORFUL REMINGTON RIFLES: *Top, two Model 66 autoloaders hold fourteen cartridges, which load through butt stock. They are made of nylon and steel, and the moving parts require no lubrication. Bottom, two Model 572 pump-action, .22-caliber rifles weigh four pounds each.* PHOTO BY ALEX HENDERSON

chucks and red squirrels, the porcupines, and the predatory hawk species—all of which are more commonly called varmints.

SMALL-GAME CARTRIDGES

To Daniel Wesson must go the credit for putting in the small-game hunter's hands a cartridge that time has proved to be the basis of almost every rifleman's hunting skill. In developing a new cartridge that would make an efficient weapon of the S. & W. repeating pistol (forerunner of the Volcanic pistol and rifle), Wesson worked with the "bulleted breech-cap" (BB cap) —a copper tube containing fulminate and a round ball, one of the early forms of fixed ammunition.

Wesson's first efforts resulted in a complicated cartridge consisting of a drawn copper cup into which were soldered two tiny anvils that held the priming charge. This design was impractical, but further experiment indicated that it would be a fairly simple matter to fill the small area in the folded base of the case head with fulminate. The result was a .22-caliber cartridge—made by Smith & Wesson in 1857 for their first revolver. For a century this cartridge, the .22 Short, has been virtually unchanged in size, shape, and design. To fit it for other uses, the length was increased, first to the .22 Long and later to the .22 Long Rifle—now the standard rifle cartridge, in high-speed, hollow-point-bullet loading, for most small-game shooting.

One of the early sporting rifles firing the .22 rim-fire was Remington's No. 1 Rolling Block, marketed first in 1867. The J. Stevens Arms Company also introduced a so-called "pocket rifle," with folding skeleton stock, in 1869, chambered for the .22 Short and .22 Long. Both Remington and Stevens, as well as many other makers, added several different types of .22-caliber single-shot rifles to their lines through the year 1900. Winchester's famous single-shot, drop-block action, a Browning design, brought out in 1885, was chambered for the .22 rim-fires in addition to most of the bigger cartridges.

Following the trend established in the design of big-game rifles, .22 rim-fire repeaters soon appeared. First of the pump-actions was the Colt Lightning in 1885, closely followed by the Browning-designed Winchester Model 1890, a rifle that became the most popular .22 pump gun ever put on the market. This hammer model established a pattern for small-game and plinking rifles that has changed little over the years. The present Winchester Model 62 is simply a refined version of the Model 1890, with better stock, forearm, and sights.

Marlin entered the field of .22-caliber repeaters with the Model 1891, a lever-action, tubular-magazine rifle with solid frame and side ejection. It was followed by improved designs, the Models 1892 and 1897. The '97, a takedown rifle, became one of the most popular .22's for small game. It was redesigned with a pistol grip and curved lever in 1921, becoming the Model 39, and is still in production. Marlin also produced several pump guns in .22 caliber: Models 20 and 29, which had external hammers; and two hammerless rifles, the 32 and the 38. Of these only the Model 39 lever action is now manufactured.

Remington, Winchester, and Savage also brought out hammerless pump rifles in the early 1900's. The first autoloader was produced by Winchester, in a Thomas C. Johnson design, in 1903. It fired a special .22 Automatic cartridge slightly larger than the regular rim-fire size. It was not redesigned for Long Rifle ammunition until 1933, when the Model 63 appeared.

Remington's first self-loader was the Model 16, brought out in 1914 in .22 Short, .22 Long Rifle, and .22 Winchester Special. By 1918 all these calibers had been discontinued and the rifle was

J. C. Higgins Model 33 pump-action, .22-caliber repeater.

then chambered only for the .22 Automatic cartridge, as was the Winchester Model 1903. Gradually, the Model 16 was replaced by the improved Browning Model 24 in 1922.

This is a very brief survey of early small-game and plinking rifles. Most of the guns mentioned are no longer made.

Prior to the creation of high-speed loadings in rim-fire ammunition, many more small-game cartridges were designed to fill the demand for greater power in the little rifle. The .22 Winchester Special, a fine small-game load, inside lubricated, loading a 45-grain bullet with more powder, filled the need for a low-priced cartridge with a bigger wallop than the old Long Rifle. Several manufacturers built repeating and single-shot rifles for the .25 Stevens rim-fire and the .32 Short and Long rim-fire. All of these fell by the wayside once the Long Rifle cartridge was brought to its present state of power and low trajectory in modern loadings. The high-speed versions of the .22-caliber rim-fire increase its effectiveness by about fifty per cent, making it entirely adequate for small-game shooting at normal ranges—up to seventy-five yards.

The small-game rifle, used now mostly for squirrels, rabbits, or varmints at close range, has an enviable degree of accuracy with modern loads. One-inch groups at fifty yards are commonplace with even the lowest-priced arms. The addition of a scope sight of four power (4X) makes a semi-target arm of these rifles and enormously increases the hunter's accuracy on small targets, where close holding is a must.

Cottontail rabbit. U.S. FISH AND WILDLIFE SERVICE

For all small-game shooting the .22 Long Rifle high-speed, hollow-point-bullet loading is far more effective than any other .22 rim-fire cartridge. It has the greatest power, the least drop in flight, and the mushrooming expansion of the hollow-point bullet gives great shocking effect. A fat porcupine, for example, which will take three or more of the solid-point regular loads through the body without flinching, usually will topple when this lethal pellet hits him solidly.

BOLT-ACTION RIFLES

Rifles of every conceivable type of action and loading system are available in .22 rim-fire caliber. There are bolt actions, slide actions (pump), lever actions, autoloaders (automatics), some

Mossberg Model 346B bolt-action, .22-caliber repeater.

with tubular magazines under the barrel in classic style, others loading through the butt like the old Spencer Civil War repeaters, many loading with clips of different sizes. In addition, every gun manufacturer makes single-shot models.

Bolt-action repeating .22's appeared immediately after World War I, filling a twofold need. Service men familiar with the military bolt action were partial to it, and perhaps equally important, this type of repeater could be made at far less cost than the fairly complex systems of pumps and lever actions then in vogue. Time has proved the bolt action to be one of the most reliable and accurate types of .22 rim-fire ever made.

Where speed of repeated fire is not essential, as in squirrel or varmint hunting, the bolt action does a good job. This design has the tightest breeching of all, usually the best trigger pull, and is made with a one-piece stock—all factors that increase accuracy. Most serious riflemen also agree that the bolt-action stocks are better adapted for use with the scope sight, since the combs are fuller and higher than on other types of repeaters. Most of these rifles are also drilled and tapped for mounting peep sights of standard make and have receivers grooved to accept standard tip-off scope mounts. The shooter should be able to add extra sighting equipment without help from a gunsmith.

All the bolt-action rifles fire the .22 Long Rifle cartridge. The tubular-magazine types will fire all three .22 sizes in regular and high-speed loadings. As a rule, clip loaders will handle only the

Gray squirrel. U.S. FISH AND WILDLIFE SERVICE

Long Rifle cartridge successfully, although Marlin and Mossberg have a specially designed clip for the shorter sizes of .22 ammunition.

SLIDE AND LEVER ACTIONS

Slide actions, oldest of the .22 repeaters, are very popular as a combination small-game and plinking rifle. All pump actions handle the three sizes of .22 rim-fire ammunition, which appeals to the tin-can shooter who likes Shorts because of their lower cost. In general, these are reliable guns, but the intricacy of the working parts necessitates frequent cleaning to keep them free of grit and heavy dust. The slide actions give a very satisfactory rate of sustained fire and hold anywhere from fifteen to twenty

cartridges. While their accuracy is somewhat less than that of the bolt actions, they are good enough for most small-game hunting.

Marlin currently makes the only lever-action .22 rim-fire rifles: the old favorite Model 39 and its most recent version, the Mountie. The latter is a twenty-inch-barrel carbine design with straight grip stock. Model 39's have a tubular magazine of large capacity and a visible hammer. They can be taken down into a compact unit for packing in a suitcase or duffel bag. Marlin's latest lever action is the Model 56, a hammerless design with an extremely short lever throw, a clip-type magazine, and solid frame.

AUTOLOADERS

The autoloader is by far the most popular action with the plinker and the small-game hunter who likes to take rabbits on the run. Although it fires as fast as the trigger can be pulled, it is not a true automatic; it simply reloads itself for each successive shot.

Most autoloaders function properly only with the Long Rifle cartridge, since the energy required to move the breech mechanism and depress the action spring is calculated on the basis of this cartridge. Notable exceptions are: the Remington Models 550 and 552, the J. C. Higgins Model 31, and the Mossberg Models 350K, 352K, all of which handle all three sizes of .22 rim-fires. The magazine systems vary: there are tubular types under the barrel or in the butt

WINCHESTER .22-CALIBER RIFLES: *Left to right, Model 62 pump action; Model 52 Sporter bolt action; Model 63 autoloader (Long Rifle cartridge only); and Model 77 autoloader, with tubular magazine.*
PHOTO BY JOSEPH BURNS

stock, and clip magazines in various capacities.

Many manufacturers put out at least one single-shot, .22-caliber rifle. Savage's Model 15 and Winchester's Model 67 are also made in a boy's rifle that has a shorter stock and barrel than the regular models. All single-shots have extra safety devices to make them less hazardous in the hands of inexperienced shooters.

SHOTGUNS

Squirrels and rabbits are fair game for the shotgun shooter; in fact it is likely that more shot shells are fired at cottontail and snowshoe rabbits each year than at all other small game combined. The upland-game gun referred to in Chapter 13 is as good a choice for this purpose as any, with the .410 gauge in the Winchester Model 42 or Remington Model 11-48 rated as the sportiest weapons in this class. A fine arm for the casual small-game hunter is the Savage Model 24, a combination gun that fires both the .22 Long Rifle and .410-gauge three-inch shell.

The 20 gauge in a variety of single-shot and bolt-action repeaters makes a good choice in a small-game gun for the furred species. The Winchester Model 37 and the Stevens Model 94, both break-open, single-barreled shotguns, are made in special adaptations for youngsters in 20 and .410 gauge. The relatively low cost of the small-gauge repeaters in bolt action, in both tubular- and clip-magazine type, makes it practical for every hunter to own one for his squirrel, rabbit, and crow shooting.

The young hunter of the nineteenth century could never have imagined the variety, simplicity, and accuracy of today's sporting firearms. But, then, the sons of frontiersmen always had a living target to shoot at. All too often nowadays the best the younger generation can find is an occasional rabbit and a lot of tin cans.

CHAPTER FIFTEEN **VARMINTS**

Too many rocks and too many logs,

Too many rocks to catch ground hogs!

FOLK SONG

The long-range shooting of small, non-game animals is the only hunting sport that has no tradition dating back to pioneer times. Although Americans have always killed pests, in the days of the frontier they did not make it a specialized activity. The wildcat, mountain lion, skunk, raccoon, and various other "critters" were grouped as varmints (*vermin,* colloquially) and shot for the welfare of game and domestic animals.

Today, varmint shooting is carried on with enormous enthusiasm because of the challenge to marksmanship that the woodchuck (also called ground hog or marmot), the prairie dog, coyote, fox, and jackrabbit present. These fairly small targets are not considered a sporting proposition unless taken at 200 yards or more, usually with a small-caliber, high-velocity rifle delivering the ultimate in accuracy.

A typical varmint hunt gets under way when a chuck, at 300 yards—invisible to all but the keenest eye—is spotted with binoculars. The skilled shooter then carefully estimates his range and checks the wind by observing how the weeds and grass bend. He settles down in a prone position, sets his chuck-rest to support his rifle—or

uses a pillow for the purpose—calculates the exact amount of bullet fall and wind drift over the distance, possibly resets the scope sight, and then squeezes off the trigger to fire a carefully hand-loaded cartridge. The odds are that the chuck, almost a fifth of a mile off, will fall dead.

Shooting woodchucks, as a game in itself, began early in the century, when the first high-velocity loads appeared. The old-timers used the Schuetzen type of rifle on a Remington, Winchester, Stevens, Ballard, or other single-shot action, usually chambered for the old .25/21, .25/25, .28/30, and .32/40. Flat trajectory was still a hope for the future, for most of the early varmint shooting was done at less than 200 yards. Medium-powered cartridges such as the .25/20 and the .32/20 were considered proper for the sport, particularly after high-speed, light-bullet loadings in these calibers flattened the trajectory and increased the killing range. Two fairly good varmint loads appeared before 1920, the .22 Hi-Power and the .250/3000 Savage, but the rifles for which they were made—the lever-action 99's—left something to be desired at long range. Since chuck shooters wanted the greatest

PAGES 250 AND 251: *Farm country of New England, with open meadows and rolling hills, is woodchuck-hunters' paradise. The farm pest is vulnerable to power of Super Custom Coltsman rifle, .243 caliber, with Colt 4X scope and mount. Glasses are Bushnell 9X binocular.* PHOTO BY ROBERT MOTTAR

ABOVE: *Although fox most often is hunted with dogs and killed with a shotgun, this view of mounted animal on stone wall illustrates magnification power of long-range rifle's telescope. A scope is essential in shooting woodchuck, the sporting varmint hunter's main target.*
PHOTO BY OZZIE SWEET. COURTESY OF SPORTS ILLUSTRATED

WINCHESTER RIFLES FOR VARMINT SHOOTERS: *Left to right,
Model 70 standard grade, in .220 Swift caliber,
with Monte Carlo stock and Lyman 4X Challenger scope.
Model 70 target rifle, .243 caliber, with heavy
barrel, special stock, and Lyman Supertarget scope.*

PHOTO BY JOSEPH BURNS

possible accuracy, they preferred the bolt-actions and heavy single-shot rifles.

Development of the .22 Hornet in the early 30's by reworking the old .22 Winchester Center-Fire cartridge, gave the sport the impetus it needed. Here was a tiny cartridge, highly accurate, safe to shoot in farm country, with sufficient power to drop a chuck at 200 yards and a trajectory flat enough to minimize guesswork. On impact with almost any solid object, the little high-speed bullet would disintegrate, without ricochet. Another thing in its favor was that the sound of the report was low enough so that a farmer working in his fields would not be likely to worry about ricochet and, consequently, the safety of his stock.

At first this cartridge was available only in custom-built rifles for which the varmint shooter hand-loaded ammunition. But when it came into widespread use, all the ammunition companies put commercial loads on the market. Strangely enough, no commercial arms maker built a rifle to fire the cartridge, although four different brands of .22 Hornet ammunition were available.

In 1933, Winchester chambered its Model 54 bolt action for the Hornet, and Savage Arms its Model 19H. The Savage rifle was a cross between the Model 23, chambered for the popular chuck loads (the .25/20 and .32/20), and the 19 N.R.A. target rifle. It was the first attempt to put a special varmint rifle on the market. It had a target type of stock designed primarily for prone shooting—the varmint hunter's basic shooting position — and was drilled and tapped to take telescope sight bases, something of a novelty in a hunting rifle in the early 30's. The Model 19H has since been replaced by the Savage Model 340, currently made in .30/30, .222 Remington, and .22 Hornet.

Not content with the .22 Hornet as issued, the chuck hunter at once began to design more powerful cartridge cases of .22 caliber, shooting the Hornet bullet but at higher speeds. One of the best of these "wildcats" was the .22 Lovell, essentially a necked-down .25/20 Stevens Single Shot holding more powder than the Hornet case and giving the 45-grain bullet a speed of about 3,000 feet per second at the muzzle. This was a custom job and no commercial rifle has ever been chambered for it. The .22 Lovell and its successor, the .22R Lovell, however, came very close to being the ideal chuck hunter's load for shooting in farm country.

The Lovell inspired a wave of new designs in wildcat varmint loads that is steadily increasing. Every conceivable standard cartridge, up to the .300 H & H Magnum, has been necked down to take .22-caliber bullets, and custom-built varmint rifles have been chambered to fire them. The commercial ammunition makers have blithely ignored most of the wildcat loads created by hand-loading varmint shooters. In response to the demand, however, several .22-caliber varmint cartridges have been marketed, some influenced by laymen's designs, others developed in company laboratories.

In the late 30's, Winchester put on the market the .218 Bee, a cartridge chambered in the Model 65, and the .219 Zipper, chambered in the Model 64. The .218 Bee was simply a necked-down version of the old .25/20 Repeater caliber (as distinguished from the .25/20 Stevens Single Shot—a much longer case); the .219 Zipper was a necked-down modification of the early .25/35 Winchester. However, varmint shooters despised these rifles because they were lever actions. Consequently, the rifles have since disappeared, although the cartridges, still in production, are sought by varmint hunters who own custom-built rifles that can take them.

To Lyle Kilbourne, loading-tool expert with the Lyman Gunsight Corporation, Middlefield,

Western coyote, or brush wolf, offers varmint shooter some of his longest-range chances on the open country of plains and prairie.
PHOTO BY WILLIAM VANDIVERT

Connecticut, goes the credit for a big assist in varmint-load design for American hand loaders. Kilbourn improved the ballistics of the .22 Hornet and the .219 Zipper by enlarging the chambers of the rifles that were used for these calibers, then firing factory-loaded ammunition in them. The expanded cases became the basis for reloaded cartridges of more power. Flatter trajectory was obtained at nominal expense by rechambering a standard barrel. These loads are now classified as the K-Hornet and K-Zipper. This system of "wildcatting" has another advantage: it permits the use of regular factory loads in these rifles if no reloads are on hand.

Remington has developed a chuck cartridge for use up to 300 yards or more. Starting with no preconceived case design, the firm's ballistics engineers evolved a load firing a .22-caliber, 50-grain bullet at around 3,200 feet per second. This rimless cartridge—practically a miniature of the .30/06—is called the .222 Remington. It is superbly accurate and, in a good bolt-action rifle, is capable of putting all its shots into a two-inch group at 200 yards. In an effort to pro-

The species marmot has three main branches: the woodchuck, below, who lives at low elevations, generally in the East, and who is smaller than either the yellow-bellied marmot who lives in the hill country of Midwest, or the big, hoary, whistling marmot of the northwest mountains. All three hibernate. Long-range rifles necessary to kill them include Savage Model 340, .222 Remington caliber, and Marlin Varmint King, .222 Remington.

PHOTOS BY WILLIAM VANDIVERT, BELOW, AND
FISH AND WILDLIFE SERVICE

duce a new military cartridge of small caliber for a light autoloading carbine, Remington has also brought out the .222 Magnum — an even more powerful version of the .222.

Remington's Model 722 Varmint rifle is chambered for both of these cartridges. Several other varmint rifles also are available in the regular .222 Remington loading: the previously mentioned Savage Model 340, the Marlin Varmint King (built on Sako action), and various foreign-made rifles such as the regular Sako line, manufactured in Finland. Remington also turns out its Model 760 slide-action rifle in this caliber.

For varmint shooting in areas where the loud report of a powerful rifle does not alarm the community, still other cartridges are available. In prairie and western mountain country, for instance, a hunter can do almost as he pleases in burning powder. For this terrain a cartridge that will produce kills at 400 yards or more when used in a rifle equipped with a target scope is Winchester's .220 Swift, the speediest .22 caliber on the market and a universal favorite since 1936. Its somewhat light, 48-grain bullet does, however, leave something to be desired for the longest-range shooting, since velocity falls off rapidly and wind gets in its disconcerting side-drift. To overcome some of these un-

desirable effects, Winchester developed the .243, a necked-down counterpart of the .308, loaded with a 6-mm bullet of eighty grains. Remington's contribution in this field is the .244, which fires a 6-mm bullet of seventy-five grains; the cartridge is made by necking down the .257 Roberts, one of the better long-range, .25-caliber loads. The ballistics of the .243 Winchester and the .244 Remington are quite similar, as both have a muzzle velocity of 3,500 fps or more. These are superbly accurate loads with ample power for bigger game than the western rock chuck or coyote, particularly in their heavier bullet loadings: one hundred grains for the .243 and ninety grains for the .244.

In the field of the longest-range varmint shooting, Weatherby's .257 Magnum stands out markedly above all others. With the 87-grain bullet this cartridge gives 3,950 fps, by all odds the flattest-shooting load commercially available. Few, if any, wildcat cartridges can exceed the extraordinary long-range accuracy and power of this .25-caliber design which is based on the .300 H & H Magnum case.

Since varmint shooting is usually a leisurely sport that calls for careful calculation and deliberate marksmanship, a special rifle is required. The light weight of the deer or big-game rifle is no particular advantage here, for the rifle is transported in the hunter's car. Steady holding and better accuracy are fostered by use of a heavier rifle, ranging in weight from a minimum of eight pounds to a possible maximum of twelve pounds, less the scope sight. Stock design is influenced by the fact that shooting is done while the gunner is prone, although the design is not so extreme as to preclude comfortable holding in the sitting or offhand position. The cheekpiece and Monte Carlo comb are highly practical additions to the scope-fitted rifle. Trigger pull is sharp and fairly light—never more than five pounds—with no perceptible creep. Speed of repeated fire means almost nothing, as varmint shooting is normally a one-shot operation. A miss and the target is quickly away. Therefore, the bolt action with medium-weight barrel and target type of stock is ideal. Winchester's Model 70 Varmint rifle in .243 caliber is an example of the special weapon in commercial form.

But no true varmint shooter is satisfied for long with a commercial job. Altering stocks, improving barrel-bedding, rechambering to a wildcat load—all are part of the happy tinkering that is a way of life to the hunter who delights in bagging non-game critters at a range farther than the unaided eye can see them.

257

CHAPTER SIXTEEN **MARKSMANSHIP**

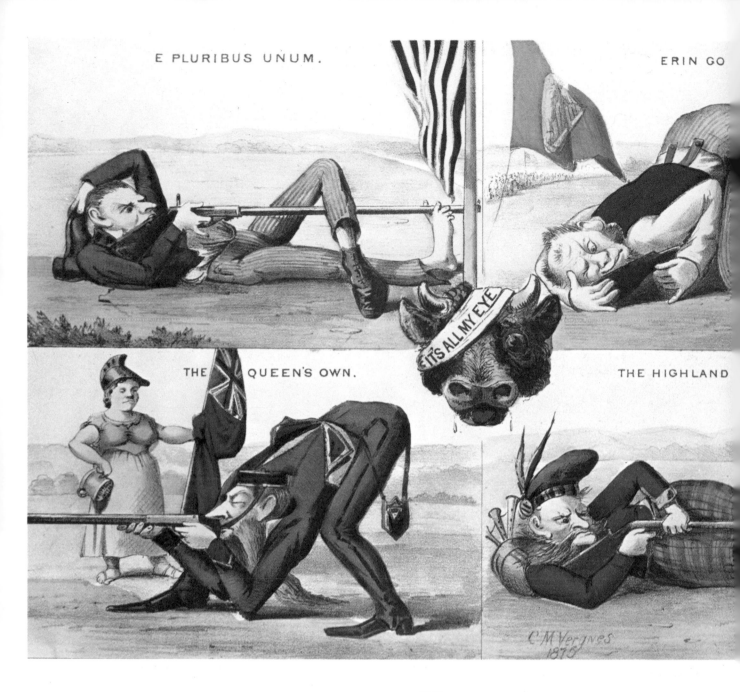

THE QUEEN'S OWN.

THE HIGHLAND

C.M Vergnes
1875

PAGES 258 AND 259: GUNS FOR SHOOTING PAPER
AND CLAY TARGETS: *Colt Python target revolver, with
ribbed barrel, large grips, comes in .38 Special or .357
Magnum. Remington Model 11-48 skeet gun is 28 gauge.*
PHOTO BY ROBERT MOTTAR

ABOVE: *Contemporary caricatures of old-time target
shooters exaggerates positions sometimes used
in competitive marksmanship.* LITHOGRAPH BY CURRIER
AND IVES, FROM HARRY T. PETERS COLLECTION, MUSEUM
OF CITY OF NEW YORK

The measure of a man in early America was not
only how many rails he could split but how well
he could shoot at the mark. Skilled riflemen
achieved the stature of today's home-run hitters.
Regional competition among the experts drew
enormous crowds to bet on the matches—crowds
that would compare favorably with the masses
of bettors at the pari-mutuel windows of a big
race track today.

Enthusiasm reached World Series proportions
in 1874 at Creedmore, Long Island. The newspapers that covered this First International
Rifle Match between the Irish Wimbledon

Dinner finished, the men smoked fraternally,

then went out to celebrate the day by shooting at a mark.

BERNARD DE VOTO

champions and the Americans described the shooting style of each member of the six-man teams, reproduced the targets they shot at, and predicted the outcome of the contest. As it turned out, the Americans won, but only because one of the Irishmen fired a bullet at an American target, a mistake that cost the Irish a possible four points. The final score: Americans, 934; Irish, 931.

It was a notable achievement, with the Americans (who had never before fired at a range of more than 500 yards) successfully blasting at targets 800, 900, and 1,000 yards distant. They used specially built target-model versions of buffalo guns: the Remington and the Sharps .44-caliber breechloaders, both known as Creedmore models. The precision shooting that was demonstrated at Creedmore did not become possible until the percussion system of ignition was well-established in the 1840's. Although some remarkable shooting had been done with Kentucky flintlocks, they could not be counted on for fast, positive firing after the trigger was squeezed—a drawback that made consistent accuracy impossible. These "turkey rifles," developed for match shooting toward the end of the eighteenth

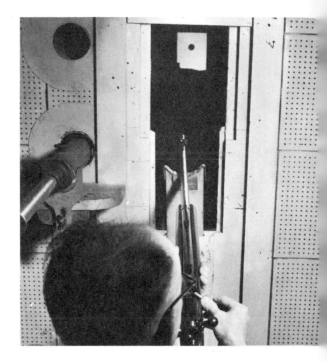

ABOVE: *Expert rifleman targets
.22-caliber Model 52 match
rifle on Winchester range. Not until targeteer
approves rifle is it ready for shipment.*
PHOTO BY HANK AUBIN

LEFT: *Famous Winchester target rifles are, left
to right, Model 70, .30/06 caliber, and
Model 52, .22 caliber.* PHOTO BY JOSEPH BURNS

ABOVE RIGHT: *While a little Negro boy proudly
exhibits victim of an earlier round, the other
participants in this festive Hudson Valley
turkey shoot concentrate on next shot. Manservant
gets in last-moment kibitzing, two bystanders
place a side bet, and a little girl covers her ears
to ward off the sound of exploding black powder.
Genre scene painted in 1836 was hung two
years later in National Academy.*
PAINTING BY CHARLES DEAS.
COURTESY PAUL MELLON AND
SPORTS ILLUSTRATED

century, had exceptionally heavy, octagonal barrels, thirty-eight to forty inches long, full stocks, double-set triggers, and, frequently, "tube sights." The latter resembled the modern target telescopes, but had no lenses. The tube, however, kept sunlight from distorting the shooter's view of his sights. (Telescope sights were not used until between 1835 and 1840.)

Following the development of percussion locks, the next improvement in target rifles came in 1840 when Alvan Clark, a telescope-lens maker of Cambridge, Massachusetts, invented the false muzzle. This device, also known as a bullet starter, enabled a marksman to seat a conical bullet directly in line with the rifling.

In the hands of skilled shooters, this was all the muzzle-loaders of the black-powder era needed to run up incredibly high scores. Even with smokeless powder, their scores were not surpassed until recently, and then only by riflemen using ultra-special bench-rest rifles, meticulously created hand loads, and the finest telescopic sighting equipment.

In 1859, forty-three years after he helped Remington build his first rifle, Morgan James, the gunsmith of Utica, New York, fired a ten-shot group at 220 yards with every bullet striking well within a circle the size of a silver dollar. James also put nine shots into a half-inch group 110 yards away. Another marksman, George Ferris, using a James-built rifle, fired forty shots at 440 yards into a five-inch area.

These were outstanding examples of good shooting, but the most significant displays of a rifle made by James occurred early in the Civil War. In 1861, at Weehawken, New Jersey, Colonel Hiram Berdan, who had been recruiting his famous regiment of Sharpshooters, wanted to emphasize what a long-range marksman could do to a man-sized target. Berdan, in prone posi-

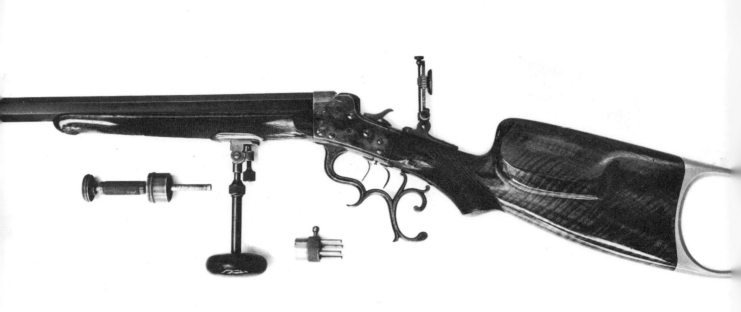

*Remington-Schuetzen match rifle, with double-set
triggers, rear Vernier sight, palm rest.*

GUN: WILLIAM FLORENCE. PHOTO BY ROBERT MOTTAR

tion, leveled his thirty-two-pound, .48-caliber
rifle, and, squinting down a full-length telescope,
fired at a dummy of Jefferson Davis 220 yards
away. Repeatedly he hit "Jeff's" head, and when
spectators called for the eye or the nose, Berdan
obliged. He finished off the display by punching
bullets through the buttons of the coat. His men
also were fantastically good shots, and it is little
wonder, since no man was admitted to the regiment unless he could shoot an average of five
inches from the bull's-eye on ten consecutive
shots from a distance of six hundred feet. But
Berdan was not satisfied with turkey rifles for
military marksmen. He wanted Sharps' breechloaders. He took his men to Washington, and
their prowess filled the newspapers. When the
word reached the President, he decided to see for
himself. With three of his Cabinet and a clutch
of top-ranking generals, he visited Berdan's
camp. Seizing the opportunity, Berdan repeated

his Weehawken show. Lincoln was convinced
that the best was none too good for Berdan's
regiment, and an order for breechloaders was
given the next day.

Others besides James who made black-powder rifles, now highly valued as collector's items,
included William Billinghurst, Edwin Wesson,
P. A. Reinhart, John Sherry, Norman Brock-
way, and Horace Warner. They all had something in common with today's gunmaker: they
spent countless hours of painstaking care building their super-accurate weapons. They were
motivated by more than love; a rifle maker's
business flourished, then as now, only when his
rifles won important matches.

MODERN TARGET RIFLES

Today, when match victory comes only by
placing shots in a charmed inner circle called the

*Ruger Black Hawk, above, is popular with big-game hunters,
and a marksman's gun when loaded with .38 Special mid-range target
loads. Ruger's top-grade target pistol is the .22-caliber
Mark I automatic, below.* PHOTOS BY DAVID STECHER

TOP: *Colt Python, engraved by Alvin A. White.*
GUN, COURTESY P. R. PHILLIPS
MIDDLE: *Smith & Wesson Heavy Masterpiece.*
BOTTOM: *High Standard Sentinel.*

X-ring, shooters need highly specialized rifles. Some use custom-made guns, while others, for ranges up to 200 yards, shoot the Winchester Model 52 or the Remington Model 40X. The factory-built rifle often used for 1,000 yards is the Winchester Model 70 in Target, National-Match, and Bull-Gun grades, in .30/06 and .300 Magnum.

The young target shooter has a choice of lighter and less expensive rifles: Remington Model 521TL and Model 513T, and Winchester Model 75 Target. All are stocked for four-position shooting, rigged with slings, and mounted with micrometer rear sights.

LEFT, COLT TARGET AND PLINKING GUNS: *Top to bottom, Match Target automatic, .22 caliber; Frontier Scout, .22 caliber; Python, .357 Magnum and .38 Special; Officer's Model, .38 Special, .22 Long Rifle.*
PHOTO BY EDWARD SAXE

HANDGUNS

To Ira Paine goes much of the credit for establishing the handgun as an accurate arm. In the 1880's, firing a single-shot Stevens, he was the top marksman in the United States. When he went to Europe he ran into trouble until he changed to the weapon his competitors were using, the .44 Smith & Wesson Russian revolver.

Although Paine's reputation was enhanced by his revolver shooting—he ran up scores that are envied by first-class shooters today—the single-shot, .22-caliber pistol remained for many years the established match weapon. Shooting experts had long recognized the efficiency of the six gun as a weapon of high firepower against man-sized targets in war or Indian fighting, but as an instrument of precision shooting it was generally held in contempt. "Buffalo Bill" Cody, in his many exhibitions, attempted to popularize it, but marksmen were well aware that his aerial shooting of glass balls was done with cartridges loaded with bird shot, rather than with bullets.

It was not until Smith & Wesson and Colt began building special target revolvers with adjustable sights more than fifty years ago that the revolver became the chief competition arm. Actions in all subsequent special guns are noticeably smoother than in comparable service guns.

THE PLINKER'S HANDGUN

Besides gun-club marksmen there is a small army of revolver and pistol enthusiasts that uses the handgun to shoot small game and plink at tin cans, Bustible Bull's-eyes, and small-game silhouettes. They use .22's, which generally have fixed sights and are, therefore, less expensive and less delicate than adjustable-sight guns.

Bill Ruger, president of Sturm-Ruger, began a trend in the .22 field in 1950 by making a shrewd guess that TV-indoctrinated shooters would buy a single-action handgun that looked like a western hero's pistol. He took a "hog-leg" design, engineered it for better performance and greater durability, labeled it the Single-Six and put it on the market. Sales were phenomenal. Colt followed Ruger's lead with the Frontier Scout, a .22-caliber, scaled down, lightweight version of the old Peacemaker. Not to be outdone, High Standard modified its Sentinel, and produced the Double-Nine—a gun that looks like a single-action but is a nine-shot, double-action revolver. In 1956 Ruger bolstered his lead on the field with the Lightweight Single-Six and in 1958 he introduced the .22 Bearcat.

Plinkers and small-game shooters also use .22 automatics, generally in the four-and-a-half-inch barrel length—a size that fits easily in a shoulder holster. A disadvantage of this pistol is that it functions as an autoloader only with the cartridge for which it is chambered—usually the

.22 Long Rifle. Revolvers, on the other hand, accept all three .22 sizes.

CLAY-TARGET SHOOTING

An entirely different aspect of markmanship got under way in 1831 at the Sportsmen's Club of Cincinnati when a shotgun was fired at a pigeon released from a trap. This new range shooting at a live target worked simply: a line was drawn on the ground about forty yards from the trapped pigeon; the bird was freed, and the gunner allowed two shots to bring it down before it reached the line. This form of trapshooting, however, did not last long. Humane societies managed to get it outlawed in most states, and gunners in areas where it was legal could not long afford the cost of live birds.

But banging away on a range with a shotgun had captured the imagination of sportsmen. An attempt to meet the demand for artificial targets was made in 1876 by Captain William Bogardus, one of the country's best shots at live birds. His trap, powered by the energy of a wagon spring, sent glass balls spinning thirty-five feet in the air. Bits of flying glass, however, proved to be something of a hazard, and in the 1880's targets made of clay were substituted for the glass balls. Unfortunately, they did not always break when hit. (For that matter, neither do today's "clay" targets, but the pitch, asphaltum, and limestone dust of which they are made will make a tiny puff of black smoke if hit by at least one pellet.)

REMINGTON TARGET GUNS: *Left to right, Model 870 12-gauge trap gun, with ventilated rib, large slide handle, straight stock, recoil pad; Model 58 Sportsman 12-gauge autoloader, a popular skeet shooters' gun; Model 40X Rangemaster, .22 Long Rifle caliber, single shot, heavy barrel.*
PHOTO BY ALEX HENDERSON

Gunners fire at clay birds, thrown from concealed traps.
Informal practice here simulates shooting pheasants in cornfield.
PHOTO BY OZZIE SWEET

With the coming of the clay target, shooters found a relatively inexpensive way to keep shooting all year, regardless of season or the scarcity of game. The artificial birds are tough enough to stand normal handling in shipping, break readily when struck by two or three pellets and, best of all, simulate the rapid flight of many native game birds. Also, their design enables them to be thrown in any direction, at any vertical angle up to ninety degrees, and their flight can be accurately controlled.

Besides trapshooting, the clay bird has led to skeet shooting, handtrapping, tower-shooting, and grouse walks. Nationally, trap and skeet have a tremendous following among people who just love to shoot.

For straight trapshooting, a special gun is necessary. Since the bird leaves the traphouse sixteen yards from the shooter, it is usually twenty-five yards away before a shot can be made. The bird is small and usually presents only its edge for a target, so it takes a dense pattern to break it up. A small-gauge, open-bored field gun will not do unless the gunner is a really fast shot.

The trap gun has a long barrel and a pair of sights—for accurate aiming—and a straight stock with high comb, both of which tend to reduce recoil. Since the gun is always mounted deliberately and lined up on the traphouse before a call is made for the bird, there is time to get set, to snuggle down on the comb, and to aim.

Most trapshooters compete in matches for money or prizes—as well as for sport—and consequently their guns are usually show pieces. All of them are carefully bored and choked to put the greatest amount of fine shot, usually #7½ or #8, into a thirty-inch circle at forty yards.

Skeet shooting is another highly competitive clay-target sport that has a large following in this country. It differs greatly from trap-shooting in layout, method, and type of gun involved.

The skeet shooter breaks his targets at about twenty-two yards and has to be ready for birds traveling toward him and away from him, at high and low angles. In addition, two birds at a time are thrown in four sets of pairs in each round. Because skeet is designed to simulate shooting conditions in the field, it demands fast shooting. The gunner is not permitted to mount his gun and, indeed, it is not certain exactly how soon his bird will appear after he calls for it. Electric timers may release the bird at any time within three seconds.

The major difference between the trap and the skeet gun is in barrel length and boring. Skeet guns are not sighted, so there is no need for a long barrel. A gunner points ahead of the target and makes a fast lead as he fires. As it takes a very wide pattern of shot to hit a fast-moving target at a tricky angle, open bores bring better results. Ranges are short, so fine shot—usually #9—is the usual load.

It is possible to do a job on a skeet field with a regular upland gun, but for the devotee a specially designed gun is necessary. The standard field gun is too light for consistent swinging in a one-hundred-bird match, and no one can stand the pounding from a light 12 gauge in all-day shooting. Both problems were solved by making skeet-gun models of repeaters, equipping them with a recoil-compensating device attached to the muzzle and either an adjustable choke or changeable choke tubes, and by adding weight to the stock and forearm of double guns.

Nothing has contributed more to the popularity of small-gauge shotguns than skeet shooting. Unlike trap, where the 12 gauge reigns supreme, skeet shooting is done with gauges right down to the 28 and .410. The 28's survival as an American gun, in fact, is the result of demand by skeet shooters.

For many shooters, both trap and skeet are

out of reach. Either there are no fields within easy distance or the cost of shooting is more than the shooter can afford. Also, many beginners are embarrassed to step out on a regular field with experienced shooters. The answer is hand-trapping. It is the best way to learn to handle a shotgun. There is no pressure of competition, no hurrying to avoid holding up the next squad of shooters, which happens on both skeet and trap fields. All it takes is two people, a gun of simple type, a hand-trap, plenty of shells and birds, and a safety area of at least two hundred yards. Hand-trap shooters use break-open single-barreled guns or bolt actions in the small gauges—20 or 28—although, obviously, any gauge can be used. Later on, they often switch to the .410.

GUNS IN THE LAND OF THE FREE

Some four hundred and fifty years have passed since the gun was brought to the shores of America. It was a primitive weapon then, but for all its crudity it embodied a permanent idea and no one ever lost patience with it. By now it has outlasted all its quaint contemporaries. Pike and halberd, arbalest and long-bow, saber and cutlass—all the killing tools of those first armor-clad adventurers except the gun have become curiosities today.

The gun has always marched apace with the times. To every demand upon it—for greater range, greater power, greater accuracy—it has responded. Its original form has proved to be a true conception, endlessly adaptable. Today it is a precision instrument of infinite variations and capabilities, accommodating to the requirements of the shooter, although demanding in return the coordinated skills of hand and eye—and the respect—that enable it to do its best.

These facts are also true elsewhere in the world. All nations and all people have quickly seen, or learned, the efficacy of the gun. But the great difference has been that only in America has everyone traditionally and constitutionally been free to possess and use it. This freedom has made the gun an agent of American history to an extraordinary degree. Undeniably, the strength of the gun has been employed to conquer and control and change the course of other nations as well. But essentially these were military actions conducted by men whose right to bear arms was foreclosed when their enlistment ended. Except for the landed aristocracy, the gentlemen fowlers, and the king's foresters, the gun and its power to make the weak the equal of the strong have generally been forbidden to the citizenry.

In America, and later the United States, the gun has had prime military uses in repelling or subduing enemies, but it has also been an implement of social and economic change. And this was possible only because the milieu was favorable to the gun and to its common, everyday use.

As the northeastern quarter of the vast New World emerged from colonialism, in part with the gun's help, George Washington proclaimed that "to be prepared for war is one of the most effective means of preserving the peace." Many nations, before and since, have subscribed to this notion, but relatively few since classic times have accepted Washington's calm assumption

WINCHESTER CLAY-TARGET GUNS: *Left to right, Model 50 skeet autoloader, 12 gauge, also made in 20 gauge; Model 42 skeet, .410 gauge; Model 21 skeet double, 12, 16, 20 gauge, with beavertail fore end, selective single trigger and ejectors; Model 12 trap pump action, 12 gauge, with extension slide handle, high-comb straight stock, recoil pad. All but Model 21 have ventilated ribs.*
PHOTO BY JOSEPH BURNS

that the policy was best executed by a citizen army—"provided with uniform arms and so far accustomed to the use of them, that the Total strength of the Country might be called on at a Short Notice on any very interesting Emergency." It has always been an accepted article of faith that the nation's shield would be the skilled marksman, an ever-ready Minute Man.

Of course, many forces bore on the evolution of the United States, of which the freedom to keep arms was only an element and an expression of intent. Yet it was as logical as it was unusual. The early Americans had to shoot well to stay alive. Along the restless, advancing boundaries of the New World, food and clothing were often obtainable only by the gun. War was frequent enough to maintain the gun in readiness, but even during the years of peace there was local, individual conflict with Indians and purposeful, workaday shooting that spurred the shooter to keep his eye sharp and his trigger finger steady. The casual fun of the turkey shoot and the Rendezvous was rooted in reason.

Later, the gun was instrumental in establishing the West. Much of the shooting was aimless and inconclusive, and frequently the deaths were meaningless, yet many a fusillade had the effect of casting a vote for one way of life as against another. And, certainly, the buffalo hunters striving to satisfy a consumer market were eventually a political and social force greater than they knew. Probably more than the U. S. Cavalry, they ruined the Indian.

It is easy to claim too much. Probably no one is prepared to say that the course of history would have been vastly otherwise had the role of the gun been different or less. Nonetheless, it is tempting to think of the path the Revolu-

Author aims a Ruger Black Hawk, .357 Magnum.
PHOTO BY JERRY TIFFANY

tion might have taken had the British utilized Major Ferguson's repeater. It is interesting to consider whether the westward movement could have been stalled or contained or diverted in any way by Indians with better arms and better aim. It is engaging—if fruitless—to speculate on the consequences of Burr's missing Hamilton, of long rifles failing to do their duty at New Orleans, of a General Ripley becoming an eager convert to breechloaders and repeaters.

Or, more than any of these, what might have happened if, for reasons of national policy, the people's constitutional freedom to "keep and bear arms," guaranteed by the Bill of Rights, had been infringed by amendment or repeal. It might have been, but it never has and, strangely, it is somehow inconceivable that it should be.

We are still a nation of gun-toters. The ever-new weapons of mass obliteration have diminished the shoulder arm and handgun. Yet the love of shooting and the regulated but unquestioned right to shoot persist. There are 15,000,000 hunters in the field each autumn. Other millions shoot the year around on the target range, the skeet and trap fields, and in the endless pursuit of varmints.

It can perhaps be proved that controlled shooting has been one of our more effective conservation techniques, that our wildlife thrives, in harmonious balance with its environment, because of selective hunting. And it can be argued that superior marksmanship is a healthy discipline to be instilled in youth, as well as a national asset in the dark night of war. But these considerations are after the fact. The motivation is everything. In a nation with a short tradition as time is counted, the gun has itself become traditional, a continuing thread that reminds us of what we were and how we came to be what we are. This is reason enough for its cherished place in the land of the free.

BASIC GUN DATA

MODEL 70 BOLT ACTION HIGH POWER

MODEL 77 .22 RIM-FIRE AUTOLOADER

MODEL 12 PUMP ACTION

MODEL 94 LEVER ACTION HIGH POWER

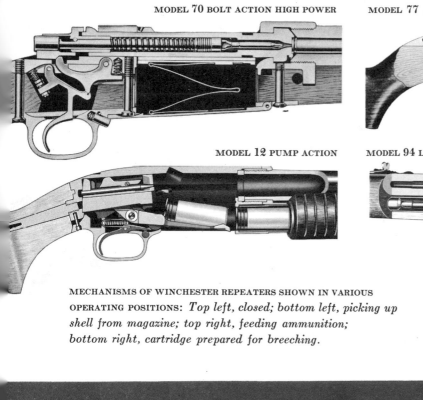

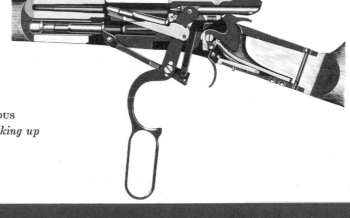

MECHANISMS OF WINCHESTER REPEATERS SHOWN IN VARIOUS
OPERATING POSITIONS: *Top left, closed; bottom left, picking up
shell from magazine; top right, feeding ammunition;
bottom right, cartridge prepared for breeching.*

POST AND APERTURE

IMPROVED

MODIFIED

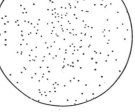

OPEN REAR AND BEAD

PEEP REAR AND BEAD

SIGHTS

*Metallic sights for target
and hunting rifles. Top
sketches show sights held
at base of bull's-eye.
Sketch, at right, shows how
hunters can cover
vital area with bead.*

FULL

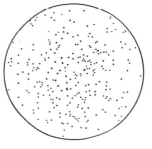

CHOKES

*Open- or improved-cylinder
boring has wide spread
for short ranges; modified
boring, an all-around
pattern for general hunting;
full-choke boring, longest
range for wildfowl and trap.*

BASIC GUN DATA CONTINUED

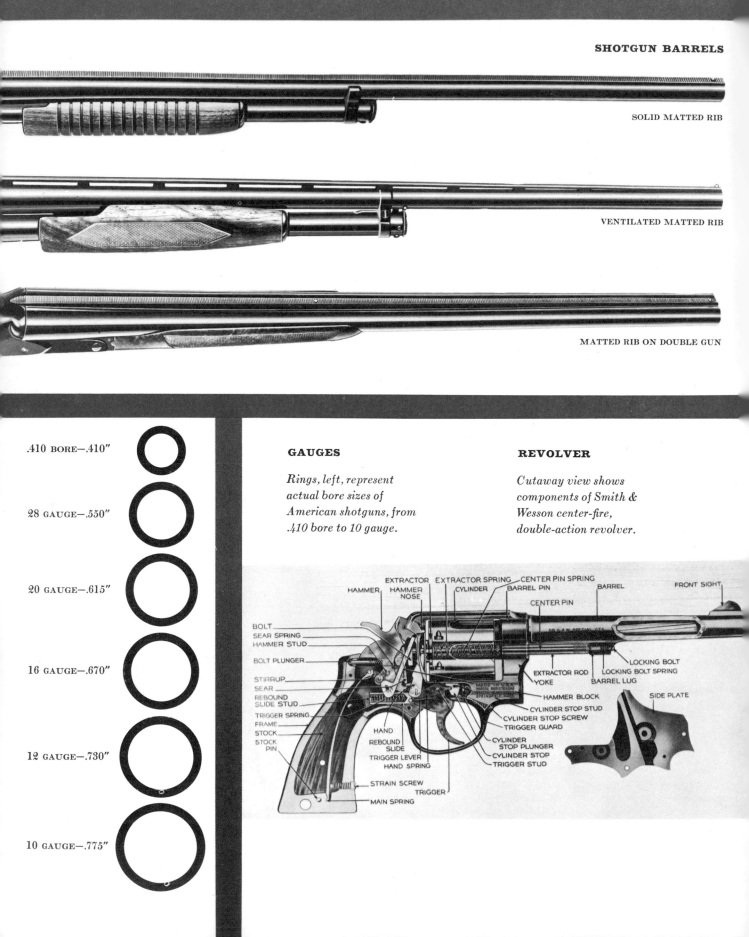

SHOTGUN BARRELS

SOLID MATTED RIB

VENTILATED MATTED RIB

MATTED RIB ON DOUBLE GUN

.410 BORE—.410″

28 GAUGE—.550″

20 GAUGE—.615″

16 GAUGE—.670″

12 GAUGE—.730″

10 GAUGE—.775″

GAUGES

Rings, left, represent actual bore sizes of American shotguns, from .410 bore to 10 gauge.

REVOLVER

Cutaway view shows components of Smith & Wesson center-fire, double-action revolver.

HAMMER
EXTRACTOR
HAMMER
NOSE
EXTRACTOR SPRING
CYLINDER
CENTER PIN SPRING
BARREL PIN
BARREL
FRONT SIGHT
CENTER PIN

BOLT
SEAR SPRING
HAMMER STUD
BOLT PLUNGER

STIRRUP
SEAR
REBOUND
SLIDE STUD
TRIGGER SPRING
FRAME
STOCK
STOCK
PIN

HAND
REBOUND
SLIDE
TRIGGER LEVER
HAND SPRING

STRAIN SCREW
MAIN SPRING

EXTRACTOR ROD
YOKE

HAMMER BLOCK
CYLINDER STOP STUD
CYLINDER STOP SCREW
TRIGGER GUARD
CYLINDER
STOP PLUNGER
CYLINDER STOP
TRIGGER STUD
TRIGGER

LOCKING BOLT
LOCKING BOLT SPRING
BARREL LUG

SIDE PLATE

BIBLIOGRAPHY

ALBAUGH, WILLIAM A., III. and SIMMONS, EDWARD N.
Confederate Arms. Harrisburg, Stackpole, 1957.

ASKINS, COL. CHARLES
The Shotgunner's Book. Harrisburg, Stackpole, 1958.

BAKELESS, JOHN
Lewis and Clark: Partners in Discovery.
New York, William Morrow, 1947.

BEEBE, LUCIUS and CLEGG, CHARLES
The American West. New York, E. P. Dutton, 1955.

BILLINGTON, RAY ALLEN
Westward Expansion. New York, Macmillan, 1949.

BRUCE, ROBERT V.
Lincoln and the Tools of War. New York, Bobbs-Merrill, 1956.

CHAMBERLAIN, SAMUEL E.
My Confession. New York, Harper and Brothers, 1956.

CHAMPLAIN, SAMUEL de
Works. Toronto, Champlain Society, 1922-1936.

CONARD, HOWARD LEWIS
*Uncle Dick Wootton, The Pioneer Frontiersman of the
Rocky Mountain Region*. Chicago, Lakeside Press,
R. R. Donnelley and Sons, 1957.

EDWARDS, WILLIAM B.
The Story of Colt's Revolver. Harrisburg, Stackpole, 1953.

FULLER, CLAUD E.
The Breechloader in the Service. Topeka, ARCA, 1933.
The Rifled Musket. Harrisburg, Stackpole, 1958.
The Whitney Firearms. Huntington, West Virginia,
Standard Publications, 1946.

GLUCKMAN, ARCADI
United States Muskets, Rifles and Carbines.
Buffalo, Otto Ulbrich, 1948.
United States Martial Pistols and Revolvers.
Buffalo, Otto Ulbrich, 1939.

HANSON, CHARLES E., Jr.
The Northwest Gun. Lincoln, Nebraska
State Historical Society, 1955.

HICKS, MAJ. JAMES E.
U.S. Firearms. La Canada, California,
James E. Hicks and Son, 1957.

JOHNSON, CHARLES
*A General History of the Lives and Adventures of the
most Famous Highwaymen (and) a Genuine Account of the Voyages
and Plunders of the Most Notorious Pirates*. London, 1736.

KARR, CHARLES L. Jr. and KARR, CAROLL L.
Remington Handguns. Harrisburg, Stackpole, 1951.

KEITH, ELMER
Sixguns by Keith. Harrisburg, Stackpole, 1955.
Shotguns by Keith. Harrisburg, Stackpole, 1950.

LEACH, DOUGLAS EDWARD
*Flintlock and Tomahawk: New England
in King Philip's War*. New York, Macmillan, 1958.

LEWIS, B. R.
Small Arms and Ammunition in the United States Service.
Washington, D. C., Smithsonian Institution, 1956.

MAYER, JOSEPH R.
Flintlocks of the Iroquois. Rochester, Rochester
Museum of Arts and Sciences, Research Records, 1943.

McCRACKEN, HAROLD
Portrait of the Old West. New York, McGraw-Hill, 1952.
Frederic Remington. Philadelphia, J. B. Lippincott, 1947.
Charles Russell. New York, Doubleday, 1957.

McHENRY, ROY C. and ROPER, WALTER F.
Smith and Wesson Handguns. Huntington, West
Virginia, Standard Publications, 1945.

PARSONS, JOHN E.
The First Winchester. New York, William Morrow, 1955.
Henry Deringer's Pocket Pistol. New York, William Morrow, 1952.
The Peacemaker and Its Rivals. New York, William Morrow, 1950.
Smith and Wesson Revolvers. New York, William Morrow, 1957.

PARSONS, JOHN E. and du MONT, JOHN S.
Firearms in the Custer Battle. Harrisburg, Stackpole, 1953.

PETERSON, HAROLD L.
Arms and Armor in Colonial America.
Harrisburg, Stackpole, 1956.
Arms and Armor of the Pilgrims. Plymouth, Massachusetts,
Plimoth Plantation and Pilgrim Society, 1957.

ROBERTS, NED
Muzzle-Loading Cap Lock Rifle.
Harrisburg, Stackpole, 1952.

RUSSELL, CARL P.
Guns on the Early Frontiers.
Berkeley, University of California, 1957.

SANDOZ, MARI
The Buffalo Hunters. New York, Hastings House, 1954.

SAWYER, CHARLES WINTHROP
Firearms in American History. Boston, The Author, 1910-1920.

SERVEN, JAMES E.
Colt Firearms. Santa Ana, California, The Author, 1954.

SMITH, WINSTON O.
The Sharps Rifle. New York, William Morrow, 1943.

STEVENS, WILLIAM O.
Pistols at Ten Paces. Boston, Houghton Mifflin, 1940.

TAYLOR, JOHN
Pondoro, Last of the Ivory Hunters.
New York, Simon and Schuster, 1955.

WELLMAN, PAUL I.
The Indian Wars of the West. New York, Doubleday, 1954.
The Trampling Herd. New York, Carrick and Evans, 1939.

WILLIAMSON, HAROLD F.
Winchester, The Gun that Won the West.
Washington, D. C., Combat Forces Press, 1952.

WINANT, LEWIS
Firearms Curiosa. New York, Greenberg, 1955.
Pepperbox Firearms. New York, Greenberg, 1952.

Quotations used as chapter headings came from the following books: Chapter 1—*The Generall Historie of Virginia*, John Smith, Glasgow, J. MacLehose and Sons, 1907; Chapter 4—*The Frontier in American History*, Frederick J. Turner, New York, Henry Holt, 1921; Chapter 8—*Hunting Grounds of the Great West*, Richard Irving Dodge, London, 1877; Chapter 10—From *African Game Trails* by Theodore Roosevelt with permission of Charles Scribner's Sons; Chapter 11—From *Outdoor Pastimes of an American Hunter* by Theodore Roosevelt with permission of Charles Scribner's Sons; Chapter 12—"Long Island Pond Shooting," Lynn Bogue Hunt, from *Duck Shooting Along the Atlantic Tidewater*, Eugene Connett, ed., New York, William Morrow, 1947; Chapter 13—"The Brave Quail," Robert Ruark, from *Field and Stream Anthology*, New York, Henry Holt, 1955; Chapter 15—*Folk Song U.S.A.*, John A. and Alan Lomax, ed., New York, Duell, Sloan and Pearce, 1947; Chapter 16—*Across the Wide Missouri*, Bernard De Voto, Boston, Houghton Mifflin, 1947.

INDEX

Italic numbers refer to illustrations.

INDEX

Italic numbers refer to illustrations.

INDEX

Italic numbers refer to illustrations.